Danish
phrase book

Berlitz Publishing Company, Inc.

Princeton   Mexico City   Dublin   Eschborn   Singapore

How best to use this phrase book

● We suggest that you start with the **Guide to pronunciation** (pp. 6–9), then go on to **Some basic expressions** (pp. 10–15). This gives you not only a minimum vocabulary, but also helps you get used to pronouncing the language. The phonetic transcription throughout the book enables you to pronounce every word correctly.

● Consult the **Contents** pages (3–5) for the section you need. In each chapter you'll find travel facts, hints and useful information. Simple phrases are followed by a list of words applicable to the situation.

● Separate, detailed contents lists are included at the beginning of the extensive **Eating out** and **Shopping guide** sections (Menus, p. 38, Shops and services, p. 97).

● If you want to find out how to say something in Danish, your fastest look-up is via the **Dictionary** section (pp. 164–189). This not only gives you the word, but is also cross-referenced to its use in a phrase on a specific page.

● If you wish to learn more about constructing sentences, check the **Basic grammar** (pp. 159–163).

● Note the **colour margins** are indexed in Danish and English to help both listener and speaker. And, in addition, there is also an **index in Danish** for the use of your listener.

● Throughout the book, this symbol ☛ suggests phrases your listener can use to answer you. If you still can't understand, hand this phrase book to the Danish-speaker to encourage pointing to an appropriate answer. The English translation for you is just alongside the Danish.

Copyright © 1993 Berlitz Publishing Company, Inc.,
400 Alexander Park, Princeton, NJ 08540, USA
9-13 Grosvenor St., London W1X 9FB UK

Second revised edition–10th printing - June 2000

ISBN 2-8315-7732-2
Printed in Spain

Contents

Guide to pronunciation   6

Some basic expressions   10

Arrival   16

16	Passport control	19	Where is . . . ?
16	Customs	19	Hotel reservation
18	Baggage—Porter	20	Car hire (rental)
18	Changing money	21	Taxi

Hotel—Accommodation   22

23	Checking in—Reception	28	Difficulties
25	Registration	29	Laundry—Dry cleaner's
26	Hotel staff	30	Hairdresser—Barber
27	General requirements	31	Checking out
28	Telephone—Post (mail)	32	Camping

Eating out   33

34	Eating habits	49	Game and poultry
34	Meal times	50	Potatoes
35	Danish cuisine	51	Vegetables and noodles
36	Asking and ordering	52	Sauces and garnishes
38	What's on the menu?	53	Herbs and spices
40	Breakfast	54	Cheese
41	Starters (Appetizers)	55	Fruit and nuts
42	Open sandwiches	56	Desserts—Pastries
43	Salads	57	Drinks
43	Egg dishes	60	Nonalcoholic drinks
44	Smörgåsbord	61	Complaints
44	Soups and stews	62	The bill (check)
45	Fish and seafood	63	Snacks—Picnic
47	Meat		

Travelling around 65

65	Plane	73	Bus
66	Train	74	Boat service
67	Inquiries	74	Bicycle hire
68	Tickets	75	Car
69	Reservation	76	Asking the way
69	On the train	77	Parking
71	Baggage and porters	78	Breakdown—Road
72	Underground (subway)		assistance
72	Coach (long-distance bus)	79	Road signs

Sightseeing 80

81	Where is . . . ?	84	Religious services
82	Admission	85	Countryside
83	Who—What—When?	85	Landmarks

Relaxing 86

86	Cinema (movies)—Theatre	89	Sports
88	Opera—Ballet—Concert	90	On the beach
88	Nightclubs—Discos	91	Winter sports

Making friends 92

92	Introductions	94	Invitations
94	The weather	95	Dating

Shopping guide 97

98	Shops and services	118	Electrical appliances
100	General expressions	119	Grocer's
104	Bookshop—Stationer's	120	Household articles
106	Camping equipment	121	Jeweller's—Watch-
107	Chemist's (drugstore)		maker's
111	Clothing	123	Optician
111	Colour	124	Photography
112	Fabric	126	Tobacconist's
113	Size	127	Souvenirs
115	Clothes and accessories	127	Records—Cassettes
117	Shoes	128	Toys

Your money: banks—currency ... 129

130	At the bank	131	Business terms

At the post office ... 132

133	Telegrams	134	Telephoning

Doctor ... 137

137	General	143	Prescription—Treatment
138	Parts of the body		
139	Accident—Injury	144	Fee
140	Illness	144	Hospital
141	Women's section	145	Dentist

Reference section ... 146

146	Countries	152	Greetings
147	Numbers	153	Time
149	Year and age	154	Abbreviations
150	Seasons	155	Signs and notices
150	Months	156	Emergency
151	Days and date	156	Lost property
152	Public holidays	157	Conversion tables

Basic grammar ... 159

Dictionary and index (English—Danish) ... 164

Danish index ... 190

Map of Denmark ... 192

Acknowledgements
We are particularly grateful to Sven Ove Nathan and Gitta Muller for their help in the preparation of this book, and to Dr. T. J. A. Bennett who devised the phonetic transcription.

Guide to pronunciation

You'll find the pronunciation of the Danish letters and sounds explained below, as well as the symbols we're using for them in the transcriptions.

The imitated pronunciation should be read as if it were English except for any special rules set out below. It is based on Standard British pronunciation, though we have tried to take into account General American pronunciation as well. Of course, the sounds of any two languages are never exactly the same; but if you follow carefully the indications supplied here, you'll have no difficulty in reading our transcriptions in such a way as to make yourself understood.

In the transcriptions, syllables written in **bold type** should be stressed.

Consonants

Letter	Approximate pronunciation	Symbol	Example	
b, f, l, m, n, v	as in English			
c	1) before **e, i, y, œ** and **ø**, like **s** in **s**it	c	**citron**	seet**roān**
	2) before **a, o, u** and a consonant, like **k** in **k**ite	k	**café**	kafē
d	1) when at the end of the word after a vowel, or between a vowel and unstressed **e** or **i**, like **th** in **th**is*	d	**med**	mɛdh
	2) otherwise, as in English	d	**dale**	dāler

---

*The letter **d** is not pronounced in **nd** and **ld** at the end of a word or syllable (*guld* = **gool**), or before unstressed **e** or before **t** or **s** in the same syllable (*plads* = **plass**).

g	1) at the beginning of a word or syllable, as in **go**	g	**glas**	glas
	2) when at the end of a word after a long vowel or before unstressed **e**, usually like **y** in **yet** occasionally like **ch** in Scottish lo**ch**); sometimes mute after **a, e, o**	y	**sige**	sēēyer
hv	like **v** in view	v	**hvor**	vōār
j, hj	like **y** in **yet**	y	**ja**	yǣ
k	1) between vowels, generally like **g** in go	g	**ikke**	igger
	2) otherwise like **k** in **kite**	k	**kaffe**	kahfer
l	always as in leaf, never as in bell	l	**vel**	vehl
ng	as in sing, never as in finger, unless **n** and **g** are in separate syllables	ng ngg	**ingen** **ingre-diens**	**ing**ern inggray-dee**ehnss**
p	1) between vowels, generally like **b** in **b**it	b	**stoppe**	sto**b**ber
	2) otherwise like **p** in **p**ill	p	**pude**	poodher
r	pronounced in the back of the throat, as in French, at the beginnings of words, but otherwise often omitted	r	**rose**	rōāsser
s	always as in see (*never* as in ri**s**e)	s	**skål** **ventesal**	skawl vehnder-saal
sj	usually like **sh** in **sh**eet (but may also be pronounced like the **ss y** in pa**ss y**ou)	sh	**sjælden**	**sh**ehlern
t	1) between vowels, generally like **d** in **d**o	d	**lytte**	lew**d**er
	2) otherwise like **t** in **t**o (at the end of a word often mute)	t	**torsk**	toarsk

PRONUNCIATION

Vowels

A vowel is generally long in stressed syllables when it's the final letter or followed by only one consonant. If followed by two or more consonants, or in unstressed syllables, the vowel is generally short.

a					
a	1) when long, like **a** in car	ā	**klare**	**klā**rer	
	2) when short, more like **a** in cart	a	**hat**	hat	
e	1) when long, as **e** in the French "**les**" but longer	Ē	**flere**	**flĒ**rer	
	2) when short, like the **i** in h**i**t	E	**fedt**	fEt	
	3) when short, also like **e** in m**e**t	eh	**let**	leht	
	4) when unstressed, like **a** in **a**bove	er*	**hjælpe**	**yehl**per	
i	1) when long, like **ee** in b**ee**	ēē	**ile**	**ēē**ler	
	2) when short, between **a** in pl**a**te and **i** and p**i**n	ee	**liter**	**lee**derr	
		i	**drikke**	**dri**gger	
o	1) when long, like the **oa** sound in b**oa**t before you bring your lips together to finish the word	ōa	**pol**	p**ōa**l	
	2) when short, more or less the same sound	oa	**bonde**	**boa**ner	
	3) when short, also like **o** in l**o**t	o	**godt**	god	
u	1) when long, like **oo** in p**oo**l	ōō	**frue**	fr**ōō**er	
	2) when short, like **oo** in l**oo**t	oo	**nu**	noo	
y	put your tongue in the position for the **ee** of b**ee**, but round your lips as for the **oo** of p**oo**l	ēw	**nyde**	**nēw**dher	
		ew	**lytte**	**lew**der	

---

* This **r** should not be pronounced when reading this transcription.

Udtale

æ	1) when long, like **ai** in air	$\overline{æ}$	**sæbe**	**sæber**
	2) when short, like **e** in get	æ	**ægte**	**œhgter**
ø	put your lips together to whistle but make a noise with your voice instead, can be long or short	$\overline{ø}$	**frøken**	**frøgern**
		ø	**øl**	**øl**
å	1) when long, like **aw** in saw	$\overline{aw}$	**åben**	**awbern**
	2) when short, like **o** in on	aw	**på**	**paw**

Note: In or after long vowels, many Danish speakers use a glottal stop (like the Cockney pronunciation of water as wa'er). You will be understood perfectly well without it, so we have not shown this distinctive sound in our transcriptions.

Diphthongs

av, af	like **ow** in n**ow**	ow	**hav**	**how**
ef, ej, ij, eg	like **igh** in s**igh**	igh	**nej**	**nigh**
ev	like **e** in g**e**t followed by a short **oo** sound	eh°°	**levned**	**leh°°nerdh**
ou, ov	like **o** in g**o**t followed by a short **oo** sound	o°°	**sjov**	**sho°°**
øi, øj	like **oi** in **oi**l	oi	**øje**	**oier**
øv	like **ur** in h**ur**t followed by a short **oo** sound	ø°°	**søvnig**	**sø°°nee**

Pronunciation of the Danish alphabet

A	$\overline{a}$	K	$\overline{koa}$	U	$\overline{oo}$
B	$b\overline{e}$	L	ehl	V	$v\overline{e}$
C	$s\overline{e}$	M	ehm	W	**dob**behltv$\overline{e}$
D	$d\overline{e}$	N	ehn	X	ehks
E	$\overline{e}$	O	$\overline{oa}$	Y	$\overline{ew}$
F	æf	P	$p\overline{e}$	Z	seht
G	$g\overline{e}$	Q	$\overline{koo}$	Æ	$\overline{æ}$
H	hoa	R	ær	Ø	$\overline{ø}$
I	$\overline{ee}$	S	ehs	Å	$\overline{aw}$
J	yoath	T	$t\overline{e}$		

Some basic expressions

Yes.	**Ja.**	ya
No.	**Nej.**	nigh
Please.	**Vær så venlig.**	vær sāw **vehn**lee
Thank you.	**Tak.**	tak
Thank you very much.	**Mange tak.**	**mang**er tak
That's all right/ You're welcome.	**Det er i orden/Åh, jeg be'r.**	dE ehr ee **ord**ern/āw yigh bEr

Greetings *Hilsner*

Good morning.	**God morgen.**	goadh**mōā**ern
Good afternoon.	**God dag.**	goadh**dai**
Good evening.	**God aften.**	goadh**af**dern
Good night.	**God nat.**	goadh**nat**
Goodbye.	**Farvel.**	far**vehl**
See you later.	**På gensyn/Vi ses.**	paw **gehn**sewn/vee sEs
Hello/Hi!	**Hej!**	high
This is Mr./Mrs./ Miss . . .	**Det er hr./fru/ frk. . . .**	dE ehr herh/froo/**frö**gern
How do you do? (Pleased to meet you.)	**God dag. (Det glæder mig at træffe Dem.)**	goadh**dai**. (dE **glæ**dherr migh ah **træf**er dehm)
How are you?	**Hvordan har De det?**	vor**dan** har dee dE
Very well, thanks. And you?	**Tak, godt. Og hvordan har De det?**	tak god. oa vor**dan** har dee dE
How's life?	**Hvordan går det?**	vor**dan** gawr dE
Fine.	**Tak, godt.**	tak god

I beg your pardon?	**Undskyld.**	**oon**skewl
Excuse me. (May I get past?)	**Undskyld. (Kan jeg komme forbi?)**	**oon**skewl. (kan yigh **komer** for**bee**)
Sorry!	**Beklager!**	beh**klaer**

Questions *Spørgsmål*

Where?	**Hvor?**	vōar
How?	**Hvordan?**	vor**dan**
When?	**Hvornår?**	vor**nawr**
What?	**Hvad?**	vadh
Why?	**Hvorfor?**	vor**for**
Who?	**Hvem?**	vehm
Which?	**Hvilken?**	**vil**kern
Where is ...?	**Hvor er ...?**	vōar ehr
Where are ...?	**Hvor er ...?**	vōar ehr
Where can I find/ get ...?	**Hvor kan jeg finde/få ...?**	vōar kan yigh **finn**er/faw
How far?	**Hvor langt?**	vōar langt
How long?	**Hvor længe?**	vōar **læng**er
How much/How many?	**Hvor meget/Hvor mange?**	vōar **migh**ert/vōar **mang**er
How much does this cost?	**Hvor meget koster det her?**	vōar **migh**ert **kos**derr dɛ hehr
When does ... open/ close?	**Hvornår åbner/ lukker ...?**	vor**nawr** āwbnerr/**loog**gerr
What do you call this/that in Danish?	**Hvad kalder man det her/det der på dansk?**	vadh **kal**err man dɛ hehr/dɛ dehr paw dahnsk
What does this/that mean?	**Hvad betyder det her/det der?**	vadh ber**tewdh**err dɛ hehr/dɛ dehr

Do you speak ...? *Kan De tale ...?*

Do you speak English?	**Kan De tale engelsk?**	kan dee **täler ehng**erlsk
Does anyone here speak English?	**Er der nogen her, der kan tale engelsk?**	ehr dehr **nōā**ern hehr dehr kan **täler ehng**erlsk
I don't speak (much) Danish.	**Jeg kan ikke tale det (ret meget) dansk.**	yigh kan **igg**er **täler** dᴇ (reht **migh**ert) dansk
Could you speak more slowly?	**Kan De tale lidt langsommere?**	kan dee **täler** leet **lang**somerrer
Could you repeat that?	**Kan De gentage det?**	kan dee **gehn**täer dᴇ
Could you spell it?	**Kan De stave det?**	kan dee **staver** dᴇ
How do you pronounce this?	**Hvordan udtaler man det her?**	vor**dan oodh**tälerr man dᴇ hehr
Could you write it down, please?	**Kan De være rar og skrive det ned?**	kan dee **vä**rer rar oa **skreev**er dᴇ nehdh
Can you translate this for me/us?	**Kan De oversætte det her for mig/os?**	kan dee o°°**errseh**der dᴇ hehr for migh/os
Could you point to the ... in the book, please?	**Kunne De være rar og vise os ... i bogen?**	**koo**ner dee **vä**rer rar oa **vēē**ser os ... ee **boa**ern
word	**ordet**	**ōā**rerdh
phrase	**vendingen**	**vehn**ingern
sentence	**sætningen**	**seht**ningern
Just a moment.	**Lige et øjeblik.**	**lēē**er eht **oier**blik
I'll see if I can find it in this book.	**Jeg vil se, om jeg kan finde det i denne bog.**	yigh vil sᴇ om yigh kan **finn**er dᴇ ee **deh**ner bô
I understand.	**Jeg forstår det.**	yigh for**stawr** dᴇ
I don't understand.	**Jeg forstår det ikke.**	yigh for**stawr** dᴇ **igg**er
Do you understand?	**Kan De forstå det?**	kan dee for**staw** dᴇ

Can/May ...? *Kan/Må ...?*

Can I have ...?	**Kan jeg få ...?**	kan yigh faw
Can we have ...?	**Kan vi få ...?**	kan vee faw
Can you show me ...?	**Kan De vise mig ...?**	kan dee **vēē**ser migh

I can't.	**Jeg kan ikke.**	yigh kan **igger**
Can you tell me ...?	**Kan De sige mig ...?**	kan dee **see**er migh
Can you help me?	**Kan De hjælpe mig?**	kan dee **yehl**per migh
Can I help you?	**Kan jeg hjælpe Dem?**	kan yigh **yehl**per dehm
Can you direct me to ...?	**Kan De vise mig vejen til ...?**	kan dee **vees**er migh **vigh**ern til

Do you want ...? *Ønsker De ...?*

I'd like ...	**Jeg vil gerne ...**	yigh veel **gehr**ner
We'd like ...	**Vi vil gerne ...**	vee veel **gehr**ner
What do you want?	**Hvad ønsker De?**	vadh **øns**gerr dee
Could you give me ...?	**Kan De give mig ...?**	kan dee **gee**ver migh
Could you bring me ...?	**Kan De lade mig få ...?**	kan dee **ladh**er migh faw
Could you show me ...?	**Kan De vise mig ...?**	kan dee **vees**er migh
I'm looking for ...	**Jeg ser efter ...**	yigh sɛr **ehf**der
I'm searching for ...	**Jeg leder efter ...**	yigh **ledh**er **ehf**der
I'm hungry.	**Jeg er sulten.**	yigh ehr **sool**dern
I'm thirsty.	**Jeg er tørstig.**	yigh ehr **tørs**dee
I'm tired.	**Jeg er træt.**	yigh ehr træt
I'm lost.	**Jeg er faret vild.**	yigh ehr **får**erdh veel
It's important.	**Det er vigtigt.**	dɛ ehr **vig**teet
It's urgent.	**Det haster.**	dɛ **has**derr

It is/There is ... *Det er/Der er ...*

It is ...	**Det er ...**	dɛ ehr
Is it ...?	**Er det ...?**	ehr dɛ
It isn't ...	**Det er ikke ...**	dɛ ehr **igger**

Here it is.	**Her er det.**	hehr ehr dE
Here they are.	**Her er de.**	hehr ehr dee
There it is.	**Der er det.**	dehr ehr dE
There they are.	**Der er de.**	dehr ehr dee
There is/There are ...	**Der er ...**	dehr ehr
Is there/Are there ...?	**Er der ...?**	ehr dehr
There isn't/aren't ...	**Der er ikke ...**	dehr ehr **igger**
There isn't/aren't any.	**Der er ikke nogen.**	dehr ehr **igger** nōāern

It's ... *Det er ...*

beautiful/ugly	**smukt/grimt**	smōōkt/grimt
better/worse	**bedre/værre**	**behdh**rer/**vehr**er
big/small	**stort/lille**	stoart/**leel**er
cheap/expensive	**billigt/dyrt**	beeleet/dēwrt
early/late	**tidligt/sent**	teedhleet/sɛnt
easy/difficult	**nemt/svært**	nehmt/svært
free (vacant)/ occupied	**ledigt/optaget**	lehdheet/**opt**äerdh
full/empty	**fuldt/tomt**	foolt/tomt
good/bad	**godt/dårligt**	god/**daw**leet
heavy/light	**tungt/let**	toongt/leht
here/there	**her/der**	hehr/dehr
hot/cold	**varmt/koldt**	varmt/kolt
near/far	**i nærheden/langt væk**	ee **nærh**ēdhern/langt væk
next/last	**næste/sidste**	næsder/**sees**der
old/new	**gammelt/nyt**	**gam**erlt/newt
old/young	**gammel/ung**	**gam**erl/oong
open/shut	**åbent/lukket**	**āwb**ernt/**loog**gerdh
quick/slow	**hurtigt/langsomt**	**hoort**eet/**lang**somt
right/wrong	**rigtigt/forkert**	**rig**teet/for**kehrt**

Quantities *Mængde*

a little/a lot	**en smule/en masse**	ehn smooler/ehn maser
few/a few	**få/et par stykker**	faw/eht par **stewg**gerr
much/many	**meget/mange**	**migh**ert/**mang**er
more/less (than)	**mere/mindre (end)**	**meh**rer/**mind**rer ehn
enough/too	**nok/for**	nok/for
some/any	**nogen**	nōāern

Prepositions *Præpositioner*

above	**ovenpå**	o°°ernpaw
after	**efter**	ehfder
at	**ved**	vehdh
before (time)	**før**	før
behind	**bagved**	ba**v**ehdh
below	**nedenunder**	**nehdh**ernoonerr
between	**mellem**	**meh**lerm
down/downstairs	**ned/nedenunder**	nehdh/**nehdh**ernoonerr
during	**i løbet af**	ee l**ö**berdh ah
for	**for**	for
from	**fra**	fra
in/inside	**i/indenfor**	ee/**i**nernfor
near	**nær**	nær
next to	**ved siden af**	vehdh **seedh**ern ah
on	**på**	paw
outside	**udenfor**	**oo**dhernfor
since	**siden**	**seedh**ern
through	**gennem**	**geh**nerm
to	**til**	til
towards	**mod**	moadh
under	**under**	**oon**err
until	**indtil**	**in**til
up/upstairs	**op/ovenpå**	op/o°°ernpaw
with	**med**	mehdh
without	**uden**	**oo**dhern

A few more useful words *Nogle flere nyttige ord*

and	**og**	oa
but	**men**	mehn
never	**aldrig**	**al**dree
none	**ingen**	**ing**ern
not	**ikke**	**ig**ger
nothing	**ikke noget**	**ig**ger n**oa**ert
now	**nu**	noo
only	**kun**	koon
or	**eller**	**ehl**er
perhaps	**måske**	**mos**gE
soon	**snart**	snart
then	**så**	saw
too (also)	**også**	**oss**aw
very	**meget**	**migh**ert
yet	**endnu**	eh**noo**

16

Arrival

Passport control *Paskontrol*

You've arrived. Whether you've come by ship or plane, you'll have to go through passport and customs formalities. There's certain to be somebody around who speaks English.

Here's my passport.	**Her er mit pas.**	hehr ehr meet pas
I'll be staying ...	**Jeg skal blive her ...**	yigh skal bl**ee**er hehr
a few days	**et par dage**	eht par d**ae**r
a week	**en uge**	ehn **oo**er
2 weeks	**2 uger**	toa **oo**err
a month	**en måned**	ehn m**aw**nerdh
I don't know yet.	**Jeg ved det ikke endnu.**	yigh vehdh dE **ig**ger eh**noo**
I'm here on holiday.	**Jeg er her på ferie.**	yigh ehr hehr paw **feh**ryer
I'm here on business.	**Jeg er her i forretninger.**	yigh ehr hehr ee for**reht**ningerr
I'm just passing through.	**Jeg er her kun på gennemrejse.**	yigh ehr hehr koon paw **gehn**ermrighser

If things become difficult:

I'm sorry, I don't understand.	**Undskyld, jeg kan ikke forstå det.**	**oon**skewl yigh kan **ig**ger for**staw** dE
Does anyone here speak English?	**Er der nogen her, der kan tale engelsk?**	ehr dehr n**oa**ern hehr dehr kan **tāl**er **ehng**erlsk

Told *Customs*

After collecting your baggage at the airport (*lufthavnen—* **loofhownern**), you have a choice: use the green exit if you have nothing to declare. Or leave via the red exit if you have items to declare (in excess of those allowed).

Told goods to declare	**Toldfrit** nothing to declare

The chart below shows customs allowances for items of personal use.*

Cigarettes	Cigars	Tobacco	Spirits (Liquor)	Wine
1) 400 or 100 or 500 g.			1 l. and	2 l.
2) 800 or 200 or 1 kg.			10 l. and	90 l.
3) 200 or 50 or 250 g.			1 l. and	2 l.

1) Visitors from outside the EC
2) Visitors arriving from EC countries with non-tax-free items
3) Visitors arriving from EC countries with tax-free goods from an EC country or goods obtained outside the EC

I have nothing to declare.	**Jeg har ikke noget at fortolde.**	yigh har **igg**er n**oā**ert ah for**tol**er
I have ...	**Jeg har ...**	yigh har
a carton of cigarettes	**en karton cigaretter**	ehn kar**tong** sigga**rehd**err
a bottle of whisky	**en flaske whisky**	ehn **flasg**er "whisky"
It's for my personal use.	**Det er til eget brug.**	dɛ ehr til **igh**erdh br$\overline{oo}$
It's a gift.	**Det er en gave.**	dɛ ehr ehn **gav**er

Må jeg se Deres pas?	Your passport, please.
Har De noget at fortolde?	Do you have anything to declare?
Vær venlig at åbne denne taske.	Please open this bag.
De skal betale told for det her.	You'll have to pay duty on this.
Har De mere bagage?	Do you have any more luggage?

* All allowances are subject to change.

Baggage—Porter *Bagage—Drager*

Porters are few and far between, so best make use of the free luggage trolleys.

Porter!	**Drager!**	dra**err**
Please take (this/my) ...	**Vær rar og tag (denne/min)** ...	vehr rar oa ta (**dehner/meen**)
luggage	**bagage**	bag**å**sher
suitcase	**kuffert**	koo**ffert**
(travelling) bag	**taske/holdall**	tasger/"holdall"
That one is mine.	**Den der er min.**	dehn dehr ehr meen
Take this luggage ...	**Tag denne bagage** ...	ta **dehner** bag**å**sher
to the bus	**til bussen**	til **boo**sern
to the luggage lockers	**til bagageboksene**	til bag**å**sher **boks**erner
to the taxi	**til taxa'en**	til **tak**saern
How much is that?	**Hvor meget bliver det?**	v**ō**ar **migh**ert bl**ēē**err dɛ
There's one piece missing.	**Der mangler noget.**	dehr **mang**lerr n**ō**aert
Where are the luggage trolleys (carts)?	**Hvor er bagagevognene?**	v**ō**ar ehr bag**å**shervoanerner

Changing money *Veksling af penge*

You'll find a bank at the Copenhagen Airport and at most provincial airports too. In Copenhagen the exchange office at the Central Railway Station (*hovedbanegården*—**hoa**erbæner-gawrern) stays open every day of the week from 7 a.m. to 9 p.m.

Where's the nearest currency exchange office?	**Hvor er det nærmeste valutakontor?**	v**ō**ar ehr dɛ **nær**merster val**oo**takont**ō**ar
Can you change these traveller's cheques (checks)?	**Kan De indløse disse rejsechecks?**	kan dee **inl**øser **dees**er **righ**ser "cheques"
I want to change some dollars/pounds.	**Jeg ønsker at veksle nogle dollars/pund.**	yigh **øns**gerr at **vehks**ler n**ō**aler "dollars"/poon

BANK—CURRENCY, see page 129

| Can you change this into Danish crowns? | **Kan De veksle det her til danske kroner?** | kan dee **vehks**ler dɛ hehr til **dan**sker **kroa**ner |
| What's the exchange rate? | **Hvad er kursen?** | vadh ehr **koors**ern |

Where is ...? *Hvor er ...?*

Where is the ...?	**Hvor er ...?**	vōar ehr
booking office	**billetkontoret**	beel**lehd**kont**ōar**edh
duty (tax)-free shop	**den toldfri (skattefri) butik**	dehn **tol**free (**skadd**erfri) boo**tik**
newsstand	**aviskiosken**	a**vees**kiosgern
restaurant	**restauranten**	rehstoa**rang**ern
How do I get to ...?	**Hvordan kommer jeg til ...?**	vor**dan** ko**merr** yigh til
Is there a bus into town?	**Kører der en bus ind til byen?**	**kø**rerr dehr ehn boos in til **bew**ern
Where can I get a taxi?	**Hvor kan jeg få en taxa?**	vōar kan yigh faw ehn **tak**sa
Where can I hire (rent) a car?	**Hvor kan jeg leje en bil?**	vōar kan yigh **ligh**er ehn beel

Hotel reservation *Værelsesbestilling*

At Copenhagen main railway station you can make hotel reservations at the office marked *P*. Larger provincial towns offer similar facilities.

Do you have a hotel guide (directory)?	**Har De en hotelfortegnelse?**	har dee ehn hoa**tehl**for**tighn**erlser
Could you reserve a room for me?	**Kan De reservere et værelse til mig?**	kan dee rehsehr**vēr**er eht **vær**erlser til migh
in the centre	**i centrum**	ee **sen**troom
near the railway station	**nær ved jernbane-stationen**	nær vehdh **jehrn**bāner-sta**shon**ern
a single room	**et enkeltværelse**	eht **ehn**kerldvær**erl**ser
a double room	**et dobbeltværelse**	eht **dobb**erldvær**erl**ser
not too expensive	**ikke for dyrt**	**igg**er for dewrt
Where is the hotel/ guesthouse?	**Hvor er hotellet/ pensionatet?**	vōar ehr hoa**tehl**erdh/ pangshoa**nad**erdh
Do you have a street map?	**Har De et gadekort?**	har dee eht **gādh**erkort

HOTEL/ACCOMMODATION, see page 22

Car hire (rental) *Biludlejning*

There are car hire firms at Copenhagen Airport and at most provincial airports and terminals. Tourist information bureaux have lists of firms, otherwise look up under *Autoudlejning* in the trade telephone directory. You'll need to provide a current national or international driving licence (*førerbevis*) and be over 20 years of age (25 for some firms). Most agencies require a cash deposit, which is waived if you present a recognized credit card.

I'd like to hire (rent) a car.	Jeg vil gerne leje en bil.	yigh veel **gehr**ner **ligh**er ehn beel
small	lille	**leel**er
medium-sized	mellemstor	**mehl**ermstoar
large	stor	stoar
automatic	med automatisk gear	mehdh owto**ma**tisk geer
I'd like it for a day/ a week.	Jeg vil gerne have den en enkel dag/en uge.	yigh veel **gehr**ner ha dehn ehn **ehn**kerl dai/ehn **ōō**er
Are there any week-end arrangements?	Findes der nogle weekendtilbud?	**fin**ners dehr **nōā**ler "week-end"**til**bōōdh
Do you have any special rates?	Har De nogle særtakster?	hår dee **nōā**ler **sær**taksderr
What's the charge per day/week?	Hvad koster det pr. dag/uge?	vadh **kos**derr dɛ pehr dai/**ōō**er
Is mileage included?	Er det med kilometerpenge?	ehr dɛ mehdh keeloam**ē**derpehnger
What's the charge per kilometre?	Hvor meget koster det pr. kilometer?	**vōā**r **migh**ert **kos**derr dɛ pehr keeloam**ē**derr
I'd like to leave the car in ...	Jeg vil gerne levere bilen tilbage i ...	yigh veel **gehr**ner leh**vē**rer **bee**lern **til**bäer i
I'd like full insurance.	Jeg vil gerne have fuld forsikring.	yigh veel **gehr**ner ha fool for**seek**ring
How much is the deposit?	Hvor meget skal jeg betale i depositum?	**vōā**r **migh**ert skal yigh ber**tä**ler ee deh**poa**seetoom
I have a credit card.	Jeg har kreditkort.	yigh har kreh**dit**kort
Here's my driving licence.	Her er mit kørekort.	hehr ehr meet **kø**rerkort

CAR, see page 75

Taxi *Taxa*

Cabs can be hailed in the street or ordered by phone. They are recognized by a *Taxi* or *Taxa* sign. You'll find taxi ranks at airports, railway stations and at various points in the cities. All cabs are metered and the fare is inclusive of tip. Rates may differ from place to place, so it's best to ask the approximate fare beforehand.

Where can I get a taxi?	**Hvor kan jeg få en taxa?**	vōar kan yigh faw ehn **tak**sa
Where is the taxi rank (stand)?	**Hvor er der en taxaholdeplads?**	vōar ehr dehr ehn **tak**sa **hol**erplas
Could you get me a taxi?	**Kan De få fat på en taxa for mig?**	kan dee faw fat paw ehn **tak**sa for migh
What's the fare to ...?	**Hvad koster det til ...?**	vadh **kos**derr dE til
How far is it to ...?	**Hvor langt er der til ...?**	vōar langt ehr dehr til
Take me to ...	**Kør mig til ...**	kør migh til
this address	**denne adresse**	**deh**ner ah**dreh**ser
the airport	**lufthavnen**	**looft**hownern
the town centre	**byens centrum**	**bew**erns **sehn**troom
the ... Hotel	**Hotel ...**	ho**atehl**
the railway station	**jernbanestationen**	**jehrn**bānersta**shon**ern
Turn ... at the next corner.	**Drej til ... ved det næste hjørne.**	drigh til ... vehdh dE **næs**der **yør**ner
left/right	**venstre/højre**	**vehn**strer/**hoi**rer
Go straight ahead.	**Kør lige ud.**	kør **lee**er ōodh
Please stop here.	**Stands her.**	stans hehr
I'm in a hurry.	**Jeg har travlt.**	yigh har trowlt
Could you drive more slowly?	**Kan De køre lidt langsommere?**	kan dee **kø**rer leet **lang**somerrer
Could you help me carry my luggage?	**Kan De hjælpe mig med at bære bagagen?**	kan dee **yehl**per migh mehdh at **bæ**rer ba**gā**shern
Could you wait for me?	**Kan De vente på mig?**	kan dee **vehn**der paw migh
I'll be back in 10 minutes.	**Jeg kommer tilbage om 10 minutter.**	yigh **kom**err til**bā**er om tee mi**noo**derr

TIPPING, see inside back-cover

Hotel—Other accommodation

Early reservation is essential in most tourist centres during the high season. If you arrive without a booking, look for the Room Reservation Service, at the office marked *P*, at the Central Railway Station in Copenhagen.

There are free publications listing different accommodation in Denmark. Hotels are not graded by stars as in some other countries, but normally the price level is a fair guide to the standard.

Bondegårdsferie (**boa**nergāwrsfehreeer)	A popular farmhouse holiday with board, lodging and farm life included in the price.
Kro (kroa)	Similar to a country inn in England; this can be modest or luxurious, combining good personal service with hearty food.
Motel (moa**tehl**)	Motels are becoming more widespread in Denmark, with improving services. Lists of recommended motels are available from tourist information offices.
Missionshotel (mee**shons**hoatehl)	A modest establishment offering comfortable accommodation and good service at fair prices.
Pensionat (pangshoa**nad**)	This is a boarding-house, and the price of the room usually includes full- or half-board. These can be booked through the Accommodation Bureau.
Sommerhus (**som**erhōōs)	This "summer cottage" may be a bungalow, private house or apartment in a holiday region. Further information is available from local tourist offices.
Vandrerhjem (**van**dreryehm)	A youth and family hostel found all over Denmark. To obtain a membership card, contact your own national Youth Hostels Association. Beds may be in dormitories.
Ungdomsherberg (**oong**domshehrbehr)	A student hotel, with relaxed restrictions on night-time closure and regulations.
Can you recommend a hotel/guesthouse?	**Kan De anbefale et hotel/pensionat?**	kan dee **an**berfāler eht hoatehl/pangshoa**nad**
Are there any self-catering flats (apartments) vacant?	**Er der nogle lejligheder ledige med eget køkken?**	ehr dehr **noa**ler **ligh**leehedherr **led**hēeer mehdh **ighert køggern**

Checking in—Reception *Ankomst—Reception*

My name is ...	**Mit navn er ...**	meet nown ehr
I have a reservation.	**Jeg har bestilt værelse.**	yigh har ber**stilt vær**erlser
We've reserved 2 rooms/an apartment.	**Vi har bestilt 2 værelser/en lejlighed.**	vee har ber**stilt** to **vær**erlserr/ehn **ligh**leehehdh
Here's the confirmation.	**Her er bekræftelsen.**	hehr ehr ber**kræf**derlsern
Do you have any vacancies?	**Har De nogle ledige værelser?**	har dee **no**aler l**ɛd**eēer **vær**erlserr
I'd like a ...	**Jeg vil gerne have et ...**	yigh veel **gehr**ner ha eht
single room	**enkeltværelse**	**ehn**kerldv**ær**erlser
double room	**dobbeltværelse**	**do**berldv**ær**erlser
We'd like a room ...	**Vi vil gerne have et værelse ...**	vee veel **gehr**ner ha eht **vær**erlser
with twin beds	**med to senge**	mehdh toa **sehn**ger
with a double bed	**med dobbeltseng**	mehdh **do**berldsehng
with a bath	**med bad**	mehdh badh
with a shower	**med brusebad**	med **broo**serbadh
with a balcony	**med altan**	mehdh al**tan**
with a view	**med udsigt**	mehdh **oodh**sigt
at the front	**mod gaden**	moadh **gādh**ern
at the back	**mod gården**	moadh **gāw**ern
It must be quiet.	**Det skal være roligt.**	dɛ skal **vær**er **roal**eet
Is there ...?	**Er der ...?**	ehr dehr
air conditioning	**klimaanlæg**	**klēē**ma **an**læg
a conference room	**et mødelokale**	eht **mø**dherlokāler
a gymnasium	**en gymnastiksal**	ehn gewmna**steek**sal
a laundry service	**tøjvask**	**toi**vask
a private toilet	**toilet på værelset**	toa**let** paw **vær**erlserdh
a radio/television in the room	**radio/fjernsyn på værelset**	**radio/fyehrn**sewn paw **vær**erlserdh
room service	**service på værelset**	"service" paw **vær**erlserdh
a swimming pool	**svømmebasin**	**svø**mmerbassæng
washing machine	**en vaskemaskine**	ehn **vasg**ermaskeener
hot/running water	**varmt/rindende vand**	varmt/**reen**erner van

CHECKING OUT, see page 31

| Could you put an extra bed/a cot in the room? | Kan De sætte en ekstra seng/ barneseng op på værelset? | kan dee **sædd**er ehn **ehk**stra sehng/**barn**ersehng op paw **vær**erlserdh |

How much? *Hvor meget?*

What's the price ...?	Hvad koster det...?	vadh **kos**derr dE
per day	pr. dag	pehr dai
per week	pr. uge	pehr **ōō**er
for bed and breakfast	for et værelse og morgenmad	for eht **vær**erlser oa **mōa**ernmadh
excluding meals	uden måltider	**ōō**dhern **mawl**teedherr
for full board (A.P.)	for helpension	for **hehl**pangshon
for half board (M.A.P.)	for halvpension	for **hal**pangshon
Does that include ...?	Er ... inkluderet?	ehr ... inkloo**dēr**erdh
breakfast	morgenmad	**mōa**ernmadh
service	service	"service"
value-added tax (sales tax)	moms	moms
Is there any reduction for children?	Er det billigere for børn?	ehr dE **beelēē**eerrer for børn
Do you charge for the baby?	Koster det noget for babyen?	**kos**derr dE **nōa**ert for "baby"ern
That's too expensive.	Det er for dyrt.	dE ehr for dewrt
Do you have anything cheaper?	Har De noget billigere?	har dee **nōa**ert beel**ēē**eerrer
Is electricity included in the rental?	Er elektriciteten iberegnet i lejen?	ehr ehlehktrisi**teht**ern **ī**berrighnerdh ee **ligh**ern

How long? *Hvor længe?*

We'll be staying ...	Vi bliver her ...	vee **blēē**err hehr
overnight only	en enkel nat	ehn **ehnk**erl nat
a few days	et par dage	eht par **dae**r
a week (at least)	i (mindst) en uge	ee (meenst) ehn **ōe**r
I don't know yet.	Jeg ved det ikke endnu.	yigh vehdh dE **igg**er eh**noo**

NUMBERS, see page 147

Decision *Beslutning*

May I see the room?	**Kan jeg se værelset?**	kan yigh sE **væ**rerlserdh
That's fine. I'll take it.	**Det er godt. Jeg tager det.**	dE ehr god. yigh tar dE
No. I don't like it.	**Jeg kan ikke lide det.**	yigh kan **igg**er li dE
It's too ...	**Det er for ...**	dE ehr for ...
cold/hot	**koldt/varmt**	kolt/varmt
dark/small	**mørkt/lyst**	mørkt/lewst
noisy	**støjende**	**stoi**erner
I asked for a room with a bath.	**Jeg bad om et værelse med bad.**	yigh bädh om eht **væ**rerlser mehdh badh
Do you have any-thing ...?	**Har De noget ...?**	har dee no͞aert
better	**bedre**	**behdh**rer
bigger	**større**	**stør**rer
cheaper	**billigere**	**bee**le͞eerrer
quieter	**roligere**	ro͞ale͞eerrer
Do you have a room with a better view?	**Har De et værelse med en bedre udsigt?**	har dee eht **væ**rerlser mehdh ehn **behdh**rer o͞odhsigt

Registration *Indskrivning*

Upon arrival at a hotel or guesthouse you'll be asked to fill in a registration form (*tilmeldelsesblanket*—**til**maylerlsserssblan-**kayt**).

Navn/Fornavn	Name/First name
Adresse (by, gade, nummer)	Home town/Street/Number
Nationalitet/Stilling	Nationality/Occupation
Fødselsdato/Fødested	Date/Place of birth
Kommer fra .../Skal videre til ...	Coming from .../Going to ...
Pasnummer	Passport number
Sted/Dato	Place/Date
Underskrift	Signature

| What does this mean? | **Hvad betyder det her?** | vadh ber**tewdh**err dE hehr |

Må jeg se Deres pas?	May I see your passport, please?
Vil De være venlig at udfylde denne tilmeldelsesblanket?	Would you mind filling in this registration form?
Underskriv venligst her.	Please sign here.
Hvor længe bliver De her?	How long will you be staying?

What's my room number?	**Hvad er nummeret på mit værelse?**	vadh ehr **noom**rerdh paw meet **vær**erlser
Will you have our luggage sent up?	**Kan jeg få bragt bagagen op?**	kan yigh faw bragt ba**gā**shern op
Where can I park my car?	**Hvor kan jeg parkere min bil?**	voār kan yigh par**kē**rer meen beel
Does the hotel have a garage?	**Har hotellet egen garage?**	har hoa**tehl**lerdh sin **igh**ern ga**rā**sher
I'd like to leave this in the hotel safe.	**Jeg vil gerne anbringe det her i hotellets boks.**	yigh veel **gehr**ner **an**breenger dE hehr ee hoa**tehl**lerdhs boks

Hotel staff *Hotelpersonale*

hall porter	**portier**	port**yE**
maid	**stuepige**	**stooe**r**pēē**er
manager	**direktør**	direh**ktør**
porter	**hotelkarl**	hoa**tehl**kal
receptionist	**receptionist**	rehsehp**sho**nist
switchboard operator	**telefonist**	tehlerfo**nist**
waiter	**tjener**	ty**Ē**nerr
waitress	**frøken**	**frø**gern

Address the waiter as *tjener* (**tyEnnerr**) and the waitress as *frøken* (**frøgern**).

TELLING THE TIME, see page 153

General requirements *Almindelige forespørgsler*

The key to room ..., please.	**Nøglen til værelse ..., tak.**	noilern til **væer**erlser ... tak
Could you wake me at ... please?	**Kan De vække mig klokken ...?**	kan dee **væg**ger migh **klog**gern
May we have breakfast in our room, please?	**Kan vi få morgenmaden på værelset?**	kan vee faw **mōa**ernmadhen paw **væer**erlserdh
Is there a bath on this floor?	**Findes der bad på denne etage?**	**fin**ners dehr badh paw **deh**ner eh**tā**sher
What's the voltage?	**Hvad er spændingen?**	vadh ehr **spæn**ingern
Where's the shaver socket (outlet)?	**Hvor er stikkontakten til barbermaskinen?**	vōar ehr **stik**kontakdern til **bā**behrmaskeenern
Can you find me a ...?	**Kan De skaffe mig en ...?**	kan dee **skaf**fer migh ehn
babysitter	**babysitter**	"babysitter"
secretary	**sekretær**	sεkreh**tær**
typewriter	**skrivemaskine**	**skree**vermaskeener
May I have a/an/some ...?	**Kan jeg få ...?**	kan yigh faw
ashtray	**et askebæger**	eht **as**gerbæer
bath towel	**et badehåndklæde**	eht **bādh**erhawnklædher
(extra) blanket	**et (ekstra) tæppe**	eht (**ehk**stra) **tæb**er
envelopes	**nogle konvolutter**	**nōa**ler konvo**loodd**err
(more) hangers	**nogle (flere) bøjler**	**nōa**ler (**flē**rer) **boi**lerr
hot-water bottle	**en varmedunk**	ehn **vār**merdoonk
ice cubes	**nogle isterninger**	**nōa**ler **ēes**tehrningerr
needle and thread	**nål og tråd**	**nāw**l oa **trāw**dh
(extra) pillow	**en (ekstra) pude**	ehn (**ehk**stra) **pōo**dher
reading lamp	**en læselampe**	ehn **læs**erlamper
soap	**noget sæbe**	**nōa**ert **sæ**ber
writing paper	**noget brevpapir**	**nōa**ert breh°°pa**pēer**
Where's the ...?	**Hvor er ...?**	vōar ehr
bathroom	**badeværelset**	**bādh**ervæererlserdh
dining-room	**spisesalen**	**spēe**sersälern
emergency exit	**nødudgangen**	**nødh**oodhgangern
hairdresser's	**frisøren**	free**sōr**ern
lift (elevator)	**elevatoren**	ehleh**vā**toarern
Where are the toilets?	**Hvor er toilettet?**	vōar ehr toa**leh**derdh

BREAKFAST, see page 38

Telephone—Post (Mail) *Telefon—Post*

Can you get me Ålborg 12-34-56-78?	**Kan jeg få Ålborg 12 34 56 78?**	kan yigh faw **awlb**oar toal **fēēe**rotrehdhver **sehks**ohaltrehs **oad**er
Do you have any stamps?	**Har De frimærker?**	har dee **free**mærkerr
Would you post this for me, please?	**Vil De poste det her for mig?**	veel dee **post**er dɛ hehr for migh
Are there any letters for me?	**Er der nogle breve til mig?**	ehr dehr **nōā**ler **breh°°**er til migh
Are there any messages for me?	**Er der nogen besked til mig?**	ehr dehr **nōā**ern ber**skɛdh** til migh
How much is my telephone bill?	**Hvor stor er min telefonregning?**	**vōā**r stoar ehr meen tehleh**foan**righning

Difficulties *Vanskeligheder*

The ... doesn't work.	**... virker ikke.**	... **veer**gerr **igg**er
air conditioning	**klimaanlægget**	**klēē**ma **an**lehgerdh
bidet	**bidetet**	beed**ɛ**erdh
fan	**ventilatoren**	vehntee**la**toarern
heating	**varmen**	**vär**mern
light	**lyset**	**lews**erdh
radio	**radioen**	**ra**dioern
television	**fjernsynet**	**fyehrn**sewnerdh
The tap (faucet) is dripping.	**Vandhanen drypper.**	**van**hänern **drewbb**err
There's no hot water.	**Der er ikke noget varmt vand.**	dehr ehr **igg**er **nōā**ert varmt van
The washbasin is blocked.	**Håndvasken er stoppet.**	**hawn**vaskern ehr **stobb**erdh
The window is jammed.	**Vinduet kan ikke åbnes.**	**veendōō**erdh kan **igg**er **āwb**ners
The curtains are stuck.	**Gardinerne hænger fast.**	gär**deen**erner **hæng**err fast
The bulb is burned out.	**Lyspæren er gået.**	**lews**pǣrern ehr **gaw**erdh
My bed hasn't been made up.	**Min seng er ikke blevet redt.**	meen sehng ehr **igg**er **bleh°°**erdh reht

POST OFFICE AND TELEPHONE, see page 132

The ... is broken.	... er i uorden.	... ehr ee ōoordern
blind	rullegardinet	roolergardēenerdh
lamp	lampen	lampern
plug	stikket	stiggerdh
shutter	skodderne	skodherner
switch	kontakten	kontakdern
Can you get it repaired?	Kan De få det repareret?	kan dee faw dE rehparērerdh

Laundry—Dry cleaner's *Vaskeri—Kemisk rensning*

Where's the nearest laundry/dry-cleaner's?	Hvor er der nærmeste vaskeri/renseri?	vōar ehr dehr nærmerster vaskerree/rensserree
I'd like these clothes ...	Jeg vil gerne have dette tøj ...	yigh veel gehrner ha dehder toi
cleaned	kemisk renset	kEmisk rehnserdh
ironed	strøget	stroierdh
pressed	presset	prehserdh
washed	vasket	vasgerdh
When will they be ready?	Hvornår er det færdigt?	vornawr ehr dE færdeet
I need them ...	Jeg har brug for det ...	yigh har brōo for dE
today	i dag	ee dai
tonight	i aften	ee afdern
tomorrow	i morgen	ee mōaern
Can you ... this?	Kan De ... det her?	kan dee ... dE hehr
mend	reparere	rehparērer
patch	lappe	lapper
stitch	sy	sew
Can you sew on this button?	Kan De sy denne knap?	kan dee sew dehner knap
Can you get this stain out?	Kan De fjerne denne plet?	kan dee fjehrner dehner pleht
Is my laundry ready?	Er min vask klar?	ehr meen vask klar
This isn't mine.	Det her er ikke mit.	dE hehr ehr igger meet
There's something missing.	Der mangler noget.	dehr manglerr nōaert
There's a hole in this.	Der er gået hul i det her.	dehr ehr gawerdh hool ee dE hehr

Hairdresser—Barber *Damefrisør—Herrefrisør*

Is there a hairdresser/ beauty salon in the hotel?	**Findes der en damefrisør/ skønhedssalon på hotellet?**	finners dehr ehn **da**merfreesør/ **skøn**hehdhssallong paw hoat**ehl**lerdh
Can I make an appointment for Thursday?	**Kan jeg komme på torsdag?**	kan yigh **kom**er paw **toars**dai
I'd like a cut and blow dry.	**Jeg vil gerne have mit hår klippet og føntørret.**	yigh veel **gehr**ner ha meet hawr **klip**perdh oa **føn**tørrerdh
I'd like a haircut, please.	**Jeg vil gerne have mit hår klippet.**	yigh veel **gehr**ner ha meet hawr **klip**perdh
bleach	**en blegning**	ehn **bligh**ning
blow-dry	**en føntørring**	ehn **føn**tørring
colour rinse	**en farveskylning**	ehn **fär**verskewlning
dye	**en farvning**	ehn **fär**vning
face pack	**en ansigtsmaske**	ehn **an**seegtsmasger
hair gel	**en hårgele**	ehn **hawr**shehlE
manicure	**en manicure**	ehn manee**kew**rer
permanent wave	**en permanent**	ehn pehrma**nehnt**
setting lotion	**en setting lotion**	ehn "setting lotion"
shampoo and set	**håret vasket og sat**	**hawr**rerdh **vas**gerdh oa sat
with a fringe (bangs)	**med pandehår**	mehdh **pan**erhawr
I'd like a shampoo for ... hair.	**Jeg vil gerne have en shampoo til ... hår.**	yigh veel **gehr**ner ha ehn "shampoo" til ... hawr
normal/dry/greasy (oily)	**normalt/tørt/fedtet**	nor**malt**/tørt/f**E**derdh
Do you have a colour chart?	**Har De et farvekort?**	ha dee eht **fär**verkort
Don't cut it too short.	**Klip det ikke for kort.**	klip dE **igg**er for kort
A little more off the ...	**Lidt mere ...**	leet **meh**rer
back	**bagtil**	**bä**teel
neck	**ved halsen/i nakken**	vehdh **hal**sern/ee **nagg**ern
sides	**i siderne**	ee **seedh**erner
top	**øverst oppe**	**øv**erst **opp**er
I don't want any hairspray.	**Jeg vil ikke have hårlak.**	yigh veel **igg**er ha **hawr**lak

DAYS OF THE WEEK, see page 151

I'd like a shave.	**Jeg vil gerne barberes.**	yigh veel **gehrn**er **bā**behrers
Would you trim my ..., please?	**Vil De være venlig at studse mit ...?**	veel dee **vær**er **vehn**lee ah **stooss**er meet
beard moustache sideboards (sideburns)	**skæg** **overskæg** **kindskæg**	skæg o°°erskæg **kin**skæg

Checking out *Afrejse*

May I have my bill, please?	**Må jeg bede om regningen?**	maw yigh bε om **righn**ingern
I'm leaving early in the morning.	**Jeg skal afsted i morgen tidlig.**	yigh skal ah**stehdh** ee **mōā**ern **teed**lee
Please have my bill ready.	**Vær venlig og gør regningen klar.**	vær **vehn**lee oa ao gør **righn**ingern klar
We'll be checking out around noon.	**Jeg rejser ved tolvtiden.**	yigh **righ**serr vehdh **tolt**eedhern
I must leave at once.	**Jeg skal afsted med det samme.**	yigh skal ah**stehdh** mehdh dε **sam**mer
Is everything included?	**Er alt iberegnet?**	ehr alt iber**righn**erdh
Can I pay by credit card?	**Kan jeg betale med kreditkort?**	kan yigh ber**tāl**er mehdh kreh**dit**kort
I think there's a mistake in the bill.	**Jeg tror, der er en fejl i regningen.**	yigh troar dehr ehr ehn fighl ee **righn**ingern
Can you get us a taxi?	**Kan De skaffe os en taxa?**	kan dee **skaff**er os ehn **tak**sa
Could you have our luggage brought down?	**Kunne vi få bagagen ned?**	**koon**er vee faw ba**gā**shern nehdh
Here's the forwarding address.	**Her er vores adresse til omadressering.**	hehr er voars ah**drehs**er til **oam**adrehsehring
You have my home address.	**De har min hjemmeadresse.**	dee har meen **jehm**meradrehser
It's been a very enjoyable stay.	**Vi har nydt opholdet meget.**	vee har newt **op**holerdh **migh**ert

TIPPING, see inside back-cover

Camping *Camping*

Camp sites are found all over Denmark. You need a Danish or international camping pass to use a site, though a guest pass is issued if necessary. If you wish to camp on private property, ask the owner for permission.

Is there a camp site near here?	**Er der en campingplads i nærheden?**	ehr dehr ehn **kam**pingplas ee **nær**hēdhern
Can we camp here?	**Kan vi kampere her?**	kan vee kamp**ē**rer hehr
Do you have room for a tent/caravan (trailer)?	**Har I plads til et telt/en campingvogn?**	har ee plas til eht tehlt/ehn **kam**pingvoan
What's the charge ...?	**Hvad koster det ...?**	vadh **kos**derr DE
per day	**pr. dag**	pehr dai
per person	**pr. person**	pehr pehr**soan**
for a car	**for en bil**	for ehn beel
for a tent	**for et telt**	for eht tehlt
for a caravan (trailer)	**for en campingvogn**	for ehn **kam**pingvoan
Is there/Are there (a) ...?	**Er der .../Findes der ...**	ehr dehr/**finners** dehr
drinking water	**drikkevand**	**drigger**van
electricity	**elektricitet**	ehlehktrisi**teht**
playground	**en legeplads**	ehn **ligher**plas
restaurant	**en restaurant**	ehn resto**arang**
shopping facilities	**indkøbsmuligheder**	inkøbsmoolihehdher
swimming pool	**et svømmebasin**	eht **svøm**merbassæng
Where are the showers/toilets?	**Hvor er bruserne/toiletterne?**	vōar ehr **brōō**serner/toa**leht**terner
Where can I get butane gas?	**Hvor kan jeg få flaskegas?**	vōar kan yigh faw **flask**ergas
Is there a youth hostel near here?	**Findes der et vandrehjem i nærheden?**	**finners** dehr eht **vand**rerjehm ee **nær**hēdhern

<table>
<tr><td>CAMPING FORBUDT
NO CAMPING</td><td>CAMPINGVOGNE FRAEBEDES
NO CARAVANS (TRAILERS)</td></tr>
</table>

CAMPING EQUIPMENT, see page 106

Camping

Eating out

Denmark offers a wide choice of eating and drinking establishments.

Bar-Pub
(bar-pōōb)

For drinks and cold meals almost round the clock (closed only between 2 and 5 in the morning). Many bars have imaginative décors from naval interiors to futuristic motifs. Most pubs are youth-oriented.

Bodega-Værtshus
(bodĒga **værtshshōōss**)

A more attractive and relaxed form of snack bar, these establishments serve drinks and a choice of perhaps a dozen simple meals. You'll find them even in smaller towns.

Café
(kahfāȳ)

Informal restaurant serving drinks and hot and cold meals. Popular with students and would-be intellectuals.

Cafeteria
(kahfertāȳreeah)

Food and drinks, often on a self-service basis. You will find cafeterias in department stores and large supermarkets. Hard liquor may not be served, but beer is generally available.

Kaffebar
(**kah**ferbahr)

Neighbourhood restaurant (sometimes a little down-at-heel) serving coffee, tea, drinks and light meals.

Pølsevogn
(**purl**sservoan)

A street-stand selling hot-dogs.

Konditori
(koandeetoa**ree**)

Pastry shops often serve coffee, tea or even a rich ice-cream dessert. If yours is a sweet tooth, this is the place to sample the best of Danish pastry.

Kro
(krōa)

A country inn, serving drinks and full meals, often having their own *kroplatte* (**kro**aplahder) as a speciality. Many are charming and romantically rustic—but, usually, the more attractive the décor the higher the prices!

Restaurant
(raystoa**rahng**)

The major cities offer a large choice of restaurants serving Danish specialities. The menu displayed outside the entrance will list the daily special *dagens ret* (**dai**ernss rayt), as well as à la carte items.

Eating habits *Sisevaner*

Denmark is known as *Nordens spisekammer*, the larder of the North, with its vast farmland. Don't turn down an invitation for a "cup of coffee" in the country: it will probably be served on a large table filled with exquisite homemade pastries. Another eye-opener will await you if you are invited to a copious Danish *koldt bord* (see page 44).

Lunch is secondary, often a cold meal—but hardly light. It might consist of *smørrebrød* (**smørr**erbrødh) (filling open-faced sandwiches—see page 42) with a glass of milk or beer. Alternatively, lunch might call for *en platte* (ehn **plad**er), a cold plate made up of six to eight Danish specialities—such as herring, fish fillet, liver paste, ham, Danish salami, possibly a rissole, a slice of beef, and cheese, all eaten with bread and butter.

Dinner, consisting of two or three substantial courses, is the main meal of the day. Soup or a cold fish dish is followed by a main course of meat, vegetables, and, inevitably, potatoes; then ice cream, doughnuts, cheese, or some *rødgrød* (**rørd**grørdh), a soft fruit jelly.

Many restaurants serve both Danish dishes and international cuisine. All over the country—sometimes on small islands or remote towns—you'll find Chinese and Japanese restaurants.

Meal times *Måltider*

Breakfast (*morgenmad*—m$\overline{o}$aernmahdh) is usually served from 7 or 8 a.m. to 10 a.m. and is usually included in the hotel arrangement.

Lunch (*frokost*—**froa**koast) is generally served from noon until 2 p.m.

Dinner (*middag*—**mid**ai) is flexible. The Danes normally have their evening meal between 6 and 8 p.m., but restaurants in all large towns serve food until late at night.

Danish cuisine *Dansk køkken*

Danish food is rightfully world-famous for its variety and rich-ness, more so than in other Scandinavian countries because of its lavish supply of dairy products and meats. Traditional dishes are enjoying a renaissance and although there is no shortage of healthy foods like yoghurt and skimmed milk and an emphasis on fresh salads, the national dish of roast pork with hot red cab-bage and browned potatoes (*brunede kartoffler*) with thick brown gravy, followed by a layer cake overflowing with whipped cream, is easily found.

Most food familiar to Anglo-Saxon tastes is available, and Danish pastries (*Wienerbrød*) are only one variety on the groaning shelves of the many patisseries (*konditori*). There are various types of delicious hard ryebreads and white (*fransk*) breads, rolls, rusks and biscuits.

Hvad ønsker De?	What would you like?
Jeg kan anbefale det her.	I recommend this.
Hvad ønsker De at drikke?	What would you like to drink?
Vi har ikke ...	We don't have ...
Ønsker De ...?	Would you like ...?

Hungry? *Sulten?*

I'm hungry/I'm thirsty.	**Jeg er sulten/jeg er tørstig.**	yigh ehr **soo**ldern/yigh ehr **tørs**dee
Can you recommend a good restaurant?	**Kan De anbefale en god restaurant?**	kan dee **an**berfåler en goadh rehstoa**rang**
Are there any inexpensive restau-rants around here?	**Er der nogle billige restauranter her i nærheden?**	ehr dehr **noa**ler **bee**leeer rehstoa**rang**err hehr ee **nær**hēdhern

If you want to be sure of getting a table in a well-known res-taurant, it may be better to book in advance.

I'd like to reserve a table for 4.	**Jeg vil gerne bestille et bord til 4.**	yigh veel **gehr**ner ber**stil**er eht boar til **feer**er

36

We'll come at 8.	**Vi kommer klokken 8.**	vee **ko**merr **klo**ggern **oa**der
Could we have a table ...?	**Kan vi få et bord ...?**	kan vee faw eht boar
in the corner	**i hjørnet**	ee **yör**nerdh
by the window	**ved vinduet**	vehdh **veen**dooerdh
outside	**udenfor**	**oo**dhernfor
on the terrace	**på terrassen**	paw tehr**ra**sern
in a non-smoking area	**for ikke-rygere**	for **ig**ger-**re**werrerr

Asking and ordering *Spørgsmål og bestilling*

Waiter/Waitress!	**Tjener/Frøken!**	**tyeh**nerr/**frö**gern
I'd like something to eat/drink.	**Jeg vil gerne have noget at spise/drikke.**	yigh veel **gehr**ner ha **noa**ert ah **spee**ser/**drig**ger
May I have the menu, please?	**Må jeg bede om spisekortet?**	maw yigh bɛ om **spee**serkorderdh
Do you have a set menu/local dishes?	**Er der en dagens ret/nogle lokale retter?**	ehr dehr ehn **daer**ns reht/loakaler **reh**derr
What do you recommend?	**Hvad kan De anbefale?**	vadh kan dee **an**berfåler
Do you have anything ready quickly?	**Har De noget, der er færdigt hurtigt?**	har dee **noa**ert dehr ehr **fær**deet **hoor**teet
I'm in a hurry.	**Jeg har travlt.**	yigh har trowlt
I'd like ...	**Jeg vil gerne have ...**	yigh veel **gehr**ner ha
Could we have a/an ..., please?	**Kan vi få ....**	kan vee faw
ashtray	**et askebæger**	eht **as**gerbæer
cup	**en kop**	ehn kop
fork	**en gaffel**	ehn **ga**ferl
glass	**et glas**	eht glas
knife	**en kniv**	ehn kneev
napkin (serviette)	**en serviet**	ehn sehrvee**eht**
plate	**en tallerken**	ehn ta**lehr**kern
spoon	**en ske**	ehn skɛ
May I have some ...?	**Må jeg bede om ...**	maw yigh bɛ om
bread	**noget brød**	**noa**ert brødh

butter	**noget smør**	noaert smør
lemon	**noget citron**	noaert seetroan
oil	**noget spiseolie**	noaert speeseroalyer
pepper	**noget peber**	noaert peber
salt	**noget salt**	noaert salt
sugar	**noget sukker**	noaert sooggerr
vinegar	**noget eddike**	noaert ehdhigger

Special diet *Særlig diæt*

Many eating places in Denmark serve food for diabetics—look
out for a smiling chef sign saying *Diabetes mad—sund mad for
alle.*

I'm on a diet.	**Jeg er på diæt.**	yigh ehr paw deeæt
I'm vegetarian.	**Jeg er vegetar.**	yigh ehr vehgeh**tar**
I don't drink alcohol.	**Jeg drikker ikke alkohol.**	yigh **drigg**err **igg**er **al**kohol
I mustn't eat food containing ...	**Jeg må ikke spise mad, der indeholder ...**	yigh maw **igg**er speeser madh dehr **in**erholerr
flour/fat	**mel/fedtstoffer**	mehl/fɛtstofferr
salt/sugar	**salt/sukker**	salt/**soogg**er
Do you have ... for diabetics?	**Er der noget ... for diabetikere?**	ehr dehr noaert ... for deeabētikerrer
cakes	**kager**	**kā**er
fruit juice	**frugtsaft**	**froogt**saft
a special menu	**en særlig menu**	ehn **sær**lee mɛnew
Do you have any vegetarian dishes?	**Er der nogle vegetariske retter?**	ehr dehr noaler vehgeh**tar**isger **rehd**err
Could I have cheese/ fruit instead of dessert?	**Kan jeg få noget ost/frugt i stedet for en dessert?**	kan yigh faw noaert ost/froogt i **stehd**herdh for ehn deh**sehrt**
Can I have an artificial sweetener?	**Må jeg få et sødemiddel?**	maw yigh faw eht **sød**hermeedherl
I'd like some more.	**Jeg vil gerne have lidt mere.**	yigh veel **gehr**ner ha leet **mehr**er
Can I have more ..., please?	**Må jeg bede om noget mere ...?**	maw yigh bɛ om noaert **mehr**er
Just a small portion.	**Kun en lille portion.**	koon ehn **leel**er por**shon**
Nothing more, thanks.	**Ikke mere, tak.**	**igg**er **mehr**er tak

What's on the menu? *Hvad er der på spisekortet?*

Most restaurants display their menu (*spisekortet*) outside. A recent innovation in restaurants is the *dagens måltid*, the meal of the day, which offers an excellent value two-course meal.

Under the headings below, you'll find alphabetical lists of dishes that might be offered on a Danish menu with their English equivalent. You can simply show the book to the waiter. If you want some fruit, for instance, let *him* point to what's available on the appropriate list. Use pages 36 and 37 for ordering in general.

	page	
Breakfast	40	**Morgenmad**
Starters (Appetizers)	41	**Forretter**
Open sandwiches	42	**Smørrebrød**
Salads	43	**Salater**
Egg dishes	43	**Ægretter**
Smörgåsbord	44	**Koldt bord**
Soups and stews	44	**Suppe- og labskovsretter**
Fish and seafood	45	**Fisk og skaldyr**
Meat	47	**Kød**
Game and poultry	49	**Vildt og fjerkræ**
Potatoes	50	**Kartofler**
Vegetables and noodles	51	**Grøntsager og nudler**
Sauces and garnishes	52	**Sovse og garnering**
Herbs and spices	53	**Urter og krydderier**
Cheese	54	**Ost**
Fruit and nuts	55	**Frugt og nødder**
Desserts—Pastries	56	**Desserter—Bagværk**
Drinks	57	**Drikkevarer**
Nonalcoholic drinks	60	**Alkoholfrie drikkevarer**
Snacks—Picnic	63	**Mellemmåltider—Medbragt mad**

Reading the menu *Læsning af spisekortet*

Dagens ret/suppe/grønsager	Dish/soup/vegetables of the day
Dagens måltid	Meal of the day
Børnemenu	Children's menu
Vegetar	Vegetarian
Køkkenchefen anbefaler ...	The chef recommends ...
Husets specialiteter	Specialities of the house
Serveres med ...	Served with ...
Vælg mellem ...	Choice of ...

ægretter	**æg**rehderr	egg dishes
burgers	"burgers"	burgers
desserter	dehs**sehrd**err	desserts
drikkevarer	driggervarerr	beverages
fisk	fisk	fish
fjerkræ	fyehrkræ	poultry
forretter	forrehderr	appetizers
forretter	forrehderr	entrees
frugt	froogt	fruit
grøntsager	grønsaer	vegetables
is	is	ice cream
kartofler	kar**tof**lerr	potatoes
kød	kødh	meat
koldt bord	kol bordh	smörgåsbord
kylling	kewling	chicken
nudler	**nood**lerr	noodles
øl	øl	beer
ost	oast	cheese
pasta	pasta	pasta
salater	sa**lād**err	salads
skaldyr	**skal**dewr	seafood
småretter	**smaw**rehderr	snacks
smørrebrød	**smør**erbrødh	open sandwich
supper	**soob**berr	soups
vildt	veelt	game
vin	vēēn	wine
vinliste	**vēēn**lisder	wine list

Breakfast *Morgenmad*

Danish breakfasts are hearty and filling. Bread rolls, meat, cheese, jam, pastries and perhaps an egg are accompanied by a glass of milk or fruit juice, followed by tea or coffee.

I'd like breakfast, please.	**Jeg vil gerne have morgenmad.**	yigh veel **gehr**ner ha **moår**rernmadh
I'll have a/an/ some ...	**Jeg vil gerne have ...**	yigh veel **gehr**ner ha
bacon and eggs	**bacon og æg**	"bacon" oa æg
boiled egg	**et æg**	eht æg
soft/hard	**blødkogt/ hårdkogt**	**blødh**koat/**hawr**koat
cereal	**cornflakes**	"cornflakes"
eggs	**æg**	æg
fried eggs	**spejlæg**	**spighl**æg
scrambled eggs	**røræg**	**rør**æg
poached eggs	**pocheret æg**	posh**Er**erdh æg
fruit juice	**juice**	"juice"
grapefruit	**grapefrugt**	"grape"froogt
orange	**appelsin**	aberl**seen**
ham and eggs	**skinke og æg**	**skeen**ger oa æg
jam	**syltetøj/marmelade**	**sew**ldertoi/marmer**lådh**er
marmalade	**appelsinmarmelade**	aberl**seen**marmerlådher
omelet	**en omelet**	ehn oamerl**eht**
pancakes	**pandekager**	**pahn**erkaaerr
porridge	**havregrød**	**howr**ergrudh
sausages	**pølser**	**purl**sserr
toast	**ristet brød**	**rees**terdh brødh
yoghurt	**yoghurt**	"yoghurt"
May I have some ...?	**Må jeg bede om ...?**	maw yigh bE om
bread	**brød**	brødh
butter	**smør**	smør
(hot) chocolate	**(varm) chokolade**	(varm) shoakoa**ladh**er
coffee	**noget kaffe**	**kaf**er
decaffeinated	**kaffeinfri**	kaffe**een**free
black/with milk	**sort/med mælk**	soart/mehdh mælk
honey	**honning**	**hon**ning
(cold/hot) milk	**(kold/varm) mælk**	(kol/varm) mælk
rolls	**rundstykker**	**roon**stewggerr
tea	**te**	teh
with milk/lemon	**med mælk/citron**	mehdh mælk/see**troan**
(hot) water	**(varmt) vand**	(varmt) van

Starters (Appetizers) *Forretter*

When you are out eating in a Danish home, it is customary to thank the hostess for the meal by saying, *Tak for mad* (tæk foar madh), to which she will reply *Velbekomme* (vElber**koam**er), which means I hope you enjoyed the meal.

When ordering à la carte, Danes generally begin with one of the many tasty starters, whereas set menus often include none.

I'd like an appetizer.	**Jeg vil gerne have en forrett.**	yigh veel **gehr**ner ha ehn **for**redh
What would you recommend?	**Hvad kan De anbefale?**	vadh kan dee **an**berfäler
agurk	a**goork**	cucumbers
ansjoser	an**shoa**serr	anchovies
artiskokker	artee**skog**gerr	artichokes
aspargeshoveder	a**spars**ho°°erderr	asparagus tips
blandet hors d'oeuvre	**blan**erdh "hors d'oeuvre"	assorted appetizers
bøftartar	**bøf**tartar	beef tartare
champignons	sham**pin**yon	mushrooms
frugtsaft	**froogt**saft	fruit juice
ananas	**an**anas	pineapple
appelsin	aberl**seen**	orange
grapefrugt	"grape"**froogt**	grapefruit
tomat	toa**mat**	tomato
fyldte tomater	**fewl**der toa**mad**err	stuffed tomatoes
gåselever	**gåws**erleh°°er	goose liver
hummer	**hoom**err	lobster
kaviar	**kav**eear	caviar
krabbekød	**krab**erkødh	crab
laks	laks	salmon
røget	**roi**erdh	smoked
gravet	**grav**erdh	cured
makrel	ma**krehl**	mackerel
marineret	maree**nē**rerdh	marinated
røget	**roi**erdh	smoked
muslinger	**moos**lingerr	mussels
oliven (fyldte)	oa**lee**vern (**fewl**der)	olives (stuffed)
radiser	rad**ee**serr	radishes
rejer	**righ**err	shrimps
rogn	roan	roe
rollmops	**rol**mops	rollmops
saltkød	**salt**kødh	salt beef slices
sild med løg	seel mehdh loi	herring with onion

sildesalat	seelersalät	herring salad
spegepølse	spigherpølser	salami
salat	salät	salad
sardiner	sardeenerr	sardines
sild	seel	herring
røget	roierdh	smoked
i lage	ee läer	soused
marineret	mahreenErerdh	marinated
skinke	skeenger	ham
tunfisk	toonfisk	tuna (tunny)
vandmelon	vanmehlon	watermelon
æg	æg	egg
hårdkogt	hawrkoat	hard-boiled
østers	ösders	oysters
ål	awl	eel
i gelé	ee shehlE	jellied
røget	roierdh	smoked

Open sandwiches *Smørrebrød*

Smørrebrød (**smør**erbrødh) literally means "buttered bread". But what an understatement! Essentially, *smørrebrød* is a large buttered open-faced sandwich generously covered with one of a variety of delicacies: veal, beef tartare, fried liver, liver paste, salmon, smoked eel, cod-roe, caviar, shrimp, herring, ham, roast beef, salad or cheese. This main layer is garnished with a variety of accessories carefully selected to emphasize taste and appearance. The entire two-storey-high *smørrebrød* presented to you tastes as delightful as it looks.

Larger restaurants have a menu of *smørrebrød* items, often with an English translation. All you have to do is to tick off each item you want, giving your choice of bread too:

franskbrød	franskbrødh	white bread
fuldkornsbrød	foolkoarnsbrødh	wholemeal
pumpernikkel-brød	poompernniggerl-brødh	black bread
rugbrød	roobrødh	rye bread

Smørrebrød is often accompanied by *snaps* (see page 58), and may be the first course of a full-course meal.

I'd like an open sandwich.	**Jeg vil gerne have en smørrebrød.**	yigh veel gehrner ha en smørerbrødh

Salads *Salater*

What salads do you have?	**Hvad slags salater har De?**	vad slagss salaterr har dE

agurksalat (ah**goork**salåt)	cucumber in vinegar dressing	
kyllingesalat (kewleengersalàt)	chicken meat, macaroni, tomato slices, green peppers, olives, green peas, lettuce and mushrooms, covered with a tomato dressing	
rødbeder (rødhbehdherr)	beetroot and diced apples in a mild dressing, possibly with horseradish	
sellerisalat (sehlerreessalåt)	celery salad with a cheese dressing or mayonnaise	

The following preparations, though styled "salads", are mainly eaten on *smørrebrød* or as appetizers:

italiensk salat (eetåleeEnsk salåt)	diced carrots and asparagus, green peas, macaroni and mayonnaise	
makrelsalat (mah**krel**salåt)	mackerel (not always smoked) in tomato sauce topped with mayonnaise	
sildesalat (seelersalåt)	marinated or pickled herring, beetroot, apple and pickles in a spicy dressing	

Egg dishes *Ægretter*

The Danes are very fond of eggs. Omelets, offered in great variety, also include the rather unusual *dessert-omelet* (deh**ssErt**-oamerlet) with jam.

I'd like a/an ...	**Jeg vil gerne have ...**	yigh veel **gehr**ner ha

et kogt æg	eht koat ehg	boiled egg
blødkogt	**blødh**koat	soft
smilende	**smee**lerner	medium
hårdkogt	**hawr**koat	hard
pocheret	poash**E**rert	poached
en omelet	ehn oamer**leht**	omelet
med champignons	mEdh **sham**peenyoan	mushroom
med ost	mEdh oast	cheese
med skinke	mEdh **skeen**ker	ham
med kyllingelever	mEdh **kew**leengerleh°°err	chicken-liver
med sukker og syltetøj	mEdh **soog**gerr oa **sewl**tertoi	sugar and jam
røræg	**rør**ceg	scrambled eggs
spejlæg	**spigh**lehg	fried eggs

æggekage (**æger**käer)	"egg cake": scrambled eggs with onions, chives, potatoes and bacon bits	
skidne æg (**skeedh**ner æg)	poached or hard-boiled eggs in a cream sauce, spiced with fish, mustard and served with rye bread, decorated with diced bacon and chives	

Smörgåsbord *Koldt bord*

The Swedish name, *smörgåsbord* ("sandwich table"), is better known than its Danish equivalent, *koldt bord* ("cold table"). Some larger restaurants specialize in this bountiful self-service buffet and in Danish homes a more modest version is prepared for special occasions.

Start at one end of the table, with herring, seafood, salads and other titbits, and return as many times as you like. In addition to fish dishes there will be a good selection of cold cuts, meat, liver paste and ham. Despite its name, *koldt bord* always includes a few hot items, including meatballs, pork sausages, soup and fried potatoes.

Aquavit and beer go particularly well with this spread. It is rare to drink wine with *koldt bord*.

Soups and stews *Suppe- og labskovsretter*

I'd like some soup.	**Jeg vil gerne have en suppe.**	yigh veel **gehr**ner ha en **soob**ber
aspargessuppe	ah**sparss**soobber	asparagus soup
champignonsuppe	sham**peen**yoan-soobber	mushroom soup
gule ærter	**goo**ler **ær**derr	split-pea soup with salt pork
hummersuppe	**hoo**mersoobber	lobster chowder
hønsekødsuppe	**høn**serkødhsoobber	chicken and vegetable soup
klar suppe med boller og grønsager	klär **soob**eer mehdh **bol**err oa **grøn**saer	vegetable soup with meatballs
æblesuppe	**æb**lersoobber	apple soup
ægte skildpaddesuppe	**æg**der **skeel**padhersoobber	turtle soup
frugtsuppe (**froogt**soobber)	"fruit soup", composed of a variety of dried fruits, served chilled or hot.	

labskoves (labsko°°s)	beef, diced potatoes, slices of carrots and onions, served with rye bread	
kråsesuppe (krāwsersoobber)	a sweet-sour chicken giblets soup, often with dried apples	
øllebrød (ōlerbrødh)	rye bread cooked with Danish beer (*hvidtøl*), sugar and lemon, served with milk and cream	

Fish and seafood *Fisk og skaldyr*

Fish is readily available everywhere. You can often watch the catch being brought in and, if you're cooking your own meals, buy in provisions from the fresh-fish market.

I'd like some fish.	**Jeg vil gerne have fisk.**	yigh veel **gehr**ner ha fisk
What kind of seafood do you have?	**Hvad slags skaldyr har De?**	vadh slags **skal**dewr har dee
aborre	ah**bor**er	perch
ansjoser	an**shōa**serr	anchovies
blåmuslinger	**blaw**mooslinger	mussels
forel	foa**rehl**	trout
gedde	**gehdh**er	pike
helleflynder	**hehl**erflewnerr	halibut
hummer	**hoom**err	lobster
karpe	**kar**per	carp
krebs	krehbs	crab
laks	laks	salmon
makrel	ma**krehl**	mackerel
pigvarre	**pig**var	turbot
rejer	**righ**err	shrimps
rødspætte	**rødh**spæder	plaice
røget sild	**roi**erdh seel	smoked herring
rogn	roan	roe
sardiner	sar**deen**err	sardine
sild	seel	herring
skrubbe	**skroob**ber	flounder
store rejer	**stoa**rer **righ**err	prawns
søtunge	**sø**toonger	sole
stør	stør	sturgeon
torsk	torsk	cod
tunfisk	**toon**fisk	tuna
ål	awl	eel
ørred	**ør**erdh	trout
østers	**øsd**ers	oysters

baked	**bagt**	bagt
fried	**stegt**	stehgt
grilled	**grillet**	**greel**erdh
marinated	**marineret**	mareen**ē**rerdh
poached	**pocheret**	posh**Ē**rerdh
sautéed	**sauteret**	sawt**Ē**rerdh
smoked	**røget**	**roi**erdh
steamed	**dampkogt**	**damp**kogt

Some fish specialities *Nogle særlige fiskeretter*

blå foreller
(blaw foa**rehl**err)
poached trout, served with boiled potatoes, melted butter, horseradish and lemon

rødspætte, stegt
(**rødh**spæder stehgt)
fried plaice served with boiled potatoes and either a parsley sauce or a mustard and herb cream dressing

rødspætter surprise
(**rødh**spæderr sewr**prees**)
"plaice surprise", fried or baked and stuffed with spinach, shrimps and asparagus tips

sild i karry
(seel ee **kā**ree)
herring with curry sauce, served with rice, leeks and dark bread

sild, røget
(seel **roi**erdh)
smoked herring on dark rye bread, garnished with a raw egg yolk, radishes and chives

torsk, kogt
(torsk kogt)
poached cod served with boiled potatoes and a mustard sauce

torskerogn, ristet
(**torsg**erroan **rees**terdh)
fried cod-roe, cold or warm, served with a mustard and herb cream dressing or potato salad

vinkogt laks med pikant sovs
(**vēēn**kogt laks mehdh **peek**ant so°°s)
salmon poached in white wine, dressed with a spicy sauce and served with salad and potatoes

ålesuppe
(**awl**ersoobber)
sweet-and-sour eel soup, with apples and prunes, served with dark rye bread

ål, stegt med stuvede kartofler
(awl stehgt mehdh **stoov**erdher kartoflerr)
fried eel with diced potatoes in a white sauce

Meat *Kød*

Danish bacon and ham are world famous, and pork is in fact the Danes' favourite meat.

beef	**oksekød**	**oks**erkødh	beef
lamb	**lammekød**	**lam**erkødh	lamb
pork	**svinekød**	**svee**nerkødh	pork
veal	**kalvekød**	**kalv**erkødh	veal

I'd like some …	**Jeg vil gerne have noget …/nogle …**	yigh veel **geh**rner ha **noa**ert …/**noa**ler	
bacon	"bacon"	bacon
bedekød	**bedh**erkødh	mutton
blodpølse	**bloadh**pølser	black pudding
brisler	**brees**lerr	sweetbreads
dyreryg	**dewr**erewg	saddle
escalope	"escalope"	escalope
frikadeller	freeka**dehl**err	meatballs
grisehoved/	**grees**erho°°erdh/	pig's head/
grisetæer	**grees**ertær	trotters
grydesteg	**grewdh**erstigh	pot roast
hamburgerryg	hambor**rewg**	gammon
kanin	ka**neen**	rabbit
kotelet	koader**leht**	chop/cutlet
nyrer	**newr**err	kidneys
oksefilet	**oks**er feelɛ	fillet
oksehale	**oks**er**häl**er	oxtail
oksemørbrad	**oks**er**mør**bradh	tenderloin
oksetyndsteg	**oks**er**tewn**stigh	sirloin
pattegris	**padd**ergrees	suckling pig
pølse	**pøl**ser	sausage
skank	skank	shank
skinke	**skeen**ger	(smoked) ham
kogt	koat	boiled
røget	**roi**erdh	smoked
spækket steg	**spægg**erdh stigh	larded roast
tunge	**toong**er	tongue
bøf (oksekød)	bøf (**oaks**erkødh)	hamburger (beef)
dansk bøf	dansk bøf	minced beef
frikadeller	freeka**dehl**err	rissoles
hakkebøf	**hagg**erbøf	minced beef patties
kalvebrissel	**käl**ver**brees**erl	veal (cutlet)
koldt kød	kolt kødh	cold cuts
kødboller	**kødh**bolerr	meatballs
lam	lam	lamb
lammebryst	**lam**erbrewst	breast
lammebov	**lam**erbo°°	shoulder

lever	**le**verr	liver
medisterpølse	mehdh**ee**sderpølser	pork sausages
oksesteg	**oks**erstigh	roast beef
ragout	ra**goo**	stew
ribbenssteg	**ribe**hnstigh	ribsteak

baked	**bagt**	bagt
barbecued	**stegt på en barbecue**	stehgt paw ehn "barbecue"
baked in grease-proof paper	**ovnstegt i folie**	o°°nstehgt ee **foal**yer
boiled	**kogt**	kogt
braised	**grydestegt**	**grewdh**erstehgt
fried	**stegt**	stehgt
grilled	**grillet**	**gree**lerdh
roast	**ovnstegt**	o°°nstehgt
sautéed	**sauteret**	sawt**ēr**erdh
stewed	**stuvet**	st**oo**erdh
very rare	**rødt**	røt
underdone (rare)	**letstegt**	**leht**stehgt
medium	**medium**	**meh**deeoom
well-done	**gennemstegt**	**gehn**ermstehgt

Some meat specialities *Nogle særlige kødretter*

If you have the opportunity to eat in a country inn, you will certainly find some of the most popular national dishes on the menu.

boller i karry
(**bol**er ee **kā**ree)
meatballs in a curry sauce, accompanied by rice

bøf med løg
(bøf mehdh loi)
minced beef and onions served with gravy, boiled potatoes and cucumbers

engelsk bøf
(**ehng**erlsk bøf)
fillet of beef with onions and boiled potatoes

flæskesteg med svær
(**flæsg**erstigh mehdh svær)
roast pork with crackling, often served with braised red cabbage, gravy and small browned potatoes

forloren skildpadde
(for**loar**ern **skeel**padher)
"mock turtle": a very traditional Danish dish consisting of meat from a calf's head with meatballs and fish balls

frikadeller	rissoles served with sweet-and-sour	
(freeka**dehl**err)	cucumber salad or red cabbage and	
	potatoes	
hamburgerryg	smoked salted saddle of pork, roasted and	
(hambor**rewg**)	served in thin slices with Cumberland sauce	
medisterpølse	spiced pork sausage, served with stewed	
(**mehdh**eesderpølser)	vegetables or sautéed cabbage and potatoes	
sprængt oksebryst	boiled, salted brisket of beef, often served	
(sprængt **okse**brewst)	with stewed cabbage	
æbleflæsk	smoked bacon with onions and sautéed	
(**æb**lerflæsk)	apple rings	

Game and poultry *Vildt og fjerkræ*

Chicken is common on menus. Game such as pheasant and grouse are offered for special occasions or holidays. Christmas calls for duck or turkey, unless family tradition demands roast pork or goose, (*gåsesteg*—**gaws**erstayg).

agerhøne	**āh**erhøner	partridge
and	an	duck
due	**dōō**er	pigeon
dyrekød	**dew**rerkødh	venison
fasan	fa**san**	pheasant
gås	gaws	goose
hare	**hār**er	hare
hareragout	**hār**erragoo	jugged hare
kalkun	kal**kōōn**	turkey
kapun	ka**poon**	capon
krikand	**krik**an	teal
kylling	**kewl**ing	chicken
bryst/ben/vinge	brewst/behn/**ving**er	breast/leg/wing
grillstegt kylling	"grill"stehgt **kewl**ing	barbecued chicken
perlehøne	**pehr**lerhøner	guinea fowl
rype	**rēw**per	grouse
skovsneppe	sko°°snehber	woodcock
ung and	oong an	duckling
vagtel	**vag**derl	quail
rensdyr	**rehns**dewr	reindeer
vildsvin	**veel**sveen	wild boar
and, stegt	roast duck stuffed with chestnuts or apples	
(an stehgt)	and prunes, served with olive or mushroom	
	sauce	
agerhøne	roast partridge served with chips (French	
(**āh**erhøner)	fries), redcurrant jam or apple sauce, and	
	horseradish	

dyreryg med Waldorf-salat (**dewr**errewg mehdh "waldorf" sa**lāt**)	saddle of venison, served with browned potatoes, poached apple halves filled with jam and accompanied by a salad of celery, walnuts and grapes
fasan, farseret (**fa**san far**sēr**erdh)	stuffed pheasant, served with a cream dressing, mushrooms, potatoes and redcurrant jam
gåsebryst, røget (**gaws**erbrewst **roi**erdh)	smoked breast of goose served with vegetables
haresteg med fløde (**hār**erstigh mehdh **flōdh**er)	roast hare, flamed in cognac and cooked in cream, vinegar and onion, served with pastry patties filled with redcurrant jelly, Duchesse potatoes and a salad
kalkunragout (kal**koon** ragoo)	jugged turkey in a sweet-and-sour gravy, served with mashed potatoes or a chestnut purée
kanin i flødepeberrod (ka**neen** ee **flōdh**erpeberroadh)	jugged rabbit in a horseradish cream dressing with roast mushroom and onions
kylling, grillstegt **kewl**ing "grill"stehgt	grilled chicken with green salad or sweet-and-sour cucumber salad and chips (French fries)
kylling med rejer og asparges (**kewl**ing mehdh **righ**er oa ah**spars**)	chicken in an asparagus sauce and garnished with shrimps

Potatoes *Kartofler*

Potatoes are grown extensively in Denmark and are a staple item in the Danish diet. They are prepared in many ways:

bagt	bagt	baked
brunede kartofler	**brōōn**erdher kar**tof**lerr	caramelized potatoes
kogte	**kog**der	boiled
nye kartofler	**new**er kar**tof**lerr	new potatoes
pommes frites	pom frit	chips (French fries)
kartoffel croquettes	kar**tof**erl kro**keh**derr	potato croquettes
kartoffelmos	kar**tof**erlmoas	mashed potatoes
kartoffelmos med æbler	kar**tof**erlmoas mehdh **æb**lerr	mashed potatoes with apple purée
kartoffelsalat	kar**tof**erl sa**lat**	potato salad (hot and cold)
stegte kartofler	**stehg**der kar**tof**lerr	sautéed potatoes

Vegetables and noodles *Grøntsager og nudler*

ærter	**ær**derr	peas
agurk	ah**goork**	cucumber
artiskokker	arteeskoggerr	artichokes
asparges	ah**spars**	asparagus
aubergine	awber**sheēn**	aubergine (eggplant)
avocado	avo**kā**doa	avocado
blandede grøntsager	blanerdher **grøn**saer	mixed vegetables
blomkål	**blom**kawl	cauliflower
bønner	**bøn**err	beans
hvide bønner	**veed**her bønerr	butter beans
grønne bønner	**grø**ner bønerr	green beans
brune bønner	**broō**ner bønerr	kidney beans
broccoli	"broccoli"	broccoli
champignoner	**sham**peenyong	mushrooms
chili	"chili"	chili
courgette	koor**sheht**terr	courgette
fennikel	**feh**neekerl	fennel
græskar	**græs**kar	pumpkin
grønne bønner	**grø**ner bønerr	French beans
gulerødder	**goōl**errødherr	carrots
julesalat	**yoōl**ersalat	endive (chickory)
kål	kawl	cabbage
kartofler	kar**tof**lerr	potatoes
kastanjer	ka**stan**yerr	chestnuts
linser	**lins**err	lentils
løg	loi	onions
majs	mighs	corn
nudler	**nood**lerr	noodles
peberfrugt	**peh**erfroogt	peppers
grøn/rød	grøn/rødh	green/red
porrer	**paw**rerr	leeks
radiser	ra**deē**serr	radishes
rødbeder	rødh**behdh**err	beetroot
roer	**roa**err	beets
rosenkål	**roas**ernkawl	Brussels sprouts
salat	sa**lat**	lettuce
selleri	**seh**lerree	celery
rice	ris	rice
græskar	**græs**kar	squash
majroer/kålrabi	**migh**roaer/kawl**rā**bee	turnips
mandelgræskar	**man**erlgræskar	vegetable marrow
søde kartofler	**sødh**er kar**tof**lerr	sweet potatoes
spinat	spi**nat**	spinach
tomater	toa**ma**derr	tomatoes

Vegetables may be served. . .

boiled	**kogt**	kogt
creamed	**tilberedt med fløde**	tilber**rehdt** mehdh **flōdh**er
diced	**skåret i terninger**	**skawr**erdh..ee **tehrning**er
mashed	**moset**	**mōās**erdh
oven-browned	**ovenstegt**	o°°**nstehgt**
steamed	**dampkogt**	**damp**kogt
stewed	**stuvet**	**stoo**erdh
stuffed	**farceret**	farsĒrerdh

Sauces and garnishes *Sovse og garnering*

Sauces are an important element in Danish cuisine and every dish has its special sauce and accompaniments. Although Danes have become more health conscious, cream still plays a big part in sauces. All the well-known French sauces are used, but there are also many particularly Danish ones.

With meat:

ansjossmør	an**shōās**smør	anchovy butter
bearnaisesovs	bɛar**nehs**so°°s	a cream dressing flavoured with tarragon and vinegar
brun sovs	broon so°°s	traditionally thick and gluey, but still a firm favourite
chutney-smør	"chutney"smør	chutney butter
flødepeberrod	**flōdh**erpeberroadh	horseradish cream dressing
persillesovs	pehr**sil**erso°°s	parsley sauce
remoulade	rehmool**āh**der	mustard and herb cream dressing
rørt smør	rørt smør	cream butter variously flavoured
æggesovs	**æg**erso°°s	egg sauce

Warm preparations:

løgsovs	loiso°°s	onion sauce
kastaniesovs	kastan**yer**so°°s	chestnut sauce, flavoured with madeira

sellerisovs	**sehl**erreeso°°s	celery-flavoured sauce with sherry
sennepssovs	**sehn**erpso°°s	mustard sauce
vildtsovs	**veelt**so°°s	sauce made with fresh cream and redcurrant jam
asier	**ah**sher	cucumbers, marinated in vinegar and sugar
græskar	**græ**skar	vegetable marrow preserved in vinegar, sugar, cloves and cinnamon
pickles	"pickles"	piccalilly
kapers	**kap**errs	capers

With salad, choose between the following dressings:

citronmarinade	see**tro**anmareenädher	lemon, oil, salt and pepper, paprika, herbs
vinaigrette-sovs	veenah**greht**so°°s	vinegar, oil, salt and pepper, mustard, and onions or garlic
ymersovs	ēwmersôs	lemon juice, spices and herbs, mixed with milk, cream or junket
stærk salatsovs (stærk sal**at**sôs)	egg yolks, vinegar or lemon juice, oil, salt and pepper or paprika, Worcester sauce, onion or garlic and dill, all mixed with whipped cream	

With desserts:

appelsinsovs	aberl**seen**so°°s	orange sauce
hvidvinssovs	veedh**veen**so°°s	white-wine sauce
råcreme (**raw**krehm)	"raw cream"—egg, sugar, whipped cream and vanilla, sometimes flavoured with sherry, liqueur or cognac	

Herbs and spices *Urter og krydderier*

anisfrø	**an**eesfrø	aniseed
basilikum	basilikum	basil
blandede urter	**blan**erdher **oord**err	mixed herbs
brøndkarse	**brøn**karser	watercress
dild	deel	dill
estragon	ehstra**gon**	tarragon

hvidløg	veedhloi	garlic
ingefær	ingerfær	ginger
kanel	kanEl	cinnamon
kapers	kaperrs	capers
kommen	komern	cumin
kryddernellike	krewdhernehleeker	clove
laurbærblad	lowerbærbladh	bay leaf
merian	mEreean	marjoram
muskatnød	mooskatnødh	nutmeg
mynte	mewnter	mint
oregano	orehgano	oregano
paprika	papreeka	paprika
peber	peɓerr	pepper
peberrod	peɓerroadh	horseradish
persille	pehrseeler	parsley
purløg	poorloi	chives
rosemarin	roasmareen	rosemary
safran	safran	saffron
salt	salt	salt
salvie	salvēēer	sage
sennep	sehnerp	mustard
skalotteløg	skaloterloi	shallot
spansk peber	spansk peɓerr	pimiento
sylteagurker	sewlderahgoorkerr	gherkins
timian	teemeean	thyme
vanilje	vaneelyer	vanilla

Cheese *Ost*

danablu	Danish blue cheese, rich
("danablu")	
danbo	a mild, firm cheese with holes, sometimes
(danboa)	flavoured with caraway seeds
elbo	a hard cheese with a delicate taste
(ehlboa)	
esrom	a strong, slightly aromatic cheese of spongy
(ehsroma)	texture
maribo	a soft, mild cheese
(mariboa)	
molbo	not unlike Edam; rich and highly flavoured
(molboa)	
mycella	similar to Danish blue cheese, but milder;
(mewsehla)	the veins are greenish-blue
samsø	a mild, firm cheese with a sweet, nutty
(samsø)	flavour

Fruit and nuts *Frugt og nødder*

Do you have any fresh fruit?	**Har De frisk frugt?**	ha dee frisk froogt
I'd like a (fresh) fruit cocktail.	**Jeg vil gerne have en (frisk) frugtsalat.**	yigh veel **gehr**ner ha ehn (frisk) **froogt**salat

abrikoser	abree**koas**err	apricots
ananas	**ananas**	pineapple
blåbær	**blaw**bær	blueberries
blommer	**blom**err	plums
citron	see**troan**	lemon
dadler	**dadh**lerr	dates
en appelsin	ehn aberl**seen**	orange
en banan	ehn ba**nan**	banana
et æble	eht **æb**ler	apple
fersken	**fehrsg**ern	peach
figner	**fee**nerr	figs
grapefrugt	"grape"froogt	grapefruit
hasselnødder	**has**erlnødherr	hazelnuts
hindbær	**heen**bær	raspberries
jordbær	**yoar**bær	strawberries
jordnødder	**yoar**nødherr	peanuts
kastanjer	kas**tan**yerr	cranberries
kirsebær	**keer**serbær	cherries
kokosnød	**koa**koasnødh	coconut
kvæde	**kvæd**her	quince
lime	"lime"	lime
mandarin	manda**reen**	tangerine
mandler	**man**lerr	almonds
melon	meh**loan**	melon
nektarin	nehkta**reen**	nectarine
pære	**pæ**rer	pear
rabarber	ra**barb**err	rhubarb
rosiner	roa**see**nerr	raisins
solbær	**soal**bær	blackcurrants
stikkelsbær	**steeg**gerlsbær	gooseberries
sultanas	**sool**tanas	sultanas
tyttebær	**tewd**erbaer	chestnuts
tørret frugt	**tø**rerdh froogt	dried fruit
valnødder	**val**nødherr	walnuts
vandmelon	**van**mehloan	watermelon
vindruer	**veen**drooer	grapes

Desserts—Pastries *Desserter—Bagværk*

Danish desserts are deservedly famous, with such classics as Danish apple cake, "veiled country maid", mousses and layer cakes. Look out especially for "Othello cake" topped with chocolate, layers of confectioner's custard and jam.

I'd like a dessert, please.	**Jeg vil gerne have en dessert, tak.**	yigh veel **gehr**ner ha en dehs**sehrt** tak
What do you recommend?	**Hvad kan De anbefale?**	vadh kan dee **an**berfäler
Something light, please.	**Noget let.**	n**ōa**ert leht
Just a small portion.	**Bare en lille portion.**	bä ehn **lee**ler por**shon**

fromage	froa**mä**sher	mousse
appelsinfromage	aberl**seen**-froamasher	orange mousse
citronfromage	seetroanfroa**mä**sher	lemon mousse
is	ēēs	ice cream
chokoladeis	shoakoa**ladh**erēēs	chocolate ice cream
jordbæris	yoarbærēēs	strawberry ice cream
kage	**kä**er	cake
flødekage	**flōdh**erkäer	cream cake
lagkage	**low**käer	layer cake
småkager	**smaw**käer	biscuits (cookies)
tørkage	**tør**käer	plain cake
karamelrand	karamehlran	caramel custard
pandekager	**pan**erkäerr	pancakes
små pandekager	smaw **pan**erkäerr	fritters

brune kager (**broo**ner **kä**er)	spicy, thin crisp brown biscuits with almond decoration; a Christmas favourite
rødgrød med fløde (**rødh**grødh mehdh **flødh**er)	fruit jelly served with cream
bondepige med slør (**boan**erpēēer mehdh slør)	"veiled country maid": a mixture of rye-bread crumbs, apple sauce, cream and sugar
æblekage med rasp og flødeskum (**æbler**käer mehdh rasp oa **flødh**erskoom)	stewed apples with vanilla served with alternating layers of biscuit-crumbs and topped with whipped cream

Drinks *Drikkevarer*

Denmark has no strict regulations governing the purchase and consumption of alcoholic beverages, but prices are high. Liquor, in particular, is heavily taxed, so make full use of the duty-free shop if you travel to Denmark by boat or plane.

Beer *Øl*

The Carlsberg and Tuborg breweries are known all over the world. But there are many others producing good, strong beer, so try some of the local brews. *Pilsner* (**pils**nerr) is a light beer, while *lager* is the term used in Denmark to denote a somewhat darker beer. Here are a few you may come across:

Skibsøl	a very dark "ship's beer" noted for its smoked-malt character
Maltøl	a very heavy beer, regarded as a tonic
Mørkt Hvidtøl	a dark, reddish brown beer; sweet and creamy
Lys Hvidtøl	a pale, sweetish, low-alcohol beer

The word "export" on the label usually indicates a beer of higher alcoholic content.

What would you like to drink?	**Hvad ønsker De at drikke?**	vadh **øns**gerr dee ah **drigg**er
I'd like a beer, please.	**Jeg vil gerne have en øl, tak.**	yigh veel **gehr**ner ha ehn øl tak
Have a beer!	**Lad os drikke øl!**	ladh os **drigg**er øl
A bottle of lager, please.	**En pilsner, tak.**	ehn **pils**ner tak
bottled beer	**flaskeøl**	flasgerøl
draught (tap) beer	**fadøl**	fadhøl
foreign brands	**udenlandsk øl**	o͞odhernlansk øl
light/dark beer	**lyst/mørkt øl**	lewst/mørkt øl
A bottle of ...	**En flaske ...**	ehn **flasg**er ...
A glass of ...	**Et glas ...**	eht glas
Half a litre of lager, please.	**Et stort glas øl.**	eht stoart glas øl

Aquavit—Snaps *Akvavit—Snaps*

Along with beer, *akvavit* (ahkva**veet**) or *snaps* (snapss) is the national drink of Denmark. Like vodka, it's distilled from potatoes, though barley is also used. The colour varies according to the herbs and spices with which the drink is flavoured.

Akvavit, often served with a beer chaser, contains about 40% pure alcohol and should be drunk ice-cold from thimble-sized glasses. It makes the perfect accompaniment to appetizers and is often served with *koldt bord*.

Wine *Vin*

Denmark is not a wine-producing country, but imported wines, mostly from France, Italy, Portugal and Spain, are widely available. Wine can be ordered by the bottle, carafe or glass. It is not usual to drink wine with *koldt bord*.

May I have the wine list?	**Må jeg bede om en vinliste?**	maw yigh bɛ om ehn **veen**lisder
I'd like a ... of red wine/white wine.	**Jeg vil gerne have ... rødvin/hvidvin.**	yigh veel **gehr**ner ha ... **rødh**veen/**veedh**veen
a bottle	**en flaske**	ehn **flasg**er
half a bottle	**en halv flaske**	ehn hal **flasg**er
a carafe	**en karaffel**	ehn karafferl
a small carafe	**en lille karaffel**	ehn **leeler** karafferl
a glass	**et glas**	eht glas
How much is a bottle of champagne?	**Hvad koster en flaske champagne?**	vadh **kos**der ehn **flasg**er "champagne"
Bring me another bottle/glass of ..., please.	**Vær rar og bring mig en flaske/et glas ... til.**	vær rar oa bring migh ehn **flasg**er/eht glas ... til
Where does this wine come from?	**Hvor kommer denne vin fra?**	voar **kom**err **dehn**er veen fra

red	**rød**	rødh
white	**hvid**	veedh
rosé	**rose**	roasᴇ
sweet	**sød**	sødh
dry	**tør**	tør
sparkling	**mousserende**	moossᴇ̄rerner
chilled	**afkølet**	owkølerdh
at room temperature	**stuetemperatur**	stoo̅ertemperatoor
Do you have open wine?	**Har De åben vin?**	har dee a̅wbern vee̅n

Other alcoholic drinks *Andre alkoholiske drikkevarer*

You can get almost all the drinks you're used to at home and the Danish and English names for most of them are the same.

After your meal, try the famous cherry liqueur, *Cherry Heering.*

I'd like a/an ...	**Jeg vil gerne have ...**	yigh veel **gehr**ner ha ...
aperitif	**en aperitif**	ehn apehree**teef**
brandy	**en brandy**	ehn "brandy"
fruit-distilled	**frugt-destilleret**	froogt-dehsteelᴇ̄rerdh
apple	**calvados**	kalva**dos**
cherry brandy	**cherry brandy**	"cherry brandy"
cognac	**en cognac**	ehn "cognac"
gin	**en gin**	ehn "gin"
liqueur	**en likør**	ehn lee**kør**
glass of port	**et glas portvin**	eht glas **poart**vee̅n
rum	**en rom**	ehn rom
vermouth	**en vermouth**	ehn **vehr**moot
vodka	**en vodka**	ehn "vodka"
whisky	**en whisky**	ehn "whisky"
neat (straight)	**tør**	tør
on the rocks	**med isterninger**	mehdh ee̅stehrningerr
with a little water	**med lidt vand**	mehdh leet van
with soda water	**med soda**	mehdh **soa**da
Give me a large gin and tonic, please.	**Jeg vil gerne ha en stor gin og tonic, tak.**	yigh veel **gehr**ner ha ehn stoar "gin" oa "tonic" tak.
Just a dash of soda, please.	**Med lidt soda.**	mehdh leet **soa**da

EATING OUT

Nonalcoholic drinks *Alkoholfrie drikkevarer*

Of course, you don't have to order wine or spirits. If you prefer, ask for a soft drink (*en læskedrik*—ehn **læs**gerdrik).

I don't drink alcohol.	**Jeg drikker ikke alkohol.**	yigh **drigg**err **igg**er **al**kohol
A bottle of mineral water, please.	**En flaske mineralvand.**	ehn **flas**ger meeneh**ral**van
apple juice	**æblesaft**	**æbler**saft
fruit juice	**frugtsaft**	**froogt**saft
grapefruit juice	**grapefrugtsaft**	"**grape**"froogtsaft
lemon juice	**citronsaft**	see**troan**saft
lemonade	**limonade**	leemoan**ädh**er
milk	**mælk**	mælk
milkshake	**en milkshake**	ehn "milkshake"
mineral water	**mineralvand**	meeneh**ral**van
fizzy (carbonated)	**dansk vand**	dansk van
still	**(almindelig) mineralvand**	(al**meen**erlee) meeneh**ral**van
orange juice	**appelsinsaft**	aberl**seen**saft
orangeade	**orangeade**	oarang**shädh**er
tomato juice	**tomatjuice**	toa**mat**"juice"
tonic water	**tonicvand**	"tonic"van

Hot beverages *Varme drikke*

The best place to go for your afternoon tea or coffee is a *konditori* (pastry shop), where you can select from a wide choice of delicious Danish pastries.

I'd like a/an ...	**Jeg vil gerne have ...**	yigh veel **gehr**ner ha
(hot) chocolate	**(varm) chokolade**	(varm) shoakoa**ladh**er
coffee	**kaffe**	**kaf**er
a pot	**en kande**	ehn **kan**er
black	**sort**	soart
decaffeinated	**kaffeinfri**	kafer**een**free
with cream	**med fløde**	mehdh **flödh**er
with milk	**med mælk**	mehdh mælk
espresso coffee	**espresso**	espresso
mokka	**mokka**	**mok**ka
tea	**te**	tɛ
cup of tea	**en kop te**	ehn kop tɛ
with milk/lemon	**med mælk/citron**	mehdh mælk/see**troan**
herb tea	**urtete**	o͞orter tɛ
iced tea	**isafkølet te**	e͞esowkölerdh tɛ

Restauranter

Complaints *Klager*

There's a plate/glass missing.	Der mangler en tallerken/et glas.	dehr **mangl**err ehn ta**lehr**kern/eht glas
I don't have a knife/fork/spoon.	Jeg har ikke fået en kniv/gaffel/ske.	yigh har **igg**er **faw**erdh en kneev/**garf**erl/skE
That's not what I ordered.	Det har jeg ikke bestilt.	dE har yigh **igg**er ber**stilt**
I asked for ...	Jeg bad om ...	yigh badh om
There must be some mistake.	Det må være en fejltagelse.	dE maw **vær**er ehn **fighl**täerlser
May I change this?	Kan jeg bytte det her?	kan yigh **bewdh**er dE hehr
I asked for a small portion (for the child).	Jeg bad om en lille portion (til et barn).	yigh badh om ehn **leel**er por**shon** (til eht barn)
The meat is ...	Kødet er ...	**kødh**erdh ehr
overdone	stegt for meget	stehgt for **migh**ert
underdone	stegt for lidt	stehgt for leet
too rare	for rødt	for røt
too tough	for sejt	for sight
This is too ...	Det her er for ...	dE hehr ehr for
bitter/salty/sweet	bittert/salt/sødt	**bid**erdh/salt/søt
I don't like this.	Jeg bryder mig ikke om det her.	yigh **brewdh**err migh **igg**er om dE hehr
The food is cold.	Maden er kold.	**madh**ern ehr kol
This isn't fresh.	Det her er ikke frisk.	dE hehr er **igg**er frisk
What's taking you so long?	Hvorfor tager det så lang tid?	**vor**for tar dE saw lang teedh
Have you forgotten our drinks?	Har De glemt vores drinks?	har dee glehmt **voar**s "drinks"
The wine doesn't taste right.	Vinen smager ikke godt.	**veen**ern **smä**er **igg**er god
This isn't clean.	Det her er ikke rent.	dE hehr ehr **igg**er rehnt
Would you ask the head waiter to come over?	Vil De bede overtjeneren om at komme herhen?	veel dee bE o°°er**tyehn**errern om ah **kom**er hehr**hen**

The bill (check) *Regningen*

Value-added tax and service charge are automatically added to your bill. Danes are not tip-minded, though after a meal out you may want to round off with an extra krone or two for good service.

I'd like to pay.	**Jeg vil gerne betale.**	yigh veel **gehr**ner ber**tāl**er
We'd like to pay separately.	**Vi vil gerne betale hver for sig.**	vee veel **gehr**ner ber**tāl**er vehr for sigh
I think there's a mistake in this bill.	**Der er vist en fejl i denne regning.**	deh ehr vist ehn fighl ee **dehn**er **righn**ning
What's this amount for?	**Hvad dækker dette beløb?**	vadh **dægg**err **dehd**er be**lōb**
Is service included?	**Er service inkluderet?**	ehr "service" inkloo**dĒr**erdh
Is the cover charge included?	**Har man beregnet for kuvert?**	har man ber**righn**erdh for koo**vehrt**
Is everything included?	**Er det hele medregnet?**	ehr dE **heh**ler **mehdh**righnerdh
Do you accept traveller's cheques?	**Tager I imod rejsecheck?**	**tā**er dee ee**moadh righs**er"cheques"
Can I pay with this credit card?	**Kan jeg betale med dette kreditkort?**	kan yigh ber**tāl**er mehdh **dehd**er krehd**it**kort
Please round it up to ...	**Vær venlig og rund det op til ...**	vær **vehn**lee oa roon dE op til
Keep the change.	**Behold byttepengene.**	ber**hol bewd**erpehngerner
That was delicious.	**Det smagte dejligt.**	dE **smag**der **digh**leet
We enjoyed it, thank you.	**Vi har nydt det.**	vee har newt dE

BETJENING INKLUDERET
SERVICE INCLUDED

TIPPING, see inside back-cover

Snacks—Picnic *Mellemmåltider—Medbragt mad*

You can buy small items at cafés, grocery shops, butchers and bakers, and in towns the *pølsevogn* (literally "sausage cars") sell excellent frankfurters in rolls with a handy paper serviette.

Give me two of these and one of those.	**Lad mig få to af dem her og en af dem der.**	ladh migh faw toa ah dehm hehr oa ehn ah dehm dehr
to the left/right above/below	**til venstre/højre ovenover/ nedenunder**	til **vehn**strer/**hoi**rer o°°ern o°°err/**nehdh**ern oonerr
It's to take away.	**Jeg tager det med mig.**	yigh tar dE mehdh migh
I'd like a piece of cake.	**Jeg vil gerne have et stykke kage.**	yigh veel **gehr**ner ha eht **stewg**ger **kā**er
fried sausage	**en grillstegt pølse**	ehn "grill"**stehgt pøl**ser
omelet	**en omelet**	ehn **oam**leht
open sandwich	**et stykke smørrebrød**	eht **stewg**ger **smør**erbrødh
with ham	**med skinke**	mehdh **skeeng**er
with cheese	**med ost**	mehdh ost
potato salad	**kartoffelsalat**	kartoferl **sa**lat
sandwich	**en sandwich**	ehn "sandwich"

Here's a basic list of food and drink that might come in useful when shopping for a picnic.

I'd like a/an/some …	**Jeg vil gerne have …**	yigh veel **gehr**ner ha
apples	**nogle æbler**	n$\overline{oa}$ler **æb**lerr
bananas	**nogle bananer**	n$\overline{oa}$ler ba**na**nerr
biscuits (Br.)	**nogle kiks**	n$\overline{oa}$ler kiks
beer	**en øl**	ehn øl
bread	**noget brød**	n$\overline{oa}$ert brødh
rye bread	**rugbrød**	**roo**brødh
white bread	**franskbrød**	**frans**brødh
butter	**lidt smør**	leet smør
cheese	**noget ost**	n$\overline{oa}$ert oast
chips (Am.)	**nogle pommes frites**	n$\overline{oa}$ler pom frit

chocolate bar	**en plade chokolade**	ehn **plå**dher shoakoa**ladh**er
coffee	**noget kaffe**	n**ōā**ert **kaf**er
cold cuts	**noget afskåret pålæg**	n**ōā**ert **ows**kawrerdh **paw**læg
cookies	**nogle småkager**	n**ōā**ler **smaw**kåerr
crisps	**nogle franske kartofler**	n**ōā**ler **frans**ger kar**tof**lerr
eggs	**nogle æg**	n**ōā**ler æg
gherkins (pickles)	**nogle syltede agurker**	n**ōā**ler **sewld**erdher ah**goor**kerr
grapes	**nogle druer**	n**ōā**ler dr**ōō**er
ham	**skinke**	**skeeng**er
ice cream	**noget is**	n**ōā**ert **ēē**s
margarine	**margarine**	marga**reen**er
milk	**noget mælk**	n**ōā**ert mælk
mustard	**noget sennep**	n**ōā**ert **sehn**erp
oranges	**nogle appelsiner**	n**ōā**ler aberl**seen**err
pepper	**noget peber**	n**ōā**ert **peb**er
roll	**et rundstykke**	eht **roon**stewgger
salt	**noget salt**	n**ōā**ert salt
sausage	**en pølse**	ehn **pøl**ser
soft drink	**en læskedrik**	ehn **læs**gerdrik
sugar	**noget sukker**	n**ōā**ert **soog**gerr
tea bags	**nogle tebreve**	n**ōā**ler t**ē**breh°°er
yoghurt	**en yoghurt**	ehn "yoghurt"
buns	**boller**	**bol**err

And for something sweet, take along a Danish pastry (*Wienerbrød*—**veen**erbrødh), or perhaps one of the following:

custard slice with jam and cream	**Napoleonskage**	napoal**Eon**skåer
Danish doughnuts	**æbleskiver**	**æb**lersk**ēē**verr
marzipan cakes	**kransekager**	**kran**serkåerr
meringues	**marengs**	ma**rehngs**

Travelling around

Plane / *fly*

Is there a flight to Rønne?	**Er der et fly til Rønne?**	ehr dehr eht flew til **rø**ner
Is it a direct flight?	**Er det et direkte fly?**	ehr dE eht **di**rehkter flew
When's the next flight to Billund?	**Hvornår afgår det næste fly til Billund?**	vor**nawr ow**gawr dE **næs**der flew til **beel**loon
Is there a connection to Viborg?	**Er der forbindelse til Viborg?**	ehr dehr for**bin**erlser til **vee**bawr
I'd like to book a ticket to Copenhagen.	**Jeg vil gerne bestille en billet til København.**	yigh veel **gehr**ner ber**stil**er ehn bee**lehd** til købern**hown**
single (one-way)	**enkeltbillet**	**ehn**kerld**beelehd̄**
return (round trip)	**returbillet**	reh**toor**beelehd
business class	**business class**	"business class"
aisle seat	**plads ved midtergangen**	plas vehdh **mid**dergangern
window seat	**vinduesplads**	**vin**doosplas
What time do we take off?	**Hvad tid letter flyet?**	vadh teed **lehd**err **flew**erdh
What time should I check in?	**Hvad tid må jeg checke ind?**	vadh teed maw yigh "check"er in
Is there a bus to the airport?	**Kører der en bus til lufthavnen?**	**kø**rerr dehr ehn boos til **looft**hownern
What's the flight number?	**Hvad er flyets nummer?**	vadh ehr **flew**erdhs **noom**mer
What time do we arrive?	**Hvad tid ankommer vi?**	vadh teed **an**komerr vee
I'd like to ... my reservation.	**Jeg vil gerne ... min bestilling.**	yigh veel **gehr**ner ... meen ber**stil**ing
cancel	**annullere**	annool**Er**er
change	**ændre på**	**æn**drer paw
confirm	**bekræfte**	ber**kræf**der

<table>
<tr><td>

ANKOMST
ARRIVAL

</td><td>

AFGANG
DEPARTURE

</td></tr>
</table>

Train *Tog*

Only the main islands and the peninsula of Jutland are served by trains, and the country's geography makes ferry boat necessary for rail connections between Sealand, the main island, and most other parts of Denmark. This introduces a pleasant element of variety into long trips.

Considerable reductions are granted to students, children (free up to four years of age), groups, families and "senior citizens". Trains and ferries have first and second-class, and long-distance night trains have sleeping-cars.

Intercity ("intercity")	long distance express; seat reservation is required when crossing the Great Belt
Lyntog (**lewn**toa)	long-distance express; seat reservation required; supplementary fare
Eksprestog (ayks**prayss**toa)	long-distance train stopping at main stations
Persontog (payr**sōān**toa)	local train stopping at all stations
Sovevogn (so°°ervoan)	sleeping car operated on international trains; individual compartments (single or double) and washing facilities
Liggevogn (**leegg**ervoan)	berth with blankets and pillows (*couchette* on long-distance coaches)
Godsvogn (**goass**voan)	guard's van (baggage car)

To the railway station *Til jernbanestationen*

Where's the railway station?	**Hvor ligger jernbanestationen?**	vōār **leeg**err jehrnbānerstashonern
Taxi!	**Taxa!**	**tak**sa
Take me to the ...	**Kør mig hen til ...**	kør migh hehn til
main railway station	**hovedbanegården**	ho°°verdhbanergawern
What's the fare?	**Hvad koster billetten?**	vadh **kosd**err bee**lehd**ern

INDGANG	ENTRANCE
UDGANG	EXIT
TIL PERRONERNE	TO THE PLATFORMS
INFORMATION	INFORMATION

Where's the ...? *Hvor er ...?*

Where is/are (the) ...?	Hvor er ...?	vo͞ar ehr
bar	baren	bārern
booking office	pladsreserveringen	plasrehsehrvēringern
currency exchange office	valutakontoret	valootakonto͞arert
left-luggage office (baggage check)	bagageop-bevaringen	bagāsheropbervāringern
lost property (lost and found) office	hittegodskontoret	heedergoskonto͞arerdh
luggage lockers	bagageboksene	bagāsherbokserner
newsstand	aviskiosken	aveeskiosgern
platform 7	perron 7	pehrong sewv
reservations office	pladsreserveringen	plasrehsehrvēringern
restaurant	restauranten	rehstoarangern
snack bar	snackbaren	snakbārern
ticket office	billetlugen	beelehdloo͞gern
waiting room	venteværelset	vehndervǣrerlserdh
Where are the toilets?	Hvor er toilettet?	vo͞ar ehr toalehderdh

Inquiries *Forespørgsler*

When is the ... train to Århus?	Hvornår kører det ... tog til Århus?	vornawr kȫrerr deht ... tô til awrho͞os
first/last/next	første/sidste/næste	fȫrsder/seesder/næsder
What time does the train to Randers leave?	Hvad tid afgår toget til Randers?	vadh teed owgawr toaerdh til raners
What's the fare to Middelfart?	Hvor meget koster det til Middelfart?	vo͞ar mighert kosderr dε til meedherlfart

TAXI, see page 21

Is it a through train?	**Er det et gennemgående tog?**	ehr dɛ eht **gehn**ermgawerner toa
Is there a connection to …?	**Er der forbindelse til …?**	ehr dehr for**bin**erlser til
Do I have to change trains?	**Skal jeg skifte tog?**	skal yigh **skee**fder toa
Is there enough time to change?	**Har jeg tid nok til at skifte?**	har yigh teed nok til at **skee**fder
Is the train running on time?	**Kører toget rettidigt?**	**kø**rerr **toa**erdh **reht**teedheet
What time does the train arrive in Roskilde?	**Hvad tid ankommer toget til Roskilde?**	vadh teed **an**komerr **toa**erdh til **ros**kiler
Is there a dining car/ sleeping car on the train?	**Er der spisevogn/ sovevogn i toget?**	ehr dehr sp**ee**servoan/ so°°ervoan ee **toa**ert
Does the train stop in Horsens?	**Standser toget i Horsens?**	**stan**serr **toa**erdh ee **hor**serns
Which platform does the train to Ribe leave from?	**På hvilket spor afgår toget til Ribe?**	paw **vil**kerdh spoar **ow**gawr **toa**erdh til **ree**ber
Which platform does the train from Elsinore arrive at?	**På hvilken perron ankommer toget fra Helsingør?**	paw **vil**kern peh**rong** **an**komerr **toa**ert fra **hehl**seengør
I'd like a time-table.	**Jeg vil gerne have en køreplan.**	yigh veel **gehr**ner ha ehn **kø**rerplan

Tickets *Billetter*

I'd like a ticket to Copenhagen.	**Jeg vil gerne have en billet til København.**	yigh veel **gehr**ner ha ehn bee**lehd** til købern**hown**
single (one-way)	**enkelt**	**ehn**kerlt
return (round trip)	**retur**	reh**toor**
first/second class	**første/anden klasse**	**førs**der/**an**ern **kla**ser
half price	**halv pris**	hal prees

De skal skifte i ...	You have to change at ...
Skift i ... og tag et nærtog.	Change at ... and get a local train.
Perron/Spor 7 er ...	Platform 7 is ...
derovre/ovenpå	over there/upstairs
til venstre/til højre	on the left/on the right
Der kører et tog til ... klokken ...	There's a train to ... at ...
Deres tog afgår fra perron 8.	Your train will leave from platform 8.
Det vil blive ... minutter forsinket.	There will be a delay of ... minutes.
Første klasse forrest/i midten/ bagerst	First class at the front/in the middle/at the rear.

Reservation *Billetbestilling*

I'd like to reserve a ...	**Jeg vil gerne bestille en ...**	yigh veel **gehr**ner be**stil**er ehn
seat (by the window)	**siddeplads (ved vinduet)**	**seedh**erplas (vehdh **vin**dooert)
berth	**køje**	**koie**
upper	**overkøje**	**o°°er**koier
middle	**køje i midten**	**koier** ee **midd**ern
lower	**underkøje**	**oon**erkoier
berth in the sleeping car	**køje i sovevognen**	**koier** ee so°°ervoanern

All aboard *Alle i toget*

Is this the right platform for the train to Odense?	**Er det den rigtige perron for toget til Odense?**	ehr dɛ dehn **reeg**teeer peh**rong** for **toa**ert til **oadh**ernsser
Is this the right train to Aarhus?	**Kører det her tog til Århus?**	**kø**rerr dɛ hehr toa til aw**hōōs**
Excuse me. Could I get past?	**Undskyld. Kan jeg komme forbi?**	**oon**skewl. kan yigh **kom**er for**bee**
Is this seat taken?	**Er denne siddeplads taget?**	ehr **dehn**er **seedh**erplas **tä**erdh

RYGERE	IKKE RYGERE
SMOKER	NONSMOKER

I think that's my seat.	**Det er vist min siddeplads.**	dE ehr vist meen **seedh**erplas
Would you let me know before we get to Roskilde?	**Vil De lade mig vide, før vi kommer til Roskilde?**	veel dee **lādh**er migh **vēēdh**er før vee **kom**err til **ros**kiler
What station is this?	**Hvad station er det her?**	vadh sta**shon** ehr dE hehr
How long does the train stop here?	**Hvor længe holder toget her?**	vōar **læng**er **hol**er **toa**erdh hehr
When do we arrive in Kolding?	**Hvornår ankommer vi til Kolding?**	vor**nawr** an**kom**err vee til **kol**ing

Sleeping / sovevognen

Are there any free compartments in the sleeping car?	**Er der nogle ledige kupeer i sovevognen?**	ehr dehr **nōa**ler **lehdh**ēēer koo**peer** ee so°°er**voa**nern
Where's the sleeping car?	**Hvor er sovevognen?**	vōar ehr so°°er**voa**nern
Where's my berth?	**Hvor er min køje?**	vōar ehr meen **koi**er
I'd like a lower berth.	**Jeg vil gerne have en underkøje.**	yigh veel **gehr**ner ha ehn **oon**er**koi**er
Would you make up our berths?	**Vil De gøre vores køjer i stand?**	veel dee **gør**er vors **koi**err ee stan
Would you wake me at 7 o'clock?	**Vil De vække mig klokken 7?**	veel dee **væg**ger migh **klog**gern sewv

Eating *I spisevognen*

There are no dining cars on Danish trains, though snacks can be obtained at the buffet bar on intercity and express trains. Most rail travel in Denmark requires taking a ferry, on which dining and/or cafeteria facilities are always provided. Ferries crossing the *Storebælt* have restaurants, serving hot and cold meals.

| Where can I get something to eat/drink? | **Hvor kan jeg få noget at spise/drikke?** | vōar kehn yigh faw nōaert aht spēēsser/drigger |

Baggage—Porters *Bagage—Dragere*

Porter!	**Drager!**	drāerr
Can you help me with my luggage?	**Kan De hjælpe mig med bagagen?**	kan dee yehlper migh mehdh bagāshern
Where are the luggage trolleys (carts)?	**Hvor er bagagevognene?**	vōar ehr bagāshervoanerner
Where are the luggage lockers?	**Hvor er bagageboksene?**	vōar ehr bagāsherbokserner
Where's the left-luggage office (baggage check)?	**Hvor er bagageopbevaringen?**	vōar ehr bagāsheropbervāringern
I'd like to leave my luggage, please.	**Jeg vil gerne efterlade min bagage.**	yigh veel gehrner ehfderladher meen bagāsher
I'd like to register (check) my luggage.	**Jeg vil gerne indskrive min bagage.**	yigh veel gehrner inskrēēver meen bagāsher

---

INDSKRIVNING AF BAGAGE
REGISTERING (CHECKING) BAGGAGE

PORTERS, see also page 18

Underground (subway) *S-tog*

Copenhagen's *S-bane* operates from 5 a.m. til 12.30 at night. Tickets are interchangeable on buses and trains. Children under 4 travel free and aged from 4–12 at half fare. Tickets must be stamped in the automatic machines on the platform before you board the train. *S-bane* stations are easily recognized by a winged *S* sign at the entrance.

Where's the nearest underground station?	**Hvor er den nærmeste S-togstation?**	voar ehr dehn **nær**merster ehs toa sta**shon**
Does this train go to ...?	**Kører det her tog til ...?**	**kø**rerr dɛ hehr toa til
Where do I change for ...?	**Hvor skal jeg skifte til ...?**	voar skal yigh **skeef**der til
Is the next station ...?	**Er den næste station ...?**	ehr den **næs**der sta**shon**
Which line should I take to ...?	**Hvilket tog skal jeg tage til ...?**	**vil**kert toa skal yigh ta til

Coach (long-distance bus) *Rutebil (Bus)*

Buses and coaches provide an extension to the rail network in serving smaller towns and remote areas. Most scheduled buses are run by the Danish State Railways (*DSB—Danske Stats- baner*), and often connect with trains and buses.

When's the next coach to ...?	**Hvornår kører den næste bus til ...?**	vor**nawr kø**rerr dehn **næs**der boos til
Does this coach stop at ...?	**Standser rutebilen i ...?**	**stan**serr **roo**derbeelern i
How long does the journey (trip) take?	**Hvor længe tager turen?**	voar **læng**er tar **too**rern

---

TIL RUTEBILERNE
TO THE BUSES

Note: Most of the phrases on the previous pages can be used or adapted for travelling on local transport.

Bus *Bus*

All major cities have excellent bus services. For a single trip you can buy your ticket on the bus. If you plan to make intensive use of the bus, you'll find it cheaper to buy a multi-journey card (*rabatkort*—rah**baht**koart). They can be purchased at railway stations and some hotels.

I'd like a booklet of tickets.	**Jeg vil gerne have et rabatkort.**	yigh veel **gehr**ner ha eht rah**baht**koart
Which bus goes to the town centre?	**Hvilken bus kører til centrum?**	**vilk**ern boos **kø**rerr til **sen**troom
Where can I get a bus to the royal palace?	**Hvor kan jeg tage en bus til Amalienbord Slot?**	vōar kan yigh ta ehn boos til ah**mailēēern**boar sloat
Which bus do I take to Lyngby?	**Hvilken bus skal jeg tage til Lyngby?**	**vilk**ern boos skal yigh ta til **lewng**bew
Where's the bus stop?	**Hvor standser bussen?**	vōar **stans**err **boos**ern
When is the ... bus to Frederiksberg	**Hvornår kører den ... bus til Frederiksberg?**	vor**nawr kø**rerr dehn ... boos til **frehdheriks**berg
first/last/next	**første/sidste/næste**	**førs**der/**sees**der/**næs**der
How much is the fare to ...?	**Hvor meget koster det til ...?**	vōar **migh**ert **kos**derr dE til
Do I have to change buses?	**Er det nødvendigt at skifte bus?**	ehr dE **nødh**vehndeet ah **skeef**der boos
How many bus stops are there to ...?	**Hvor mange stoppesteder er der til ...?**	vōar **mang**er **stopper**stehdherr ehr dehr til
Will you tell me when to get off?	**Vil De sige til, når jeg skal af?**	veel dee **sēē**er til nawr yigh skal ah
I want to get off at Langelinie.	**Jeg ønsker at stige af ved Langelinie.**	yigh **øns**gerr ah **stee**ger ah vehdh **lang**erlinyer

BUSSTOP	**STOP PÅ FORLANGENDE**
BUS STOP	REQUEST STOP

Boat service *Bådfart*

Denmark contains about 500 islands, some of which are linked by spectacular bridges. There are also regular ferry services to Norway, Sweden, England and Germany. It's advisable to reserve space for the car as well as cabins well in advance. This can be done through any travel agency.

When does the next boat for ... leave?	**Hvornår går den næste båd til ...?**	vornawr går dehn **næs**der **bāw**dh til
Where's the embarkation point?	**Ved hvilken kaj lægger båden til?**	vehdh **vil**kern kigh **læg**gerr **bāw**dhern til
How long does the crossing take?	**Hvor længe varer overfarten?**	vōar **læng**er **vā**rerr o°°erfardern
Which port(s) do we stop at?	**Hvor lægger vi til undervejs?**	vōar **læg**gerr vee til **oo**nervighs
I'd like to take a canal tour/ tour of the harbour.	**Jeg vil gerne tage på en kanaltur/ en havnerundfart.**	yigh veel **gehr**ner ta paw ehn kan**āl**tōōr/ehn **how**nerroondfart
boat	**båd**	**bāw**dh
cabin	**kahyt**	ka**hewt**
single/double	**enkelt/dobbelt**	**ehn**kerlt/**dob**erlt
deck	**dæk**	dæk
ferry	**færge**	**fæ**rer
hydrofoil	**hydrofoilbåd**	hewdroa**foil**bāwdh
life belt/boat	**redningsbælte/ redningsbåd**	**rehdh**ningsbælder/ **rehdh**ningsbāwdh
port	**havn**	hown
reclining seat	**sæde med ryglæn, man kan indstille**	**sæd**her mehdh **rewg**læn, man kan in**stil**ler
ship	**skib**	skib
steamer	**damper**	**damp**err

Bicycle hire *Cykeludlejning*

Cycles can be hired at many railway stations, but advance booking may be necessary and you'll need evidence of your identity. Organized cycling tours can be arranged through tourist offices or tour operators, with accommodation in a youth hostel, *kro* (inn) or hotel.

I'd like to hire a ... bicycle.	**Jeg vil gerne leje en ...**	yigh veel **gehr**ner **ligh**er ehn
5-gear	**cykel med gear**	**sew**gel mehdh geer

Car *Bil*

Denmark is covered with a network of very good roads. To drive your own car in Denmark you need a current driving licence and your passport: a green card is not compulsory though it is recommended. The use of seat belts (*sele*) is compulsory, including backseat belts if fitted and motorcyclists are required to wear helmets. The speed limit on motorways is 68 mph (110 km/h), 50 mph on other roads and 31 mph in built-up areas.

Where's the nearest (self-service) filling station?	**Hvor er den nærmeste benzinstation?**	voar ehr dehn **nær**merster behn**seen**stashon
Fill it up, please.	**Fuld tank.**	fool tank
Give me ... litres of petrol (gasoline).	**... liter benzin.**	... **lee**derr ben**seen**
super (premium)/ regular/unleaded/ diesel	**super/normal/ blyfri/diesel**	"super"/nor**mal**/**blew**free/ "diesel"
Please check the ...	**Vær venlig og kontroller ...**	vær **vehn**lee oa kontroa**lE**rer
battery	**batteriet**	bade**rEE**erdh
brake fluid	**bremsevæsken**	**brehm**servæsgern
oil/water	**olien/vandet**	**oa**lyern/**va**nerdh
Would you check the tyre pressure?	**Vil De være venlig at kontrollere dæktrykket?**	veel dee **vær**er **vehn**lee at kontroa**lE**rer **dæk**trewggerdh
1.6 front, 1.8 rear.	**forhjulene, baghjulene**	for**joo**lerner, bow**joo**lerner
Please check the spare tyre, too.	**Vær også venlig og kontroller reservehjulet.**	vær **os**ser **vehn**lee at kontroa**lE**rer reh**sEhr**verjoolerdh
Can you mend this puncture (fix this flat)?	**Kan De reparere denne punktering?**	kan dee rehpar**E**rer **dehn**er **poonk**tehring
Would you change the ... please?	**Vil De være rar og skifte ...?**	veel dee **vær**er rar oa **skeef**der
bulb	**pæren**	**pær**ern
fan belt	**ventilatorremmen**	vehntee**la**torrehmern
spark(ing) plugs	**tændingsrørene**	**tæn**ingsrErerner
tyre	**dækket**	**dæk**kerdh
wipers	**vinduesviskerne**	veen**doo**sveesgerner

CAR HIRE, see page 20

Would you clean the windscreen (windshield)?	**Vil De vaske forruden?**	veel dee **väs**ger forr**oo**dern

Asking the way—Directions *Spørge om vej*

Can you tell me the way to ...?	**Kan De sige mig vejen til ...?**	kan dee **see**er migh **vigh**ern til
In which direction is ...?	**Hvilken vej skal jeg køre til ...?**	**vil**kern vigh skal yigh **kør**er til
How do I get to ...?	**Hvordan kommer jeg til ...?**	vor**dan kom**er yigh til
Are we on the right road for ...?	**Er det den rette vej til ...?**	ehr dE dehn **rehd**er vigh til
How far is the next village?	**Hvor langt er der til den næste landsby?**	v**oo**ar langt ehr dehr til dehn **næs**der **lans**bew
How far is it to ... from here?	**Hvor langt er der til ... herfra?**	v**oo**ar langt ehr dehr til ... hehr**fra**
Is there a motorway (expressway)?	**Er der motorvej?**	ehr dehr **moa**torvigh
first-class main road second-class road third-class road	**hovedvej landevej bivej**	**ho°°**erdvigh **lan**ervigh **bee**vigh
How long does it take by car/on foot?	**Hvor lang tid tager det i bil/til fods?**	v**oo**ar lang teed tar dE ee beel/til foadhs
Can I drive to the centre of town?	**Kan jeg køre ind til centrum?**	kan yigh **kør**er in til **sen**troom
Is traffic allowed in the town centre?	**Må man køre inde i byens centrum?**	maw man **kør**er **in**ner ee **bew**erns **sen**troom
Can you tell me where ... is?	**Kan De sige mig, hvor ... er?**	kan dee **see**er migh v**oo**ar ... ehr
How can I find this place/address?	**Hvordan kan jeg finde frem til dette sted/denne adresse?**	vor**dan** kan yigh **fin**ner frehm til **dehd**er stehdh/ **dehn**er ah**dreh**ser
Where's this?	**Hvor er det?**	v**oo**ar ehr dE
Can you show me on the map where I am?	**Kan De vise mig på kortet, hvor jeg er?**	kan dee **vee**ser migh paw **kor**derdh v**oo**ar yigh ehr
Where are the nearest public toilets?	**Hvor er det nærmeste offentlige toilet?**	v**oo**ar ehr dE **nær**merster **of**ernl**ee**er toa**let**

De har kørt forkert.	You're on the wrong road.
Kør ligeud.	Go straight ahead.
Det ligger der til venstre/højre.	It's down there on the left/right.
overfor/bagved ...	opposite/behind ...
ved siden af/efter ...	next to/after ...
nord/syd/øst/vest	north/south/east/west
Kør til første/andet vejkryds.	Go to the first/second crossroads (intersection).
Kør til venstre ved trafiklyset.	Turn left at the traffic lights.
Kør til højre ved det næste hjørne.	Turn right at the next corner.
Det er en ensrettet gade.	It's a one-way street.
De må køre tilbage til ...	You have to go back to ...
Følg vejskiltene til Helsingør.	Follow signs for Elsinore.

Parking *Parkering*

Major towns have parking meters and zones where parking is limited. Parking discs (*parkeringsskive*) can be obtained free from police stations, garages, post offices and most banks.

Where can I park?	**Hvor kan jeg parkere?**	voar kan yigh parkērer
Is there a car park (parking lot) nearby?	**Er der en parkeringsplads her i nærheden?**	ehr dehr ehn parkēringsplas hehr ee nærhēdhern
May I park here?	**Må jeg parkere her?**	maw yigh parkērer hehr
How long can I park here?	**Hvor længe kan jeg parkere her?**	voar længer kan yigh parkērer hehr
What's the charge per hour?	**Hvad koster det pr. time?**	vadh kosderr dɛ pehr teemer
Do you have some change for the parking meter?	**Har De byttepenge til parkometeret?**	har dee bewdderpehnger til parkoamēdrerdh

Breakdown—Road assistance *Motorstop—Hjælp på vejen*

In the event of a breakdown contact FALCK, the 24-hour breakdown and towing service. Emergency telephones are available on motorways.

Where's the nearest garage?	**Hvor er det nærmeste værksted?**	vōar ehr dε **nær**merster **værk**stehdh
My car has broken down.	**Min bil har fået motorstop.**	meen beel har fāw̄erdh **moa**torstop
Where can I make a phone call?	**Hvor kan jeg telefonere?**	vōar kan yigh tehlehfoan**Ē**rer
I've had a break-down at ...	**Jeg har fået motorstop ved ...**	yigh har fāw̄erdh **moa**torstop vehdh
I'm on the Europa-road 6, about 10 km from Odense.	**Jeg er på E6, cirka 10 km fra Odense.**	yigh ayr paw ai 6, 10 keeloa**Ē**dherr nōar fpar **oad**hernser
Can you send a mechanic?	**Kan De sende en mekaniker?**	kan dee **sehn**ner ehn mehka**nee**kerr
My car won't start.	**Min bil vil ikke starte.**	meen beel veel **igg**er **star**der
The battery is dead.	**Mit batteri er fladt.**	meet badde**hree** ehr flat
I've run out of petrol (gasoline).	**Jeg er løbet tør for benzin.**	yigh ehr **lö**berdh tör for **ben**seen
I have a flat tyre.	**Jeg er punkteret.**	yigh ehr poonk**tĒ**rerdh
The engine is over-heating.	**Motoren er for varm.**	**moa**torern ehr for varm
There's something wrong with the ...	**Der er noget i vejen med ...**	dehr ehr **nō**aert ee **vigh**ern mehdh
brakes	**bremserne**	**brehms**ernerr
carburettor	**karburatoren**	karboo**ra**torern
exhaust pipe	**udstødningsrøret**	**oodh**stødhnings**rør**ert
radiator	**køleren**	**kö**lerern
wheel	**hjulet**	**jool**erdh
Can you send a breakdown van (tow truck)?	**Kan De sende en kranbil?**	kan dee **sehn**ner ehn **kran**beel
How long will you be?	**Hvornår kan De komme?**	vor**nawr** kan dee **kom**er
Can you give me an estimate?	**Kan De give mig et tilbud?**	kan dee **gēē**er migh eht til**bōō**d

Accident—Police *Ulykke—Politi*

Please call the police.	**Vær venlig og ring til politiet.**	vær **vehn**lee oa ring til poli**tierdh**
There's been an accident. It's about 2 km. from ...	**Der er sket en ulykke. Det er ca. 2 km fra**	dehr ehr skeht ehn **oo**lewgger. dε ehr **seer**ka to keeloa**meh**ter fra
Where's there a telephone?	**Hvor er der en telefon?**	v**ō**ar ehr dehr ehn tehleh**foan**
Call a doctor/an ambulance quickly.	**Ring hurtigt efter en læge/en ambulance.**	ring **hoor**teet **ehf**der ehn **læ**er/ehn amboo**langs**er
There are people injured.	**Der er nogle, der er kommet til skade.**	dehr ehr **nōa**ler deh ehr **kom**erdh til **skä**dher
Here's my driving licence.	**Her er mit kørekort.**	hehr ehr meet **kør**erkort
What's your name and address?	**Kan jeg få Deres navn og adresse?**	kan yigh faw **dehr**es nown oa ah**dreh**ser
What's your insurance company?	**Hvad er Deres forsikringsselskab?**	vadh ehr **dehr**es for**seek**ringssehlskab

Road signs *Vejskilte*

BAGRØNSET VOGNHØJDE	Height restriction
DATOPARKERING	Parking according to date*
ENSRETTET	One-way street
FALCK-ZONEN	24-hour telephone stations for emergencies
FODGØNGERE	Pedestrians
FODGØNGERE FORBUDT	No pedestrians
HOSPITAL	Hospital—Silence
JERNBANEOVERSKØRING	Railway level crossing
OMKØRSEL	Diversion, detour
OPHØR AF	End of restriction
OVERHALING FORBUDT	No overtaking
PAS PÅ	General warning notice
RABATTEN ER BLØD	Soft shoulder
RUNDKØRSEL	Roundabout (rotary)
SKOLE	School
STOPFORBUD	No stopping
UDKØRSEL	Exit
UJØVN VEJ	Poor road
VEJARBEJDE	Road works

*Night parking on one side of the street only (even numbers on even days, odd numbers on odd days).

Sightseeing

Where's the tourist office?	**Hvor er turistbureauet?**	voår ehr tooreestbewroaert
What are the main points of interest?	**Hvad er de vigtigste seværdigheder?**	vadh ehr dee **veeg**teester seh**vær**deehehdherr
We're here for ...	**Vi bliver her (kun) ...**	vee **blee**err hehr (koon)
only a few hours	**et par timer**	eht par **teem**err
a day	**en dag**	ehn dai
a week	**en uge**	ehn **ōō**er
Can you recommend a sightseeing tour/ an excursion?	**Kan De anbefale en rundtur/ en udflugt?**	kan dee **an**berfäler ehn **roont**ōōr/ehn **ōōdh**floogt
Where do we leave from?	**Hvor skal vi afsted fra?**	voår skal vee ah**stehdh** fra
Will the bus pick us up at the hotel?	**Vil bussen hente os på hotellet?**	veel **boos**ern hehnder os paw hoa**tehl**erdh
How much does the tour cost?	**Hvor meget koster turen?**	voår **migh**ert **kos**derr **tōō**rern
What time does the tour start?	**Hvad tid begynder turen?**	vadh teedh ber**gewn**err **tōō**rern
Is lunch included?	**Er frokost inkluderet?**	ehr **froa**kost inklood**ēr**erdh
What time do we get back?	**Hvad tid kommer vi tilbage?**	vadh teedh **kom**er vee til**bä**er
Do we have free time in ... ?	**Får vi tid til overs til fri disposition?**	fawr vee teedh til **o°°**ers til free disposi**shon**
Is there an English-speaking guide?	**Findes der en engelsktalende guide?**	**fin**ners dehr ehn **ehng**erlsktälernder "guide"
I'd like to hire a private guide for ...	**Jeg vil gerne have en privat guide for ...**	yigh veel **gehr**ner ha ehn pree**vat** "guide" for
half a day	**en halv dag**	ehn hal dai
a day	**en dag**	ehn dai

Where is/Where are the ...?	Hvor er ...?	vōār ehr
abbey	munkeklosteret	moonkerklostrerdh
art gallery	kunstgalleriet	koonstgalereēert
artists' quarter	kunstnerkvarteret	koonstnerkvartērerdh
botanical gardens	den botaniske have	dehn botaneesger hāver
building	bygningen	bewgningern
business district	forretning-skvarteret	forrehtningskvartērerdh
castle	borgen	bōārgern
catacombs	katakomberne	katakomberner
cathedral	domkirken	domkeergern
cemetery	kirkegården	kēērgergawrern
city centre	byens centrum	bewerns sentroom
chapel	kapellet	kapehlerdh
church	kirken	kēērgern
concert hall	koncertsalen	konsehrtsālern
court house	retsbygningen	rehtsbewgningern
downtown area	den indre by	dehn eendrer bew
embankment	dosseringen	doassehringern
exhibition	udstillingen	ōōdhstillingern
factory	fabrikken	fabriggern
fair	messen	mehsern
flea market	loppemarkedet	lobermarkerdherdh
fortress	fæstningen	fæstningern
fountain	springvandet	springvannerdh
gardens	haverne	hāverner
harbour	havnen	hownern
lake	søen	sōern
library	biblioteket	biblioatehkerdh
market	torvet	tōārverdh
memorial	mindesmærket	meenerdhsmærkerdh
monastery	klosteret	klostrerdh
monument	monumentet	moanoomenderdh
museum	museet	moosseherdh
old town	den gamle bydel	dehn gamler bewdehl
opera house	operaen	oapehräern
palace	slottet	sloderdh
park	parken	pargern
parliament building	Christiansborg (folketinget)	kreesteeansboar (folketingerdh)
planetarium	planetariet	planertārēēerdh
royal palace	Amalienborg (kongeslottet)	ammaleēērnboar (kongerslorderdh)
royal theatre	Det kongelige Teater	dE koangerleēēr teehater
ruins	ruinerne	rooēēnerner

seafront	**søbredden**	s**ö**br**E**dhern
shopping area	**indkøbscentret**	ink**ø**bssentrerdh
theatre	**teatret**	t**E**atrerdh
tomb	**gravstedet**	**grow**stehdherdh
tower	**tårnet**	**taw**rnerdh
town hall	**rådhuset**	**rawdh**hōōserdh
university	**universitetet**	ooneevehrseet**E**derdh
windmill	**vindmøllen**	**vin**mølern
zoo	**den zoologiske have**	dehn soa**loagg**eesker h**ä**ver

Admission *Adgang*

Is ... open on Sundays?	**Er ... åbent om søndagen?**	ehr ... **aw**bern om **søn**daern
What are the opening hours?	**Hvornår er der åbent?**	vorn**awr** ehr dehr **aw**bern
When does it close?	**Hvornår lukkes der?**	vorn**awr loogg**ers dehr
How much is the entrance fee?	**Hvor meget koster det i entre?**	v**oar migh**ert **kos**derr d**E** ee ang**tr**E
Is there any reduction for (the) ...?	**Er der rabat for ...?**	ehr dehr ra**bat** for
children	**børn**	børn
disabled	**handicappede**	**han**dikapperdher
groups	**grupper**	**groob**berr
pensioners	**pensionister**	pang**shon**isderr
students	**studerende**	stood**E**rehnder
Do you have a guidebook (in English)?	**Har De en brochure (på engelsk)?**	har dee ehn broa**shew**rer (paw **ehng**erlsk)
Can I buy a catalogue?	**Kan jeg købe et katalog?**	kan yigh **kø**ber eht kata**log**
Is it all right to take pictures?	**Må man fotografere her?**	maw man foatoagraf**E**rer hehr
Is there easy access for the disabled?	**Er der nem adgang for handicappede?**	ehr dehr nehm **adh**gang for **han**dikapperdher
Are there facilities/ activities for children?	**Har man særlige faciliteter/ aktiviteter for børn?**	har man s**ær**l**ēēe**r faseelee**teht**err/ akteevee**teht**err for børn

---

| **GRATIS ADGANG** | ADMISSION FREE |
| **FOTOGRAFERING FORBUDT** | NO CAMERAS ALLOWED |

Who—What—When? *Hvem—Hvad—Hvornår?*

What's that building?	**Hvad er den bygning?**	vadh ehr dehn **bewg**ning
Who was the ...?	**Hvem var ...?**	vehm var
architect	**arkitekten**	arki**tehk**tern
artist	**kunstneren**	**koonst**nerrern
painter	**maleren**	**mā**lerrern
sculptor	**billedhuggeren**	beeledhooggerern
Who built it?	**Hvem har bygget det?**	vehm har **bewg**gerdh dE
Who painted that picture?	**Hvem har malet det billede?**	vehm har **mā**lerdh dE **beel**erdher
When did he live?	**Hvornår levede han?**	vornawr **leh**verdher han
When was it built?	**Hvornår blev det bygget?**	vornawr bleh°° dE **bewg**gerdh
Where's the house where ... lived?	**Hvor ligger det hus, hvor ... boede ?**	vōar **leeg**gerr dE hoos vōar ... **boa**erdher
We're interested in ...	**Vi er interesseret i ...**	vee ehr interehss**ēr**erdh i
antiques	**antikviteter**	anteekvee**teh**terr
archaeology	**arkæologi**	arkæolo**gee**
art	**kunst**	koonst
botany	**botanik**	boata**neek**
ceramics	**keramik**	kehra**mik**
coins	**mønter**	**møn**derr
fine arts	**kunst**	koonst
furniture	**møbler**	**møb**lerr
geology	**geologi**	gEolo**gee**
handicrafts	**kunsthåndværk**	**koonst**hawndværk
history	**historie**	hi**stoar**ēēer
medicine	**medicin**	mEdi**sin**
music	**musik**	moo**sik**
natural history	**naturhistorie**	na**tōōr**histoarēēer
ornithology	**ornitologi**	ornitoaloa**gee**
painting	**malerier**	male**rēē**er
pottery	**pottemageri**	**pod**dermāerree
religion	**religion**	rehligi**oan**
sculpture	**skulptur**	skoolp**toor**
zoology	**zoologi**	soaloa**gee**
Where's the ... department?	**Hvor er afdelingen for ...**	vōar ehr **owd**ehlingern for

It's ...	Det er ...	dɛ ehr
amazing	forbløffende	forbløfferner
awful	rædsomt	rædhsomt
beautiful	smukt	smookt
gloomy	trist	treest
impressive	imponerende	impoanɛrerner
interesting	interessant	interehssant
magnificent	storartet	stoararderdh
pretty	kønt	kønt
strange	underligt	oonerleet
superb	fantastisk	fantastisk
terrifying	forfærdeligt	forfærderleet
tremendous	gevaldigt	gervaldeet
ugly	grimt	greemt

Churches—Religious services *Gudstjenester*

The majority of Danes are Protestants (Evangelical Lutheran), but in major cities there are places of worship for other denominations. Sunday services are generally held at 10 a.m. In the tourist season many churches are open for visitors. If you are interested in taking photographs, obtain permission first.

Is there a ... near here?	Ligger der en ... her i nærheden?	leegerr dehr ehn ... hehr ee nærhɛdhern
Catholic church	katolsk kirke	katoalsk keerger
Protestant church	protestantisk kirke	proderstānteesk keerger
mosque	moske	moaskɛ
synagogue	synagoge	sewnagoāer
What time is ...?	Hvad tid er ...?	vadh teedh ehr
mass/the service	messen/ gudstjenesten	mehsern/ goodstyehnerstern
Where can I find a ... who speaks English?	Hvor kan jeg finde en ..., som kan tale engelsk?	voār kan yigh finner ɛn ... som kan tāler ehngerlsk
priest/minister/ rabbi	katolsk præst/ protestantisk præst/rabiner	katoalsk præst/ proderstānteesk præst/ rabēēnerr
I'd like to visit the church.	Jeg vil gerne besøge kirken.	yigh veel gehrner bersøer keergern
I'd like to go to confession.	Jeg vil gerne gå til skrifte.	yigh veel gehrner gaw til skreefder

In the countryside *På landet*

In summer, the Danish countryside is idyllic; blue sea, lakes and fjords, green fields and forests of immense beech trees and fir. It is easy and relaxing to explore.

Is there a scenic route to ...?	**Er der en køn rute til ...?**	ehr dehr ehn køn rōoder til
How far is it to ...?	**Hvor langt er der?**	voār langt ehr dehr
Can we walk there?	**Kan vi tage derhen til fods?**	kan vee ta dehr**hehn** til foadhs
What kind of ... is that?	**Hvad for ... er det?**	vadh for ... ehr dᴇ
animal	**et dyr**	eht dewr
bird	**en fugl**	ehn fool
flower	**en blomst**	ehn blomst
tree	**et træ**	eht træ

Landmarks *Landemærker*

bridge	**en bro**	ehn bro
cliff	**en klippe**	ehn **kleeb**er
farm	**en bondegård**	ehn **boan**ergawr
field	**en mark**	ehn mark
footpath	**en fodsti**	ehn **foadh**stee
forest	**en skov**	ehn sko°°
garden	**en have**	ehn **hä**ver
hill	**en bakke**	ehn **bagg**er
house	**et hus**	eht hoos
island	**en ø**	ehn ø
lake	**en sø**	ehn sø
meadow	**en eng**	ehn ehng
path	**en sti**	ehn stee
pond	**en dam**	ehn dam
river	**en flod**	ehn floadh
road	**en vej**	ehn vigh
sea	**et hav**	eht how
spring	**en kilde**	ehn **keel**er
valley	**en dal**	ehn dal
village	**en landsby**	ehn **lans**bew
wall	**en mur**	ehn mōor
waterfall	**et vandfald**	eht **van**fal
wood	**en skov**	ehn sko°°

ASKING THE WAY, see page 76

Seværdigheder

Relaxing

Cinema (movies)—Theatre *Biograf—Teater*

Cinema tickets can usually be bought in advance. Foreign films are shown with the original soundtrack and Danish subtitles.

You can find out what's on from newspapers and bill-boards.

What's on at the cinema tonight?	**Hvad går der i biografen i aften?**	vadh gawr dehr ee beeoa**graf**ern ee **af**dern
What's playing at the ... Theatre?	**Hvad spiller man på ... teatret?**	vadh **speel**err man paw ... tEatrerdh
What sort of play is it?	**Hvad slags stykke er det?**	vadh slags **stewgg**er ehr dE
Who's it by?	**Hvem har skrevet det?**	vehm har **skreh**°°erdh dE
Can you recommend a ...?	**Kan De anbefale ...?**	kan dee **an**berfåler
good film comedy musical	**en god film et lystspil en musical**	ehn goadh film eht **lewst**spil ehn "musical"
Where's that new film directed by ... being shown?	**Hvor går den nye film af ...?**	vo͞ar gawr dehn **new**er film af
Who's in it?	**Hvem spiller i den?**	vehm **speel**err ee dehn
Who's playing the lead?	**Hvem spiller hovedrollen?**	vehm **speel**err ho°°erdhrolern
Who's the director?	**Hvem er instruktør?**	vehm ehr instrook**tør**
At which theatre is that new play by ... being performed?	**På hvilket teater går det nye stykke af ...?**	paw **vil**kert tEaterr gawr dE **new**er **stewgg**er af

What time does it begin?	**Hvornår begynder det?**	vornawr bergewnerr dE
Are there any seats for tonight?	**Er der flere pladser tilbage til i aften?**	ehr dehr flErer plasserr tilbāer til ee afdern
How much are the seats?	**Hvor meget koster billetterne?**	vōar mighert kosderr beelehderner
I'd like to reserve 2 seats for the show on Friday evening.	**Jeg vil gerne bestille 2 billetter til forestillingen fredag aften.**	yigh veel gehrner berstiler to beelehderr til foresteelingern frEdai afdern
Can I have a ticket for the matinée on Tuesday?	**Kan jeg få en billet til eftermiddags-forestillingen på tirsdag?**	kan yigh faw ehn beelehd til ehfdermidas-forerstilingern paw tirsdai
I'd like a seat in the stalls (orchestra).	**Jeg vil gerne have en plads i parkettet.**	yigh veel gehrner ha ehn plas ee parkehtterdh
Not too far back.	**Ikke for langt tilbage.**	igger for langt tilbāer
Somewhere in the middle.	**Et eller andet sted i midten.**	eht ehler annehdh stehdh ee meeddern
How much are the seats in the circle (mezzanine)?	**Hvor meget koster billetterne på balkonen?**	vōar mighert kosderr beelehderner paw balkongern
May I have a programme, please?	**Må jeg bede om et program?**	maw yigh bE om eht program
Where's the cloakroom?	**Hvor er garderoben?**	vōar ehr gārderrōabern

---

Der er desværre udsolgt. I'm sorry, we're sold out.

Der er kun nogle få pladser tilbage på balkonen. There are only a few seats left in the circle (mezzanine).

Må jeg se Deres billet? May I see your ticket?

Det er Deres plads. This is your seat.

DAYS OF THE WEEK, see page 151

Opera—Ballet—Concert *Opera—Ballet—Koncert*

The Royal Theatre of Copenhagen has a grand tradition, especially for the ballet and plays by classic writers such as Holberg. There are plenty of concerts and the modern hall of the broadcasting company (*radiokoncertsal*) offers classical and modern programmes.

Can you recommend a(n) ...?	**Kan De anbefale en ...?**	kan dee **an**berfäler ehn
ballet	**ballet**	ball**eht**
concert	**koncert**	kon**sehrt**
opera	**opera**	**oa**pehrä
Where's the opera house/the concert hall?	**Hvor er operaen/ koncertsalen?**	vōar ehr **oa**pehräern/ kon**sehrt**sälern
What's on at the opera tonight?	**Hvad går der i operaen i aften?**	vadh gaw dehr ee **oa**pehräern ee **af**dern
Who's singing/ dancing?	**Hvem synger/ danser?**	vehm **sewng**err/**dans**err
Which orchestra is playing?	**Hvilket orkester spiller?**	**vil**kert or**keh**ster **spee**lerr
What are they playing?	**Hvad spiller man?**	vadh **spee**lerr man
Who's the conductor/ soloist?	**Hvem er dirigenten/ solisten?**	vehm ehr deeree**gehn**dern/ soa**lees**dern

Nightclubs—Discos *Natklubber—Diskoteker*

There are numerous clubs, bars and discos, many with floor shows and most offering snacks and beer.

Can you recommend a good nightclub?	**Kan De anbefale en god natklub?**	kan dee **an**berfäler ehn goadh **nat**kloob
Is there a floor show?	**Er der et show?**	ehr dehr eht "show"
Is evening dress required?	**Er det nødvendigt at være selskabsklædt?**	ehr dɛ nødh**vehn**deet ah **vär**er **sehl**skabsklæt
Where can we go dancing?	**Hvor kan vi gå hen og danse?**	vōar kan vee gaw hehn oa **dans**er
Is there a disco- theque in town?	**Findes der et diskotek i byen?**	**fin**ners dehr eht diskoat**ēk** ee **be**wern

Sports *Sport*

Danes are as keen on sport as the other Scandinavians and you'll have plenty of opportunity for engaging in all types of sporting activity, as well as spectating. For an active holiday Denmark can offer cycling, riding, sailing, fishing, tennis, golf and skating.

Is there a football (soccer) match anywhere this Saturday?	**Er der en fodboldkamp et eller andet sted nu på lørdag?**	ehr dehr ehn **fodh**boldkamp eht **ehl**lerr annerdh stehdh noo paw **lør**dai
Which teams are playing?	**Hvilke hold spiller?**	vilker hol **spee**lerr
Can you get me a ticket?	**Kan De skaffe mig en billet?**	kan dee **skä**fer migh ehn bee**lehd**

basketball	**basketball**	"basketball"
boxing	**boksning**	**boks**ning
car racing	**bilvæddeløb**	beel**væd**herløb
cycling	**cykling**	**sew**gling
football (soccer)	**fodbold**	**foad**bold
horse racing	**hestevæddeløb**	**hehs**dervædherløb
(horse-back) riding	**ridning**	**reedh**ning
skiing	**skiløb**	**ski**løb
swimming	**svømning**	**svøm**ning
tennis	**tennis**	"tennis"
volleyball	**volleyball**	"volleyball"

I'd like to see a boxing match.	**Jeg vil gerne se en boksekamp.**	yigh veel **gehr**ner sɛ ehn **boks**erkamp
What's the admission charge?	**Hvad koster billetten?**	vadh **kos**derr beel**ehd**ern
Where's the nearest golf course?	**Hvor ligger den nærmeste golfbane?**	vo͞ar **lee**gerr dehn **nær**merster **golf**bäner
Where are the tennis courts?	**Hvor ligger tennisbanerne?**	vo͞ar **lee**gerr "tennis" **bä**nerner
What's the charge per ...?	**Hvad koster det pr. ...?**	vadh **kos**derr de pehr
day/round/hour	**dag/runde/time**	dai/**roon**der/**teem**er

Can I hire (rent) rackets?	**Kan jeg leje en ketsjer?**	kan yigh **ligh**er ehn **keht**sher
Where's the race course (track)?	**Hvor er væddeløbsbanen?**	vōar ehr **vædh**erløbsbānern
Is there any good fishing/hunting around here?	**Findes der et godt sted, hvor man kan fiske/gå på jagt her i nærheden?**	**finn**ers dehr eht god stehdh vōar man kan **fisg**er/gaw paw yagt hehr ee **nær**hēdhern
Do I need a permit?	**Skal man have fiskekort/jagtkort?**	skal man ha **fisg**erkort/**yagt**kort
Where can I get one?	**Hvor kan jeg få et?**	vōar kan yigh faw eht
Can one swim in the lake/river?	**Kan man gå i vandet i søen/floden?**	kan man gaw ee **van**erdh ee **sø**ern/**floadh**ern
Is there a swimming pool here?	**Findes der et svømmebasin her?**	**finn**ers dehr eht **svø**merbassæng hehr
Is it open-air or indoor?	**Er det udendørs eller indendørs?**	ehr deht **ōōdh**erndørs **ehl**er **een**erndørs
Is it heated?	**Er det opvarmet?**	ehr deht **op**varmerdh
What's the tempera-ture of the water?	**Hvor mange grader er vandet?**	vōar **mang**er **grädh**err ehr **van**erdh
Is there a sandy beach?	**Findes der en sandstrand her?**	**finn**ers dehr ehn **san**stran hehr

On the beach *På stranden*

Is it safe to swim here?	**Er det trygt at gå i vandet her?**	ehr dɛ trewgt ah gaw ee **van**erdh hehr
Is there a lifeguard?	**Findes der en livredder her?**	**finn**ers dehr ehn **lēēv**rehdherr hehr
Is it safe for children?	**Er det trygt for børnene?**	ehr dɛ trewgt for **bør**nerner
The sea is very calm.	**Havet er meget roligt.**	**how**erdh ehr **migh**ert **roa**leet
There are some big waves.	**Der er store bølger.**	dehr ehr **stoa**rer **bøl**yerr
Are there any dangerous currents?	**Findes der nogle farlige strømme?**	**finn**ers dehr **nō**aler **fā**lēēer **strø**mer
What time is high tide/low tide?	**Hvornår er der flod/ebbe?**	vor**nawr** ehr dehr floadh/**ehb**er

I want to hire (rent) a/an/some ...	**Jeg vil leje ...**	yigh veel **ligh**er
bathing hut (cabana)	**et badehus**	eht **bād**herhoos
deck chair	**en liggestol**	ehn **ligge**stoal
motorboat	**en motorbåd**	ehn **moat**orbawdh
rowing-boat	**en robåd**	ehn **roa**bawd
sailing boat	**en sejlbåd**	ehn **sighl**bawdh
skin-diving equipment	**et dykkerudstyr**	eht **dewgg**eroodhstewr
sunshade (umbrella)	**en parasol**	ehn para**sol**
surfboard	**et surfbræt**	eht "surf" bræt
water-skis	**et par vandski**	eht par **van**ski
windsurfer	**en windsurfer**	ehn "windsurfer"

PRIVAT STRAND PRIVATE BEACH
BADNING FORBUDT NO SWIMMING

Winter sports *Vintersport*

Is there a skating rink near here?	**Findes der en skøjtebane her i nærheden?**	**finn**ers dehr ehn **skoid**erbäner hehr ee **nær**hēdhern
downhill/cross-country skiing	**styrtløb/langrend**	**stewrt**løb/**lang**rehn
Are there any ski runs for ... ?	**Findes der nogle skibakker for ... ?**	**finn**ers dehr **noā**ler **ski**baggerr for
beginners	**begyndere**	ber**gew**nerer
average skiers	**middelgode skiløbere**	**midh**erlgoaer **ski**løberer
good skiers	**gode skiløbere**	**goa**er **ski**løberer
Can I take skiing lessons?	**Kan jeg få undervisning i skiløb?**	kan yigh faw **oon**erveesning ee **ski**løb
Are there any ski lifts?	**Findes der nogen skilift?**	**finn**ers dehr **noā**ern **ski**lift
I want to hire ...	**Jeg vil gerne leje ...**	yigh veel **gehr**ner **ligh**er
poles	**et par stave**	eht par **stäv**er
skates	**et par skøjter**	eht par **skoid**err
ski boots	**et par skistøvler**	eht par **ski**stølerr
skiing equipment	**noget skiudstyr**	**noā**ert **ski**oodhstewr
skis	**et par ski**	eht par ski

Making friends

Introductions *Præsentationer*

May I introduce ...?	**Må jeg præsentere ...?**	maw yigh præsehnt**Ē**rer
John, this is ...	**John, det er ...**	John dE ehr
My name is ...	**Jeg hedder ...**	yigh **hehdh**err
Pleased to meet you!	**Det glæder mig at træffe Dem!**	dE **glædh**err migh ah **træf**er dehm
What's your name?	**Hvad hedder De/du?**	vadh **hehdh**err dee/doo*
How are you?	**Hvordan har du det?**	vor**dan** har doo dE
Fine, thanks. And you?	**Tak, godt. Og hvordan har du det?**	tak god. oa vor**dan** har doo dE

Follow up *Nærmere bekendtskab*

How long have you been here?	**Hvor længe har I været her?**	vōar **læng**er har ee **vǟerdh** hehr
We've been here a week.	**Vi har været her en uge.**	vee har **vǟerdh** hehr ehn ooer
Is this your first visit?	**Er det første gang, I er her?**	ehr dE **førs**ter gang ee ehr hehr
No, we came here last year.	**Nej, vi har også været her sidste år.**	nigh vee har **oss**er **vǟerdh** hehr **sees**der awr
Are you enjoying your stay?	**Kan du lide at være her?**	kan doo li ah **vǟer** hehr
Yes, I like it very much.	**Ja, jeg kan godt lide det.**	ya yigh kan god li dE
I like the scenery a lot.	**Jeg synes vældig godt om landskabet.**	yigh sewns **væl**dee god om **lan**skåberdh
What do you think of the country?	**Hvad synes du om landet?**	vadh sewns doo om **lan**erdh
What nationality are you?	**Hvad nationalitet har du?**	vadh nashonalee**teht** har doo

* Danish has two forms of the word "you": the formal *De*, and *du* between friends. See GRAMMAR, page 173.

I'm ...	Jeg er ...	yigh ehr
American	amerikaner	amehreekānerr
British	brite	breeter
Canadian	canadier	kanadyer
English	englænder	ehnglehnerr
Irish	irlænder	eerlehnerr

Where are you staying?	Hvor bor du her?	voar boar doo hehr
Are you on your own?	Er du her alene?	ehr doo hehr alehner

I'm with my ...	Jeg er her sammen med ...	yigh ehr hehr sāmern mehdh
wife	min kone	meen koaner
husband	min mand	meen man
family	min familie	meen familyer
children	mine børn	meener børn
parents	mine forældre	meener forældrer
boyfriend/girlfriend	min kæreste	meen kærsder

father/mother	min far/mor	meen far/mor
son/daughter	min søn/datter	meen søn/dådderr
brother/sister	min bror/søster	meen bror/søsderr
uncle/aunt	onkel/tante	oangel/tander
nephew/niece	nevø/niece	nehvø/niehser
cousin	fætter/kusine	fæderr/kooseener

Are you married/single?	Er du gift/ugift?	ehr doo gift/oogift
Do you have children?	Har du børn?	har doo børn
What do you do?	Hvad laver du?	vadh lāver doo
I'm a student.	Jeg studerer.	yigh stoodērerr
What are you studying?	Hvad studerer du?	vadh stoodērerr doo
I'm here on a business trip/on holiday.	Jeg er her på forretningsrejse/på ferie.	yigh ehr hehr paw forrehtningsrighser/paw fehryer
Do you travel a lot?	Rejser du meget?	righser doo mighert
Do you play cards/chess?	Spiller du kort/skak?	speelerr doo kort/skak

COUNTRIES, see page 146

The weather *Vejret*

What a lovely day!	**Sikke et dejligt vejr!**	**sikk**er eht **digh**leet vehr
What awful weather!	**Sikke et forfærdeligt vejr!**	**sikk**er eht for**fær**derleet vehr
Isn't it cold/hot today?	**Er det ikke koldt/ varmt i dag?**	ehr dɛ **igg**er kolt/varmt ee dai
Is it usually as warm as this?	**Plejer det at være så varmt som nu?**	**pligh**err dɛ ah **vær**er saw varmt som noo
Do you think it's going to ... tomorrow?	**Tror du, det bliver ... i morgen?**	troar doo dɛ **blee**err ... ee **mō**ern
be a nice day	**dejligt vejr**	**digh**leet vehr
rain	**regnvejr**	**righn**vehr
snow	**snevejr**	**sn**ɛvehr
What's the weather forecast?	**Hvordan er vejrudsigten?**	vor**dan** ehr vehr**ōō**dhseegdern

cloud	**skyet**	**skew**erdh
fog	**tåge**	**tā**wer
frost	**frostvejr**	**frost**vehr
ice	**is**	**ee**s
lightning	**lyn**	lewn
moon	**måne**	**mā**wner
rain	**regnvejr**	**righn**vehr
sky	**himmel**	**heem**erl
snow	**snevejr**	**sn**ɛvehr
star	**stjerne**	**styehr**ner
sun	**sol**	sol
thunder	**torden**	**toar**dern
thunderstorm	**tordenvejr**	**toar**dernvehr
wind	**vind**	vin

Invitations *Indbydelser*

Would you like to have dinner with us on ...?	**Vil du spise middag sammen med os ...?**	veel doo **spee**ser mid**ai sam**ern mehdh os
May I invite you to lunch?	**Må jeg byde dig på frokost?**	maw yigh **bew**dher digh paw **fro**akost

DAYS OF THE WEEK, see page 151

Can you come round for a drink this evening?	**Kan du komme til en drink i aften?**	kan doo **kom**er til ehn drink ee **af**dern
There's a party. Are you coming?	**Vi skal have fest. Kommer du?**	vee skal ha fehst. **kom**err doo
That's very kind of you.	**Det er virkelig pænt af dig.**	dɛ ehr **virk**erleet pænt af digh
Great. I'd love to come.	**Tak, jeg vil gerne komme**	tak yigh veel **gehr**ner **kom**er
What time shall we come?	**Hvornår skal vi komme?**	vor**nawr** skal vee **kom**er
May I bring a friend?	**Må jeg tage en ven med?**	maw yigh ta ehn vehn mehdh
I'm afraid we have to leave now.	**Vi må desværre hjem nu.**	vee maw deh**svær**er yehm noo
Next time you must come to visit us.	**Næste gang må du komme og besøge os.**	**næs**der gang maw doo **kom**er oa ber**sö**er os
Thanks for the evening. It was great.	**Tak for i aften. Det var vældig hyggeligt.**	tak for ee **af**dern. dɛ var **væl**dee **hewg**gerleet

Dating *Stævnemøde*

Do you mind if I smoke?	**Har du noget imod, at jeg ryger?**	har doo **nō**aert i**moadh** ah yigh **rew**err
Would you like a cigarette?	**Vil du have en cigaret?**	veel doo ha ehn sigga**rehd**
Do you have a light, please?	**Har du en tænder?**	har doo ehn **tæn**nerr
Why are you laughing?	**Hvorfor ler du?**	vor**for** lɛr doo
Is my Danish that bad?	**Taler jeg dansk så dårligt?**	**tā**lerr yigh dansk saw **daw**leet
Do you mind if I sit here?	**Har du noget imod, at jeg sætter mig her?**	har doo **nō**aert i**moadh** ah yigh **sæd**err migh hehr
Can I get you a drink?	**Kan jeg give dig noget at drikke?**	kan yigh **gēe**er digh **nō**aert at **drig**gerr
Are you waiting for someone?	**Sidder du og venter på nogen?**	**seedh**err doo oa **vehn**derr paw **nō**aern

Are you free this evening?	**Er du fri i aften?**	ehr doo free ee **afdern**
Would you like to go out with me tonight?	**Har du lyst til at gå ud med mig i aften?**	har doo lewst til ah gaw ood mehdh migh ee **afdern**
Would you like to go dancing?	**Har du lyst til at gå ud og danse?**	har doo lewst til ah gaw ood oa **danser**
I know a good discotheque.	**Jeg kender et godt diskotek.**	yigh **kehn**err eht god diskoat**ēk**
Shall we go to the cinema (movies)?	**Skal vi gå i biografen?**	skal vee gaw ee beeoa**grafern**
Would you like to go for a drive?	**Har du lyst til en køretur?**	har doo lewst til ehn **kø**rertoor
Where shall we meet?	**Hvor skal vi mødes?**	vōar skal vee **mødh**ers
I'll pick you up at your hotel.	**Jeg vil hente dig på dit hotel.**	yigh veel **hehn**der digh paw deet hoa**tehl**
I'll call for you at 8.	**Jeg kommer klokken 8.**	yigh **kom**er **klog**gern **oad**er
May I take you home?	**Må jeg følge dig hjem?**	maw yigh **føl**yer digh yehm
Can I see you again tomorrow?	**Kan jeg se dig igen i morgen?**	kan yigh SE digh i**gehn** ee **mōa**ern
I hope we'll meet again.	**Jeg håber, vi kan ses igen.**	yigh **hāw**berr vee kan sehs i**gehn**

... and you might answer:

I'd love to, thank you.	**Tak, det vil jeg meget gerne.**	tak DE veel yigh **migh**ert **gehr**ner
Thank you, but I'm busy.	**Tak, men jeg er desværre optaget.**	tak mehn yigh ehr dehs**værr**er **op**taerdh
No, I'm not interested, thank you.	**Nej tak, jeg er ikke interesseret.**	nigh tak yigh ehr **igg**er interehss**ē**rerdh
Leave me alone, please!	**Vær rar og lad mig være i fred!**	vær rar oa ladh migh **vær**er ee frehdh
Thank you, it's been a wonderful evening.	**Tak, det har været en virkelig hyggelig aften.**	tak DE har **vær**erdh ehn **veer**kerlee **hewgg**erlee **afdern**
I've enjoyed myself.	**Jeg har moret mig.**	yigh har **moar**erdh migh

Shopping Guide

This shopping guide is designed to help you find what you want with ease, accuracy and speed. It features:

1. A list of all major shops, stores and services (p. 98).
2. Some general expressions required when shopping to allow you to be specific and selective (p. 100).
3. Full details of the shops and services most likely to concern you. Here you'll find advice, alphabetical lists of items and conversion charts listed under the headings below.

		page
Bookshop/ Stationer's	books, magazines, newspapers, stationery	104
Camping and sports equipment	useful items for camping and other leisure activities	106
Chemist's (drugstore)	medicine, first-aid, cosmetics, toilet articles	107
Clothing	clothes and accessories, shoes	111
Electrical appliances	radios, cassette recorders, shavers	118
Grocer's	some general expressions, weights, measures and packaging	119
Household articles	useful items for the house: tools, crockery, cutlery	120
Jeweller's/ Watchmaker's	jewellery, watches, watch repairs	121
Optician	glasses, lenses, binoculars	123
Photography	cameras, films, developing, accessories	124
Tobacconist's	smokers' supplies	126
Miscellaneous	souvenirs, records, cassettes, toys	127

LAUNDRY, see page 29/HAIRDRESSER'S, see page 30

Indkøbsvejledning

Shops, stores and services *Butikker, forretninger og servicevirksomheder*

Shopping hours: Generally 9 or 9.30 a.m. to 5.30 p.m., Monday to Thursday. Late-night shopping extends to 7 or 8 p.m. on Fridays, and sometimes on Thursdays also. Saturday is early closing day at noon or 2 p.m.

In Copenhagen and a few other cities, several shops open on Sunday morning — bakers', florists', *smørrebrød* shops, sweet shops and kiosks.

Note: Some shops (often food stores) are closed on Monday or Tuesday.

Where's the nearest ...?	**Hvor er den/det nærmeste ...**	vōar ehr dehn/deht **nær**merster
antique shop	**antikvitets-forretning**	anteekvee**tehts**forrehtning
art gallery	**kunstgalleri**	**koonst**galerri
baker's	**bager**	**bā**er
bank	**bank**	bank
barber's	**herrefrisør**	hehr**rer**freesør
beauty salon	**skønhedssalon**	**skøn**hehdhssalong
bookshop	**boghandel**	**boa**hanerl
butcher's	**slagter**	**slag**derr
camera shop	**fotoforretning**	**fo**toforrehtning
candy store	**chokolade-forretning**	shoakoa**lādh**erforrehtning
chemist's	**apotek**	apo**tehk**
confectioner	**konditori**	koandeetoa**ree**
dairy	**mejeri**	migher**ree**
delicatessen	**viktualieforretning**	veektooa**lēē**erforrehtning
dentist	**tandlæge**	**tan**læer
department store	**stormagasin**	**stoar**magaseen
drugstore	**apotek**	apo**tehk**
dry cleaner's	**renseri**	rehnser**ree**
electrical goods shop	**elektricitets-forretning**	ehlehk**tri**si**tehts**forrehtning
fishmonger's	**fiskehandler**	**fis**gerhanlerr
florist's	**blomsterhandler**	**blom**sterhanlerr
furrier's	**buntmager**	**boont**mayerr
greengrocer's	**grønthandler**	**grøn**hanlerr
grocer's	**købmand**	**kø**man
hairdresser's (ladies/men)	**frisør (dame-/herre-)**	free**sør** (damer-/hehrrer-)

hardware store	**isenkræmmer**	e̅e̅sernkræmerr
health food shop	**helsekostforretning**	**hehl**serkostforrehtning
hospital	**hospital**	hospi**tal**
ironmonger's	**isenkræmmer**	e̅e̅sernkræmer
jeweller's	**guldsmed**	**gools**mehdh
launderette	**møntvaskeri**	**mønt**vasgerree
laundry	**vaskeri**	vasger**ree**
library	**bibliotek**	bibleeo**tehk**
market	**marked**	**mar**kerdh
newsagent's	**bladhandler**	**bladh**hanlerr
newsstand	**aviskiosk**	ah**vees**kiosk
optician	**optiker**	**op**tigger
pastry shop	**konditori**	koandeetoa**ree**
photographer	**fotograf**	foto**graf**
police station	**politistation**	poli**ti**stashon
post office	**posthus**	**post**hoos
second-hand shop	**marskandiser**	marsgan**dees**err
shoemaker's (repairs)	**skomager**	**sko**amaerr
shoe shop	**skoforretning**	**sko**aforrehtning
watchmaker's	**urmager**	o̅o̅r**may**er
wine merchant	**vinhandler**	**veen**hanlerr

INDGANG	ENTRANCE
UDGANG	EXIT
NØDUDGANG	EMERGENCY EXIT

General expressions *Almindelige udtryk*

Where? *Hvor?*

Where's there a good ...?	**Hvor er der en god ...?**	vōar ehr dehr ehn goa
Where can I find a ...?	**Hvor kan jeg finde ...?**	vōar kan yigh finner
Where's the main shopping area?	**Hvor er forretningskvarteret?**	vōar er forrehtningskvartehrerdh
Is it far from here?	**Er det langt herfra?**	ehr dE langt hehrfra
How do I get there?	**Hvordan kan jeg komme derhen?**	vordan kan yigh komer dehrhehn

UDSALG	SALE
SØRTILBUD	SPECIAL OFFER

Service *Betjening*

Can you help me?	**Kan De hjælpe mig?**	kan dee yehlper migh
I'm just looking.	**Jeg ser mig bare omkring.**	yigh sehr migh bārer omkring
Do you sell ...?	**Sælger De ...?**	sælyerr dee
I'd like (to buy) ...	**Jeg vil gerne (købe) ...**	yigh veel gehrner kōber
Can you show me some ...?	**Kan De vise mig nogen ...?**	kan dee vēēser migh nōaern
Do you have any ...?	**Har De nogen...?**	har dee nōaern
Where's the ... department?	**Hvor er ... afdelingen?**	vōar ehr ... owdehlingern
Where is the lift (elevator)/escalator?	**Hvor er elevatoren/rulletrappen?**	vōar ehr ehlehvatorern/rōōllertrabern

That one *Den der*

Can you show me ...?	**Kan De vise mig ...?**	kan dee vēēser migh
this/that	**det her/det der**	dE hehr/dE dehr
the one in the window	**den i vinduet**	dehn ee vindōōerdh

Defining the article *Varebeskrivelse*

I'd like a ... one.	**Jeg vil gerne have en ...**	yigh veel **gehr**ner ha ehn
big	**stor**	stoar
cheap	**billig**	**bee**lee
dark	**mørk**	mørk
good	**god**	goadh
heavy	**tung**	toong
large	**stor**	stoar
light (weight)	**let**	leht
light (colour)	**lys**	lews
oval	**oval**	oa**vāl**
rectangular	**rektangulær**	**rehkt**angoolær
round	**rund**	roon
small	**lille**	**leel**er
square	**firkantet**	**fēēr**kanderdh
sturdy	**solid**	so**leedh**
I don't want anything too expensive.	**Jeg vil ikke have noget, der er for dyrt.**	yigh veel **igg**er ha **nōā**ert dehr ehr for dewrt

Preference *Hvad man hellere vil have*

Can you show me some others?	**Kan De vise mig nogle andre?**	kan dee **vēē**ser migh **nōā**ler **an**drer
Don't you have any thing ...?	**Har De ikke noget ...?**	har dee **igg**er **nōā**ert
cheaper/better	**billigere/bedre**	bee**lēē**errer/**behdh**rer
larger/smaller	**større/mindre**	**stør**rer/**min**drer

How much *Hvor meget*

How much is this?	**Hvad koster det?**	vadh **kos**der dE
How much are they?	**Hvad koster de?**	vadh **kos**der dee
I don't understand.	**Det forstår jeg ikke.**	dE for**staw** yigh **igg**er
Please write it down.	**Vær rar og skriv det ned.**	vær rar oa skreev dE nedh
I don't want to spend more than ... kroner.	**Jeg vil ikke bruge mere end ... kroner.**	yigh veel **igg**er **brōō**er **mēh**rer ehn ... **krōā**nerr

COLOURS, see page 112

Decision *Afgørelse*

It's not quite what I want.	**Det er ikke helt det, jeg vil have.**	dE er **igger** hehlt dE yigh veel ha
No, I don't like it.	**Det bryder jeg mig ikke om.**	dE **brewdh**err yigh migh **igg**er om
I'll take it.	**Jeg tager det.**	yigh tar dE

Ordering *Bestilling*

| Can you order it for me? | **Kan De bestille det til mig?** | kan dee ber**stil**er dE til migh |
| How long will it take? | **Hvor lang tid tager det?** | vōar lang teedh tar dE |

Delivery *Levering*

I'll take it with me.	**Jeg tager det med mig.**	yigh tar dE mehdh migh
Deliver it to the ... Hotel.	**Send det til ... hotellet.**	sehn dE til ... hoa**tehl**erdh
Please send it to this address.	**Vær rar og send det til denne adresse.**	vær rar oa sehn dE til **dehn**er ah**drehs**er
Will I have any difficulty with the customs?	**Vil jeg få problemer i tolden?**	veel yigh faw pro**blehm**err ee **tol**lern

Paying *Betaling*

How much is it?	**Hvor meget bliver det?**	vōar **migh**ert **blēē**er dE
Can I pay by traveller's cheque?	**Kan jeg betale med rejsechecks?**	kan yigh ber**tāl**er mehdh **righs**er"checks"
Do you accept dollars/pounds?	**Tager De dollars/pund?**	tar dee "dollars"/poon
Do you accept credit cards?	**Tager De kreditkort?**	tar dee kreh**dit**kort
Do I have to pay the VAT (sales tax)?	**Skal jeg betale moms?**	skal yigh ber**tāl**er moms
I think there's a mistake in the bill.	**Der er vist fejl i regningen.**	dehr ehr vist fighl ee **righn**ingern

Anything else? *Noget andet*

No, thanks, that's all.	**Nej tak, det er det hele.**	nigh tak dE ehr dE **hehl**er
Yes, I'd like ...	**Ja, jeg vil gerne have ...**	ja yigh veel **gehr**ner ha
Can you show me ...?	**Kan De vise mig ...?**	kan dee **vee**ser migh
May I have a bag, please?	**Kan jeg få en bærepose?**	kan yigh faw ehn **bæ**rerpoaser
Could you wrap it up for me, please?	**Kunne De pakke det ind for mig?**	**koon**er dee **pagg**er dE in for migh
May I have a receipt?	**Kan jeg få en kvittering?**	kan yigh faw ehn kveet**E**ring

Dissatisfied? *Misfornøjet*

Can you exchange this, please?	**Kunne De bytte det her for mig?**	**koon**er dee **bewd**er dE hehr for migh
I want to return this.	**Jeg vil returnere det her.**	yigh veel rehtoorn**E**rer dE hehr
I'd like a refund. Here's the receipt.	**Jeg vil gerne have pengene tilbage. Her er kvitteringen.**	yigh veel **gehr**ner ha **pehng**erner til**bæ**er. hehr ehr kveet**E**ringern

---

Kan jeg hjælpe med noget?	Can I help you?
Hvad skulle det være?	What would you like?
Hvilken ... ønsker De?	What ... would you like?
farve/form/kvalitet	colour/shape/quality
Jeg beklager, det har vi ikke.	I'm sorry, we don't have any.
Der er udsolgt.	We're out of stock.
Skal vi bestille det til Dem?	Shall we order it for you?
Tager De det med eller skal vi sende det?	Will you take it with you or shall we send it?
Skulle der være andet?	Anything else?
Det bliver ... kroner.	That's ... kroner, please.
Kassen er derovre.	The cash desk is over there.

Bookshop—Stationer's *Boghandel—Papirhandel*

In Denmark, bookshops often offer stationer's supplies too. British and American newspapers and magazines are sold at newsstands in large cities and at major railway stations.

Where's the nearest ...?	**Hvor er den nærmeste ...?**	voar ehr dehn **nær**merster
bookshop	**boghandel**	**boa**hanerl
stationer's	**papirhandel**	pa**peer**hanerl
newsstand	**aviskiosk**	ah**vees**kiosk
Where can I buy an English-language newspaper?	**Hvor kan jeg købe en engelsksproget avis?**	voar kan yigh **kø**ber ehn **ehng**erlsksproaerdh ah**vees**
Where's the guide-book section?	**Hvor står rejseførerne?**	voar stawr **righ**serførerner
Where do you keep the English books?	**Hvor står de engelske bøger?**	voar stawr dee **ehng**erlsker **bø**er
Have you any of ...'s books in English?	**Har De nogle af ...s bøger på engelsk?**	har dee **noa**ler af ... s **bø**er paw **ehng**erlsk
Do you have second-hand books?	**Har De nogle antikvariske bøger på lager?**	har dee **noa**ler ante**ekva**reesger **bø**er paw **la**er
I want to buy a/an/ some ...	**Jeg vil gerne købe ...**	yigh veel **gehr**ner **kø**ber
address book	**en adressebog**	ehn ah**dreh**serboa
adhesive tape	**noget tape**	**noa**ert "tape"
ball-point pen	**en kuglepen**	ehn **kool**erpen
book	**en bog**	ehn boa
calendar	**en kalender**	ehn ka**leh**nerr
carbon paper	**noget karbonpapir**	**noa**ert kar**bong**pa**peer**
crayons	**nogle farveblyanter**	**noa**ler **far**verblewanterr
dictionary	**en ordbog**	ehn **oar**boa
Danish-English	**dansk-engelsk**	dansk-**ehng**erlsk
pocket	**lomme-**	**lom**er-
drawing paper	**noget tegnepapir**	**noa**ert **tigh**nerpa**peer**
drawing pins	**nogle tegnestifter**	**noa**ler **tigh**nersteefderr
envelopes	**nogle kuverter**	**noa**ler koo**vehr**derr
eraser	**et viskelæder**	eht **vees**gerlædher
exercise book	**et kladdehæfte**	eht **klædh**erhæfder
felt-tip pen	**en filtpen**	ehn **feelt**pen
fountain pen	**en fyldepen**	ehn **few**lerpen
glue	**noget lim**	**noa**ert leem

grammar book	en grammatik	ehn gramateek
guidebook	en rejsefører	ehn righserførerr
ink	noget blæk	noaert blæk
black/red/blue	sort/rødt/blåt	soart/røt/blawt
(adhesive) labels	nogle (selvklæbende) etiketter	noaler (sehlklæberner) Eteekedderr
magazine	et blad/tidsskrift	eht bladh/teedhskreeft
map	et kort	eht kort
street map	gadekort	gädherkort
road map of ...	vejkort over ...	vighkort o°°er
mechanical pencil	en skrueblyant	ehn skrooerblewant
newspaper	en avis	ehn avees
American/English	amerikansk/ engelsk	amehreekansk/ehngerlsk
notebook	en notesbog	ehn noadersboa
note paper	noget brevpapir	noaert breh°°papeer
paintbox	en farvelade	ehn farverlädher
paper	noget papir	noaert papeer
paperback	en billigbog	ehn beeleeboa
paperclips	nogle clips (til papir)	noaler klips (til papeer)
paper napkins	nogle papirservietter	noaler papeerssehrveeeehderr
paste	noget klister	noaert kleesderr
pen	en pen	ehn pen
pencil	en blyant	ehn blewant
pencil sharpener	en blyantspidser	ehn blewantspeesserr
playing cards	et spil kort	eht spil kort
pocket calculator	en lommeregner	ehn lomerrighner
postcard	et postkort	eht postkort
propelling pencil	en skrueblyant	ehn skrooerblewant
refill (for a pen)	en patron (til en pen)	ehn patroan (til ehn pen)
rubber	et viskelæder	eht veesgerlädherr
ruler	en lineal	ehn leenEal
staples	nogle hæftestifter	noaler hæfdersteefderr
string	noget snor	noaert snoar
thumbtacks	nogle tegnestifter	noaler tighnersteefderr
travel guide	en rejsefører	ehn righserførerr
typewriter ribbon	et farvebånd til skrivemaskiner	eht farverbawn til skreeevermaskeenerr
typing paper	noget skrivemaskine-papir	noaert skreevermaskeener-papeer
writing pad	en skriveblok	ehn skreeverblok

Camping and sports equipment *Camping og sportsudstyr*

I'd like a/an/some ...	**Jeg vil gerne have ...**	yigh veel **gehr**ner ha
I'd like to hire a(n)/some ...	**Jeg vil gerne leje ...**	yigh veel **gehr**ner **ligh**er
air bed (mattress)	**en luftmadras**	ehn **looft**madras
backpack	**en rygsæk**	ehn **rewg**sæk
butane gas	**noget flaskegas**	nōa̅ert **flas**gergas
campbed	**en campingseng**	ehn **kam**pingsehng
(folding) chair	**en (klap)stol**	ehn **(klap)**stoal
charcoal	**noget trækul**	nōa̅ert **træ**kool
compass	**et kompas**	eht **kom**pas
cool box	**en køleboks**	ehn **kø**lerboks
deck chair	**en liggestol**	ehn **lee**gerstoal
fire lighters	**nogle ildtændere**	nōa̅ler **eelt**ænnererr
fishing tackle	**nogle fiskegrejer**	nōa̅ler **fis**gergrigher
flashlight	**en lommelygte**	ehn **lom**erlewgder
groundsheet	**et teltunderlag**	eht **tehlt**oonerla
hammock	**en hængekøje**	ehn **hæng**erkoier
ice pack	**en ispose**	ehn **ēēs**poaser
insect spray (killer)	**en insekt-spray**	ehn in**sehkt**"spray"
kerosene	**noget petroleum**	nōa̅ert peh**troal**Eoom
lamp	**en lampe**	ehn **lam**per
lantern	**en lygte**	ehn **lewg**der
mallet	**en kølle**	ehn **køl**ler
matches	**nogle tændstikker**	nōa̅ler **tæn**stiggerr
(foam rubber) mattress	**en (skumgummi) madras**	ehn **(skoom**goomee) madras
mosquito net	**et myggenet**	eht **mewg**gerneht
paraffin	**noget petroleum**	nōa̅ert peh**troal**Eoom
picnic basket	**en madkurv**	ehn **mad**koorv
pump	**en pumpe**	ehn **poom**per
rope	**et reb**	eht rehb
rucksack	**en rygsæk**	ehn **rewg**sæk
screwdriver	**en skruetrækker**	ehn **skrōō**ertræggerr
skiing equipment	**noget skiudstyr**	nōa̅ert **skee**oodhstewr
skin-diving equipment	**noget frømandsudstyr**	nōa̅ert **frø**mansoodhstewr
sleeping bag	**en sovepose**	ehn so°°**er**poaser
(folding) table	**et (klap)bord**	eht **(klap)**boar
tent	**et telt**	eht tehlt
tent pegs	**nogle teltpløkke**	nōa̅ler **tehlt**pløgger
tent pole	**en teltstang**	ehn **tehlt**stang
torch	**en lommelygte**	ehn **lom**erlewgder
windsurfer	**en windsurfer**	ehn "windsurfer"
water flask	**en vandflaske**	ehn **van**flasger

CAMPING, see page 32/HOUSEHOLD ARTICLES, see page 120

Chemist's (drugstore) *Apotek*

A Danish *apotek* (apoatɛk) doesn't stock cameras, books and the like; it is strictly a dispensary. For perfumes and cosmetics you'll have to go to a *parfumeri*.

Normal hours are 9 a.m. to 5.30 p.m. but the location of an all-night service is displayed in the windows of any chemist's shop.

This section has been divided into two parts:

1. Pharmaceutical—medicine, first-aid etc.
2. Toiletry—toilet articles, cosmetics

General *Almindeligt*

Where's the nearest (all-night) chemist's?	**Hvor er det nærmeste apotek (åbent hele natten)?**	vōar ehr dɛ **nær**merster apo**tehk** (**āw**bernt **heh**ler **nad**dern)
What time does the chemist's open/close?	**Hvornår åbner/lukker apoteket?**	vor**nawr** **āw**bnerr/**loog**gerr apo**tehk**erdh

1—Pharmaceutical *Medicin*

I'd like something for ...	**Jeg vil gerne have noget mod ...**	yigh veel **gehr**ner ha **nōa**ert moadh
a cold/a cough	**forkølelse/hoste**	for**kø**lerlser
hay fever	**høfeber**	**hø**fehberr
insect bites	**insektbid**	in**sehkt**beedh
sunburn	**solforbrænding**	**soal**forbræning
travel/altitude sickness	**køresyge/ bjergsyge**	**kø**rersēwer/**byerg**sēwer
an upset stomach	**dårlig mave**	**daw**lee **mā**ver
Can you prepare this prescription for me?	**Kan De give mig, hvad der står på recepten?**	kan de gi migh vadh dehr stawr paw reh**sehp**dern
Can I get it without a prescription?	**Kan jeg få det uden recept?**	kan yigh faw dɛ **ōo**dhern reh**sehpt**
Shall I wait?	**Skal jeg vente?**	skal yigh **vehn**der

DOCTOR, see page 137

Can I have a/an/some ...?	Kan jeg få ...?	kan yigh faw
adhesive plaster	noget hæfteplaster	noaert hæfderplasderr
analgesic	et smertestillende middel	eht smehrdesteelerner meedherl
antiseptic cream	en antiseptisk creme	ehn antiseptisk krehm
aspirin	en æske aspirin	ehn æsger "aspirin"
bandage	en bandage	ehn bandasher
elastic bandage	et elastikbind	eht elasteekbin
Band-Aids®	noget plaster	noaert plasterr
condoms	nogle kondomer	noaler kondomerr
contraceptives	nogle præventive midler	noaler prævehnteever meedhlerr
corn plasters	et ligtorneplaster	eht leetoarnerplasderr
cotton wool (absorbent cotton)	noget vat	noaert vat
cough drops	nogle hostetabletter	noaler hoasdertablehderr
disinfectant	et desinficerings-middel	eht dehsinfiserings-meedherl
ear drops	nogle øredråber	noaler örerdrawberr
eye drops	nogle øjendråber	noaler oierndrawberr
first-aid kit	en nødhælpskasse	ehn nødhyehlpskasser
gauze	noget gaze	noaert gaser
insect spray	en insektspray	ehn insehkt"spray"
iodine	noget jod	noaert yoadh
laxative	et afføringsmiddel	eht owføringsmeedherl
mouthwash	noget mundvand	noaert moonvan
nose drops	nogle næsedråber	noaler næserdrawberr
sanitary towels (napkins)	nogle hygiejnebind	noaler hewgeeighnerbin
sleeping pills	nogle sovepiller	noaler so°°erpeelerr
suppositories	nogle stikpiller	noaler steekpeeler
... tablets	nogle ...tabletter	noaler ... tablehderr
tampons	nogle tamponer	noaler tamponger
thermometer	et termometer	eht tehrmoamehderr
throat lozenges	nogle halstabletter	noaler halstablehderr
tranquillizers	et beroligende middel	eht behroaleegerner meedherl
vitamin pills	nogle vitaminpiller	noaler veetameenpeelerr

GIFT	POISON
KUN TIL UDVORTES BRUG	FOR EXTERNAL USE ONLY

2—Toiletry *Toiletartikler*

I'd like a/an/some ...	**Jeg vil gerne have ...**	yigh veel **gehr**ner ha
after-shave lotion	**noget barberlotion**	nōaert barbehr"lotion"
astringent	**en ansigtstonic**	ehn anseegts"tonic"
bath salts	**noget badesalt**	nōaert bādhersalt
blusher (rouge)	**en blusher**	ehn "blusher"
bubble bath	**noget skumbad**	nōaert skoombadh
cream	**en creme**	ehn krehm
cleansing cream	**rensecreme**	rehnserkrehm
foundation cream	**underlagscreme**	oonerlaskrehm
moisturizing cream	**fugtighedscreme**	foogteehehdhskrehm
night cream	**natcreme**	natkrehm
cuticle remover	**en neglebånds-fjerner**	ehn **nigh**lerbawnsfyehrnerr
deodorant	**en deodorant**	ehn dᴇodo**rant**
emery board	**en sandfil til neglene**	ehn **san**feel til **nigh**lerner
eyebrow pencil	**en øjenbrynsstift**	ehn oiernbrewnsteeft
eyeliner	**en eyeliner**	ehn "eyeliner"
eye shadow	**en øjenskygge**	ehn oiernskewgger
face powder	**noget pudder**	nōaert poodherr
foot cream	**en fodcreme**	ehn foadhkrehm
hand cream	**en håndcreme**	ehn hawnkrehm
lipsalve	**en læbepomade**	ehn læberpoamādher
lipstick	**en læbestift**	ehn læbersteeft
make-up remover pads	**nogle vatrondeller til at fjerne makeup med**	nōaler vatron**dehl**lerr til at fyehrner "make-up" mehdh
mascara	**en mascara**	ehn "mascara"
nail brush	**en neglebørste**	ehn **nigh**lerbørster
nail clippers	**en negleklipper**	ehn **nigh**lerkleeberr
nail file	**en neglefil**	ehn **nigh**lerfeel
nail polish	**en neglelak**	ehn **nigh**lerlak
nail polish remover	**en neglelakfjerner**	ehn **nigh**lerlakfyehrnerr
nail scissors	**en neglesaks**	ehn **nigh**lersaks
perfume	**en parfume**	ehn parfewmer
powder	**noget pudder**	nōaert poodherr
powder puff	**en pudderkvast**	ehn poodherkvast
razor	**en barbermaskine**	ehn barbehrmaskeener
razor blades	**nogle barberblade**	nōaler barbehrblādher
rouge	**noget rouge**	nōaert "rouge"
safety pins	**nogle sikkerhedsnåle**	nōaler siggerhedhsnāwler
shaving brush	**en barberbørste**	ehn barbehrbørster
shaving cream	**en barbercreme**	ehn barbehrkrehm

110

soap	et stykke sæbe	eht stewgger sæber
sponge	en svamp	ehn svamp
sun-tan cream	noget solcreme	noaert soalkrehm
sun-tan oil	noget sololie	noaert soaloalyer
talcum powder	noget talkum	noaert talkoom
tissues	nogle papir-slomme-tørklæder	noaler papeerslomer-tørklædherr
toilet paper	noget toiletpapir	noaert toalehtpapeer
toilet water	noget toiletvand	noaert toalehtvan
toothbrush	en tandbørste	ehn tanbørster
toothpaste	en tandpasta	ehn tanpasta
towel	et håndklæde	eht hawnklædher
tweezers	en pincet	ehn pinseht

For your hair *Til håret*

bobby pins	nogle hårklemmer	noaler hawrklehmerr
colour shampoo	en farveshampoo	ehn farver"shampoo"
comb	en kam	ehn kam
curlers	nogle curlere	noaler "curler"er
dry shampoo	noget tørshampoo	noaert tør"shampoo"
dye	et (hår)farvemiddel	eht (hawr)farvermeedherl
hairbrush	en hårbørste	ehn hawrbørster
hair gel	en hårgele	ehn hawrshehlE
hairgrips	nogle hårklemmer	noaler hawrklehmerr
hair lotion	noget hårvand	noaert hawrvan
hairpins	nogle hårnåle	noaler hawrnäwler
hair slide	et hårspænde	eht hawrspæner
hair spray	en hårlak	ehn hawrlak
setting lotion	en setting lotion	ehn "setting lotion"
shampoo	en shampoo	ehn "shampoo"
for dry/greasy (oily) hair	til tørt/fedtet hår	til tørt/fEterdh hawr
tint	en toning	ehn toning
wig	en paryk	ehn parewk

For the baby *Til babyen*

baby food	noget babymad	noaert "baby"madh
dummy (pacifier)	en sut	ehn soot
feeding bottle	en sutteflaske	ehn sooderflasger
nappies (diapers)	nogle bleer	noaler blEerr

Clothing *Klæder*

If you want to buy something specific, prepare yourself in advance. Look at the list of clothing on page 115. Get some idea of the colour, material and size you want. They're all listed on the next few pages.

General *Almindeligt*

I'd like …	**Jeg vil gerne …**	yigh veel **gehr**ner
I'd like … for a 10-year-old boy/girl.	**Jeg vil gerne have … til en 10-årig dreng/pige.**	yigh veel **gehr**ner ha … til ehn tee **aw**ree drehng/ peeer
I'd like something like this.	**Jeg vil gerne have noget som det her.**	yigh veel **gehr**ner ha noāert som dε hehr
I like the one in the window.	**Jeg kan lide det i vinduet.**	yigh kan li dε ee **vin**dooerdh
How much is that per metre?	**Hvor meget koster det pr. meter?**	voār **migh**ert **kos**der dε pehr **meh**terr

1 centimetre (cm) =	0.39 in.	1 inch =	2.54 cm
1 metre (m) =	39.37 in.	1 foot =	30.5 cm
10 metres =	32.81 ft.	1 yard =	0.91 m.

Colour *Farve*

I'd like something in …	**Jeg vil gerne have noget i …**	yigh veel **gehr**ner ha noāert ee
I'd like a darker/lighter shade.	**Jeg vil gerne have en mørkere/lysere nuance.**	yigh veel **gehr**ner ha ehn **mør**kerer/**lews**erer new**ang**ser
I'd like something to match this.	**Jeg vil gerne have noget, der passer til det her.**	yigh veel **gehr**ner ha noāert dehr **pass**err til dε hehr
I don't like the colour.	**Jeg kan ikke lide farven.**	yigh kan **igg**er li **far**vern

beige	**beige**	"beige"
black	**sort**	soart
blue	**blå**	blaw
brown	**brun**	broon
fawn	**lysebrun**	lewserbroon
golden	**gylden**	gewlern
green	**grøn**	grøn
grey	**grå**	graw
mauve	**lilla**	leelah
orange	**orange**	oarangsher
pink	**lyserød**	lewserrødh
purple	**violet**	vioaleht
red	**rød**	rødh
scarlet	**skarlagensrød**	skarlaernsrødh
silver	**sølvfarvet**	sølfarverdh
turquoise	**turkis**	tewrkees
white	**hvid**	veedh
yellow	**gul**	gool
light ...	**lyse-**	lewser-
dark ...	**mørke-**	mørker-

ensfarvet
(ensfarverdh)

stribet
(streeberdh)

prikket
(preeggerdh)

ternet
(tehrnerdh)

mønstret
(mønstrerdh)

Fabric *Tøjstof*

Do you have anything in ...?	**Har De noget i ...?**	har dee nōaert ee
Is that ...?	**Er det ...?**	ehr dE
handmade	**håndlavet**	hawnlaverdh
imported	**importeret**	importērerdh
made here	**lavet her**	laverdh hehr
I'd like something thinner.	**Jeg vil gerne have noget tyndere.**	yigh veel gehrner ha nōaert tewnerer
Do you have anything of better quality?	**Har De noget i en bedre kvalitet?**	har dee nōaert ee ehn behdhrer kvaleetɛt

What's it made of?	**Hvad er det lavet af?**	vadh ehr dE **laverdh ah**

cambric	**batist**	ba**tist**
camel-hair	**kamelhår**	**kamehl**hawr
chiffon	**chiffon**	shi**fong**
corduroy	**jernbanefløjl**	**yern**banerfloil
cotton	**bomuld**	**bom**ool
crepe	**crepe**	krehp
denim	**denim**	"denim"
felt	**filt**	filt
flannel	**flonel**	floa**nel**
gabardine	**gabardine**	"gabardine"
lace	**knipling**	**knip**ling
leather	**læder**	**lædh**err
linen	**lærred**	**lærer**dh
poplin	**poplin**	"poplin"
satin	**satin**	sa**tæng**
silk	**silke**	**seel**ker
suede	**ruskind**	**roo**skin
towelling	**frotté**	froa**tE**
velvet	**fløjl**	floil
wool	**uld**	ool
worsted	**kamgarn**	**kam**garn

Is it ...?	**Er det ...?**	ehr dE
pure cotton/wool	**ren bomuld/uld**	rehn **bom**ool/ool
synthetic	**syntetisk**	sewnt**tE**tisk
colourfast	**farveægte**	farver**æg**der
crease (wrinkle) resistant	**krølfrit**	**krøl**freet
Is it hand washable/ machine washable?	**Kan man vaske det i hånden/ vaskemaskinen?**	kan man **vas**ger dE ee **hawn**ern/ **vas**germaskeenern
Will it shrink?	**Kryber det?**	**krewb**err dE

Size *Størrelse*

I take size 38.	**Jeg bruger nummer 38.**	yigh **brOO**er **noom**merr **oad**erotredhver
Could you measure me?	**Kan De tage mine mål?**	kan dee ta **mee**ner mawl
I don't know the Danish sizes.	**Jeg kender ikke de danske mål.**	yigh **kehn**er **igg**er dee **dans**ger mawl

Indkøbsvejledning

Sizes can vary somewhat from one manufacturer to another, so be sure to try on shoes and clothing before you buy.

Women *Kvinder*

	Dresses/Suits					
American	8	10	12	14	16	18
British	10	12	14	16	18	20
Continental	36	38	40	42	44	46

	Stockings						Shoes			
American }							6	7	8	9
British	8½	9	9½	10	10½		4½	5½	6½	7½
Continental	0	1	2	3	4	5	37	38	40	41

Men *Mænd*

	Suits/overcoats						Shirts			
American } British	36	38	40	42	44	46	15	16	17	18
Continental	46	48	50	52	54	56	38	40	42	44

	Shoes								
American } British	5	6	7	8	8½	9	9½	10	11
Continental	38	39	40	41	42	43	44	44	45

small (S)	**lille**	**lee**ler
medium (M)	**medium**	**m**edioom
large (L)	**stor**	stoar
extra large (XL)	**ekstra stor**	**ehk**stra stoar
larger/smaller	**større/mindre**	**stø**rrer/**min**drer

A good fit? *Passer det?*

Can I try it on?	**Kan jeg prøve den?**	kan yigh **prø**ver dehn
Where's the fitting room?	**Hvor er prøverummet?**	voar ehr **prø**verroomerdh
Is there a mirror?	**Er der et spejl?**	ehr dehr eht spighl
It fits very well.	**Den passer meget godt.**	dehn **pass**err **migh**ert god
It doesn't fit.	**Den passer ikke.**	dehn **pass**err **igg**er

NUMBERS, see page 147

It's too ...	Den er for ...	dehn ehr for
short/long	kort/lang	kort/lang
tight/loose	stram/vid	stram/veedh
How long will it take to alter?	Hvor lang tid vil det tage at få den ændret?	voar lang teedh veel dɛ ta ah faw dehn ændrerdh

Clothes and accessories *Klæder og tilbehør*

I would like a/an/ some ...	Jeg vil gerne have ...	yigh veel **gehr**ner ha
bathing suit	en badedragt	ehn **bādh**erdragt
bathrobe	en badekåbe	ehn **bādh**erkawber
blouse	en bluse	ehn **blōōs**er
bow tie	en butterfly	ehn "butterfly"
bra	en behå	ehn be haw
braces	et par seler	eht par **sehl**err
cap	en kasket	ehn ka**skeht**
cardigan	en cardigan	ehn "cardigan"
coat	en frakke	ehn **fragg**er
dress	en kjole	ehn **kyoal**er
with long sleeves	med lange ærmer	mehdh **lang**er ærmerr
with short sleeves	med korte ærmer	mehdh **kord**er ærmerr
sleeveless	uden ærmer	**ōōdh**ern ærmerr
dressing gown	en slåbrok	ehn **slaw**brok
evening dress (woman's)	en aftenkjole	ehn **afd**ernkyoaler
girdle	en hofteholder	ehn **hoaf**derholerr
gloves	et par handsker	eht par **hans**gerr
handbag	en håndtaske	ehn **hawn**tasgerr
handkerchief	et lommetørklæde	eht **lom**ertørklædher
hat	en hat	ehn hat
jacket	en jakke	ehn **yagg**er
jeans	et par cowboybukser	eht par "cowboy" **boogs**err
jersey	en ulden trøje	ehn **ool**ern **troi**err
jumper (Br.)	en jumper	ehn "jumper"
kneesocks	et par knæstrømper	eht par **knæ**strømperr
nightdress	en natkjole	ehn **nat**kyoaler
pair of ...	et par ...	eht par
panties	et par trusser	eht par **troos**err
pants (Am.)	et par bukser	eht par **boogs**err
panty girdle	en roll-on	ehn "roll-on"
panty hose	et par strømpebukser	eht par **strømp**erboogserr

pullover	en pullover	ehn "pullover"
polo (turtle)-neck	højhalset	høihalserdh
round-neck	rund halsudskæring	roon halsoodhskæring
V-neck	V-hals	V-hals
with long/short sleeves	med lange/korte ærmer	mehdh langer/korder ærmerr
without sleeves	uden ærmer	oodhern ærmer
pyjamas	en pyjamas	ehn pewyamas
raincoat	en regnfrakke	ehn righnfragger
scarf	et tørklæde	eht tørklædher
shirt	en skjorte	ehn skyoarder
shorts	et par shorts	eht par "shorts"
skirt	en nederdel	ehn nehdherdehl
slip	en underkjole	ehn oonerkyoaler
socks	et par sokker	eht par sogger
stockings	et par strømper	eht par strømperr
suit (man's)	et sæt tøj	eht sæt toi
suit (woman's)	en dragt	ehn dragt
suspenders (Am.)	et par seler	eht par sehlerr
sweater	en sweater	ehn "sweater"
sweatshirt	en sweatshirt	ehn "sweatshirt"
swimming trunks	et par badebukser	eht par bādherboogserr
T-shirt	en T-shirt	ehn "T-shirt"
tie	et slips	eht slips
tights	et par strømpebukser	eht par strømperboogserr
tracksuit	en træningsdragt	ehn træningsdragt
trousers	et par bukser	eht par boogserr
umbrella	en paraply	ehn paraplew
underpants	et par underbukser	eht par oonerboogserr
undershirt	en undertrøje	ehn oonertroier
vest (Am.)	en vest	ehn vest
vest (Br.)	en undertrøje	ehn oonertroier
waistcoat	en vest	ehn vest

belt	et bælte	eht bælder
buckle	et spænde	eht spæner
button	en knap	ehn knap
collar	en flip	ehn flip
cuffs	et par manchetter	eht par manshēderr
hem	en søm	ehn søm
pocket	en lomme	ehn lomer
press stud (snap fastener)	en tryklås	ehn trewklaws
zip (zipper)	en lynlås	ehn lewnlaws

Shoes *Sko/Fodtøj*

I'd like a pair of ...	**Jeg vil gerne have et par ...**	yigh veel **gehr**ner ha eht par
boots	**støvler**	**stø**lerr
moccasins	**mokkasiner**	"moccasin"err
plimsolls (sneakers)	**lærredssko/ gymnastiksko**	**lær**erdhsskoa/ **gewm**nastikskoa
sandals	**sandaler**	sand**ā**lerr
shoes	**sko**	skoa
flat	**flade**	**flad**her
with a heel	**med hæl**	mehdh hæl
with leather soles	**med lædersåler**	mehdh **læd**hersawler
with rubber soles	**med gummisåler**	mehdh **goom**eesawler
slippers	**tøfler**	**tøf**lerr
These are too ...	**De er for ...**	dee ehr for
narrow/wide	**smalle/brede**	**smal**er/**brehd**her
big/small	**store/små**	**stoa**rer/smaw
Do you have a larger/ smaller size?	**Har De et nummer større/mindre?**	har dee eht **noom**merr **stør**rer/**mind**rer
Do you have the same in black?	**Har De det samme i sort?**	har dee dE **sam**merr ee soart
cloth	**stof**	stof
leather	**læder**	**læd**herr
rubber	**gummi**	**goom**ee
suede	**ruskind**	**roo**skin
Is it real leather?	**Er det ægte læder?**	ehr dE **æg**der **læd**herr
I need some shoe polish/shoelaces.	**Jeg har brug for noget skocreme/et par snørebånd.**	yigh har br$\overline{oo}$ for **n$\overline{oa}$**ert **sko**akrehm/eht par **snø**rerbawn

Shoes worn out? Here's the key to getting them fixed again:

Can you repair these shoes?	**Kan De reparere disse sko?**	kan dee rehpar**ēr**er **dees**er skoa
Can you stitch this?	**Kan De sy det her sammen?**	kan dee sew dE hehr **sam**ern
I want new soles and heels.	**Jeg vil have nye såle og hæle.**	yigh veel ha **new**er **saw**lerr oa **hæl**er
When will they be ready?	**Hvornår vil de være færdige?**	vor**nawr** veel dee **vær**er **fær**d$\overline{ee}$er

COLOURS, see page 112

Electrical appliances *Elektrisk udstyr*

The standard voltage is 220 AC, but some camp sites have this and 110. Plugs and sockets are different from both British and American types, so an adaptor will come in handy.

What's the voltage?	**Hvad er strømstyrken?**	vadh ehr **strømstewrgern**
Do you have a battery for this?	**Har De et batteri til det her?**	har dee eht bader**ree** til dE hehr
This is broken. Can you repair it?	**Det her er gået i stykker. Kan De reparere det?**	dE hehr ehr **gawerdh** ee **stewggerr**. kan dee rehpar**Er**er dE
Can you show me how it works?	**Kan De vise mig, hvordan det virker?**	kan dee **vēē**ser migh **vor**dan dE **veer**gerr
I'd like (to hire) a video cassette.	**Jeg vil gerne købe/ leje et videobånd?**	yigh veel **gehr**ner **kø**ber/ **ligh**er eht "video"bawn
I'd like a/an/some ...	**Jeg vil gerne have ...**	yigh veel **gehr**ner ha

adaptor	**en adapter**	ehn a**dap**ter
amplifier	**en forstærker**	ehn for**stær**gerr
bulb	**en pære**	ehn **pæ**rer
CD player	**en CD-afspiller**	en CD-**ow**speelerr
clock-radio	**et radiovækkeur**	eht radiovæg**geroo**r
electric toothbrush	**en elektrisk tandbørste**	ehn ehl**lehk**trisk **tan**børsder
extension lead (cord)	**en forlængerledning**	ehn for**læng**errlehdhning
hair dryer	**en hårtørrer**	ehn **hawr**tørrer
headphones	**hovedtelefoner**	ho°°erdhtehlerfoanerr
(travelling) iron	**et (rejse)strygejern**	eht (**righs**er)strewer**yehrn**
lamp	**en lampe**	ehn **lamper**
plug	**et stik**	eht stik
portable ...	**transportabel**	transpor**taber**l
radio	**en radio**	ehn **radio**
car radio	**bilradio**	**beel**radio
(cassette) recorder	**en (kassette) båndoptager**	ehn (kas**sehd**er) **bawn**optaer
record player	**en pladespiller**	ehn **pladher**speeler
shaver	**en barbermaskine**	ehn bar**behr**masgeener
speakers	**et par højttalere**	eht par **hoit**ålererr
(colour) television	**et (farve)fjernsyn**	eht (**farver**)**fyern**sewn
toaster	**en brødrister**	ehn **brødh**reesterr
transformer	**en transformator**	ehn transfor**mator**
video-recorder	**en videobåndoptager**	ehn "video" **bawn**optaer

Grocer's *Madvarer*

I'd like some bread, please.	**Jeg vil gerne have noget brød.**	yigh veel **gehr**ner ha **nōa**ert brødh
What sort of cheese do you have?	**Hvad slags ost har De?**	vadh slags oast har dee
A piece of ...	**Et stykke ...**	eht **stewg**ger
that one	**det der**	dE dehr
the one on the shelf	**det på hylden**	dE paw **hewl**ern
I'll have one of those, please.	**Jeg vil gerne have et af dem.**	yigh veel **gehr**ner ha eht ah dehm
May I help myself?	**Må jeg tage selv?**	maw yigh taer selv
I'd like ...	**Jeg vil gerne have ...**	yigh veel **gehr**ner ha
a kilo of apples	**et kilo æbler**	eht **keel**o **æb**lerr
half a kilo of tomatoes	**et halvt kilo tomater**	eht halt **keel**o to**mad**err
100 grams of butter	**100 gram smør**	**hun**rerdher gram smør
a litre of milk	**en liter mælk**	ehn **leed**err mælk
half a dozen eggs	**et halvt dusin æg**	eht halt doo**sin** æg
4 slices of ham	**4 skiver skinke**	feerer **skee**verr **skeeng**er
a packet of tea	**en pakke te**	ehn **pagg**er tE
a jar of jam	**et glas syltetøj/ marmelade**	eht glas **sewl**dertoi/ marmer**lad**her
a tin (can) of peaches	**en dåse ferskner**	ehn **daw**ser **fersg**nerr
a tube of mustard	**en tube sennep**	ehn **toob**er **sehn**erp
a box of chocolates	**en æske chokolade**	ehn **æsg**er shoakoa**lad**her

---

1 kilogram or kilo (kg.) = 1000 grams (g.)

100 g. = 3.5 oz.	½ kg. = 1.1 lb.
200 g. = 7.0 oz.	1 kg. = 2.2 lb.

1 oz. = 28.35 g.

1 lb. = 453.60 g.

---

1 litre (l.) = 0.88 imp. quarts = 1.06 U.S. quarts

1 imp. quart = 1.14 l.	1 U.S. quart = 0.95 l.
1 imp. gallon = 4.55 l.	1 U.S. gallon = 3.8 l.

FOOD, see also pages 63–4

Household articles *Husholdningsartikler*

aluminium foil	**aluminiums folie**	aloo**mini**ooms folyer
bottle opener	**oplukker**	op**look**ger
bucket	**spand**	span
candles	**stearinlys**	stɛa**reen**lews
clothes pegs (pins)	**tøjklemmer**	**toi**klehmerr
dish detergent	**opvaskemiddel**	op**vas**germeederl
frying pan	**stegepande**	**stigh**erpaner
matches	**tændstikker**	**tæn**steeggerr
paper napkins	**papirservietter**	pa**peer**servee**eeh**derr
paper towel	**papirhåndklæde**	pa**peer**hawnklædher
plastic bags	**plasticposer**	**pla**stikpoaserr
saucepan	**kasserolle**	kasser**roler**
tin (can) opener	**dåseåbner**	**daw**ser**awb**nerr
tea towel	**viskestykke**	**vis**gerstewgger
vacuum flask	**termoflaske**	**tehr**moflasger
washing powder	**vaskepulver**	**vas**gerpoolver
washing-up liquid	**opvaskemiddel**	op**vas**germeederl

Tools *Værktøj*

hammer	**hammer**	ham**err**
nails	**søm**	søm
penknife	**lommekniv**	**lo**merk**neev**
pliers	**tang**	tang
scissors	**saks**	saks
screws	**skruer**	**skroo**err
screwdriver	**skruetrækker**	**skroo**ertrægger
spanner	**skruenøgle**	**skroo**ernoiler

Crockery *Spisestel*

cups/mugs	**kopper/krus**	ko**berr**/kroos
plates	**tallerkner**	taler**knerr**
saucers	**underkopper**	**oon**erkoberr
tumblers	**vandglas/ølglas**	**van**glas/ølglas

Cutlery (flatware) *Spisebestik*

forks/knives	**gafler/knive**	**gaf**lerr/**knee**ver
spoons	**skeer**	**sk**eerr
teaspoons	**teskeer**	**tɛ**skeerr
(made of) plastic/ stainless steel	**(lavet af) plastic/ rustfrit stål**	(**laverdh ah**) **pla**stik/ **roost**freet stawl

Jeweller's—Watchmaker's *Guldsmed—Urmager*

Could I see that, please?	**Må jeg se det der?**	maw yigh SE dE dehr
Do you have anything in gold?	**Har De noget i guld?**	har dee nōaert ee gool
How many carats is this?	**Hvor mange karat er det her?**	vōar manger karat ehr dE hehr
Is this real silver?	**Er det ægte sølv?**	ehr dE ægder søl
Can you repair this watch?	**Kan De reparere dette ur?**	kan dee rehparĒrer dehder oor
I'd like a/an/some ...	**Jeg vil gerne have ...**	yigh veel gehrner ha
alarm clock	**et vækkeur**	eht væggeroor
bangle	**en armring**	ehn armring
battery	**et batteri**	eht baderree
bracelet	**et armbånd**	eht armbawn
chain bracelet	**armlænke**	armlænker
charm bracelet	**med vedhæng**	med vehdhhæng
brooch	**en broche**	ehn brosher
chain	**en kæde**	ehn kædher
charm	**en charm**	ehn "charm"
cigarette case	**et cigaretetui**	eht siggarehdEtooi
cigarette lighter	**en cigarettænder**	ehn siggarehdtænerr
clip	**en clips**	ehn "clips"
clock	**et ur**	eht oor
cross	**et kors**	eht kors
cuckoo clock	**et kukur**	eht kookoor
cuff links	**et par manchetknapper**	eht par mangshehtknapperr
cutlery	**noget spisebestik**	nōaert spēeserbersteek
earrings	**et par ørenringe**	eht par ōrernringer
gem	**en ædelsten**	ehn ædherlstehn
jewel box	**et smykkeskrin**	eht smewggerskrin
mechanical pencil	**en skrueblyant**	ehn skrōoerblewand
music box	**en spilledåse**	ehn speelerdawser
necklace	**en halskæde**	ehn halskædher
pendant	**et hængesmykke**	eht hængersmewgger
pin	**en nål**	ehn nawl
pocket watch	**et lommeur**	eht lomeroor
powder compact	**en pudderdåse**	ehn poodherdawser
propelling pencil	**en skrueblyant**	ehn skrōoerblewand

ring	**en ring**	ehn ring
engagement ring	**forlovelsesring**	forloaverlsersring
signet ring	**signetring**	sinEtring
wedding ring	**vielsesring**	vēēerlsersring
rosary	**en rosenkrans**	ehn roasenkrans
silverware	**noget sølvtøj**	nōaert søltoi
tie clip	**en slipseklemme**	ehn slipserklehmer
tie pin	**en slipsenål**	ehn slipsernawl
watch	**et ur**	eht oor
automatic	**automatisk**	owtomatisk
digital	**digital**	digital
quartz	**kvarts**	kvartz
with a second hand	**med sekundviser**	mehdh serkoondvēēserr
waterproof	**vandtæt**	vantæt
watchstrap	**en urrem**	ehn oorrehm
wristwatch	**et armbåndsur**	eht armbawnsoor

amber	**rav**	row
amethyst	**ametyst**	amertewst
chromium	**krom**	kroam
copper	**kobber**	koaerr
coral	**koral**	koral
crystal	**krystal**	krewstal
cut glass	**slebet glas**	slEberdh glas
diamond	**diamant**	diamand
emerald	**smaragd**	smarowd
enamel	**emalje**	Emalyer
gold	**guld**	gool
gold plate	**forgyldning**	forgewlning
ivory	**elfenben**	ehlfernbEn
jade	**jade**	yādher
onyx	**onyks**	oanewks
pearl	**perle**	pehrler
pewter	**tinlegering**	tinlehgering
platinum	**platin**	platin
ruby	**rubin**	roobin
sapphire	**safir**	safeer
silver	**sølv**	søl
silver plate	**forsølvning**	forsølning
stainless steel	**rustfrit stål**	roostfreet stawl
topaz	**topas**	topas
turquoise	**turkis**	tewrkees

Optician *Optiker*

I've broken my glasses.	**Mine briller er gået itu.**	meener breelerr ehr gawerdh itoo
Can you repair them for me?	**Kan De reparere dem for mig?**	kan dee rehparērer dehm for migh
When will they be ready?	**Hvornår vil de være færdige?**	vornawr veel dee værer færdeeer
Can you change the lenses?	**Kan De skifte linserne?**	kan dee skeefder linserner
I'd like tinted lenses.	**Jeg vil gerne have farvede linser.**	yigh veel gehrner ha farverdher linserr
The frame is broken.	**Stellet er gået i stykker.**	stehlerdh ehr gawerdh ee stewggerr
I'd like a spectacle case.	**Jeg vil gerne have et brillefutteral.**	yigh vil gehrner ha eht breelerfooderral
I'd like to have my eyesight checked.	**Jeg vil gerne, De checker mit syn.**	yigh veel gehrner dee "check"err meet sewn
I'm short-sighted/ long-sighted.	**Jeg er kortsynet/ langsynet.**	yigh ehr kortsewnerdh/ langsewnerdh
I'd like some contact lenses.	**Jeg vil gerne have et par kontaktlinser.**	yigh veel gehrner ha eht par kontaktlinserr
I've lost one of my contact lenses.	**Jeg har mistet en kontaktlinse.**	yigh har meesderdh ehn kontaktlinserr
Could you give me another one?	**Kunne jeg få en ny?**	kooner yigh faw ehn new
I have hard/soft lenses.	**Jeg har hårde/ bløde linser.**	yigh har hawrer/blødher linserr
Do you have any contact lens fluid?	**Har De kontakt- linsevæske?**	har dee kontakt- linservæsger
I'd like to buy a pair of sunglasses.	**Jeg vil gerne købe et par solbriller.**	yigh veel gehrner kōber eht par soalbreelerr
May I look in a mirror?	**Må jeg se i spejlet?**	maw yigh se ee spighlerdh
I'd like to buy a pair of binoculars.	**Jeg vil gerne købe en kikkert.**	yigh veel gehrner kōber ehn keekerdh

Photography *Fotografering*

Film is relatively inexpensive in Denmark and developing and printing are of a high quality.

I'd like a(n) ... camera.	**Jeg vil gerne have et ... kamera.**	yigh veel **gehr**ner ha eht ... **ka**mehra
automatic	**helautomatisk**	hehlowtomatisk
inexpensive	**ikke for dyrt**	**ig**ger for dewrt
simple	**enkelt**	**ehn**kerlt
Can you show me some ..., please?	**Kan De vise mig nogle ...?**	kan dee **vee**ser migh **no͞a**ler
cine (movie) cameras	**filmkameraer**	**film**kamehraerr
video cameras	**videokameraer**	"video" **kam**erraerr
I'd like to have some passport photos taken.	**Jeg vil gerne have taget nogle pasbilleder.**	yigh vil **gehr**ner ha taerdh **no͞a**ler pasbeelerdherr

Film *Film*

I'd like a film for this camera.	**Jeg vil gerne have en film til dette kamera.**	yigh vil **gehr**ner ha ehn film til **dehd**er **ka**merra
black and white	**sort/hvid**	soart/veedh
colour	**farve-**	**far**ver-
colour negative	**farvenegativ**	**far**vernehgateev
colour slide	**diapositiv**	deea**po**asitiv
cartridge	**kassette**	kas**sehd**er
disc film	**disk**	disk
roll film	**rulle**	**roo**ler
video cassette	**videobånd**	"video" bawn
24/36 exposures	**24/36 billeder**	**fe͞er**ero**te͞w**er/ **sehks**oatrehdhver **bee**lerdherr
this size	**denne størrelse**	**dehn**er **stør**rerlser
this ASA/DIN number	**dette ASA/DIN nummer**	**dehd**er ASA/DIN **noom**mer
artificial light type	**til indendørs optagelser**	til **in**erndørs op**tä**erlserr
daylight type	**til udendørs optagelser**	til **o͞odh**erndørs op**tä**erlserr
fast (high-speed)	**hurtig**	**hoor**tee
fine grain	**finkornet**	**fin**koarnerdh

Processing *Fremkaldning*

How much do you charge for processing?	**Hvad koster det at få filmen fremkaldt?**	vadh **kos**der dɛ ah faw **fil**mern **frehm**kalt
I'd like ... prints of each negative.	**Jeg vil gerne have ... aftryk af hvert negativ.**	yigh veel **gehr**ner ha ... **ow**trewk ah vehrt **neh**gativ
with a matt finish	**med mat overflade**	mehdh mat **ò**erfladher
with a glossy finish	**med højglans**	mehdh **hoi**glans
Will you enlarge this, please?	**Vil De forstørre det her?**	veel dee for**stør**rer dɛ hehr
When will the photos be ready?	**Hvornår vil billederne være færdige?**	vor**nawr** veel **beel**erdherner **vær**rer **fær**dēēer

Accessories and repairs *Tilbehør og reparationer*

I'd like a/an/some ...	**Jeg vil gerne have ...**	yigh veel **gehr**ner ha
battery	**et batteri**	eht bader**ree**
cable release	**en trådudløser**	ehn **trawdh**ōōdhløserr
camera case	**en fototaske**	ehn **foto**tasker
(electronic) flash	**en (elektronisk) flash**	ehn (ehl**ehk**tronisk) "flash"
filter	**et filter**	eht **fil**derr
for black and white	**til sort/hvid**	til soart/veed
for colour	**til farve**	til **far**ver
lens	**et objektiv**	eht **ob**yehktiv
telephoto lens	**teleobjektiv**	"tele"**ob**yehktiv
wide-angle lens	**vidvinkelobjektiv**	**veedh**vingerl**ob**yehktiv
lens cap	**et objektivdæksel**	eht **ob**yehktivdækserl
Can you repair this camera?	**Kan De reparere dette kamera?**	kan dee reh**par**ēr**er** **dehd**er **ka**mehra
The film is jammed.	**Filmen sidder fast.**	**fil**mern **seedh**err fast
There's something wrong with the ...	**Der er noget i vejen med ...**	dehr ehr **nōā**ert ee **vigh**ern mehdh
exposure counter	**tælleren**	**tæl**lerern
film winder	**fremtrækkeren**	**frehm**trækerern
lens	**objektivet**	**ob**yehktiverdh
light meter	**lysmåleren**	**lews**mawlerern
rangefinder	**afstandsmåleren**	**ow**stansmawlerern
shutter	**lukkeren**	**loog**erern

NUMBERS, see page 147

Tobacconist's *Tobakshandel*

Most international cigarette brands are readily available, as well as local ones, from tobacconists, kiosks and supermarkets. However, all cigarettes are heavily taxed.

A packet of cigarettes, please.	**En pakke cigaretter, tak.**	ehn **pagg**er sigga**rehd**err tak
Do you have any American/English cigarettes?	**Har I amerikanske/ engelske cigaretter?**	har ee amehree**kans**ger/ **ehng**erlsger sigga**rehd**err
I'd like a carton.	**Jeg vil gerne have en karton.**	yigh veel **gehr**ner ha ehn kar**tong**
Give me a/some ..., please.	**Vær rar og lad mig få ...**	vær rar oa ladh migh faw
candy	**noget slik/nogle bolsjer**	n̄o̅aert slik/n̄o̅aler **bol**sher
chewing gum	**noget tyggegummi**	n̄o̅aert **tewg**ger**goo**mee
chewing tobacco	**noget skrå**	n̄o̅aert skraw
chocolate	**noget chockolade**	n̄o̅aert shoakoa**ladh**er
cigarette case	**et cigaretetui**	eht sigga**rehd**Etooi
cigarette holder	**et cigaretrør**	eht sigga**rehd**rør
cigarettes	**nogle cigaretter**	n̄o̅aler sigga**rehd**err
filter-tipped	**med filter**	mehdh **fild**err
without filter	**uden filter**	o̅o̅dhern **fild**err
light/dark tobacco	**lys/mørk tobak**	lews/mørk tobak
mild/strong	**milde/stærke**	**meel**er/**stær**ker
menthol	**mentol-**	**men**toal-
king-size	**king-size**	"king-size"
cigars	**nogle cigarer**	n̄o̅aler si**gar**err
lighter	**en lighter**	ehn "lighter"
lighter fluid/gas	**lightervæske/- gas**	"lighter"**væs**ger/-gas
matches	**nogle tændstikker**	n̄o̅aler **tæn**stiggerr
pipe	**en pibe**	ehn **pee**ber
pipe cleaners	**piberensere**	**pee**berrehnserer
pipe tobacco	**pibetobak**	**pee**bertobak
pipe tool	**pibekradser**	**pee**berkrasserr
postcard	**et postkort**	eht **post**kort
snuff	**noget snus**	n̄o̅aert snoos
stamps	**nogle frimærker**	n̄o̅aler **free**mærgerr
sweets	**nogle bolsjer**	n̄o̅aler **bol**sherr
wick	**en væge**	ehn **væ**er

Miscellaneous *Forskelligt*

Souvenirs *Souvenirer*

Danish handicrafts cover a wide range — textiles, ceramics, glassware and toys of notable good taste. Look for hand-made costumed dolls and long-fleeced woollen rugs. Hand-made porcelain and modern-design household articles are world famous, while Georg Jensen still makes some of the world's finest silver and jewellery, and Bang & Olufsen produce audio-visual equipment of the highest quality. Other practical purchases include stylish furniture and antiques.

Here are some ideas for your shopping:

applied arts	**kunsthåndværk**	**koonst**thawnværk
aquavit	**akvit**	akva**veet**
amber	**rav**	row
antiques	**antikviteter**	anteekveet**ē**derr
candles	**stearinlys**	st**ear**eenlewss
ceramics	**keramik**	kehra**meek**
costumed doll	**en dukke i folkedragt**	ehn **doog**ger ee **foal**kerdragt
embroidery	**broderi**	broader**ree**
furniture	**møbler**	**mö**blerr
gadget	**en sjov, lille ting**	ehn sho°° **leel**er teeng
glassware	**en glasting**	ehn **glas**teeng
hand-painted	**håndmalet**	**hawn**mälert
modern	**moderne**	moad**Ē**rner
knitwear	**strikvarer**	**streek**värerr
lamp	**en lampe**	ehn **lamp**er
poster	**en plakat**	ehn **plah**kāt
shag-rug	**et rya-tæppe**	eht **rēwa**-taiber
woollen	**uldent**	**oo**lernt
stamps	**frimærker**	**free**mærkerr
textiles	**tekstilvarer**	t**ek**steelvärerr
hand-printed	**håndtryk**	**hawn**trewg

Records—Cassettes *Plader—Kassetter*

I'd like a ...	**Jeg vil gerne have ...**	yigh veel **gehr**ner ha
cassette	**en kassette**	ehn kas**sehd**er
video cassette	**en videokassette**	ehn **vi**deokassehder
compact disc	**en CD**	ehn sE dE

L.P. (33 rpm)	en LP (33 omdrejninger)	ehn ehl pE (trehotrehdhver omdrighninger)
E.P. (45 rpm)	en EP (45 omdrejninger)	ehn Eh pE (fehmoa førrer omdrighninger)
single	en single	ehn "single"

Do you have any records by ...?	Har De nogle plader med ...?	har dee nōāler pladherr mehdh
Can I listen to this record?	Kan jeg høre denne plade?	kan yigh hØrer dehner pladher
chamber music	kammermusik	kamermoosik
classical music	klassisk musik	klasisk moosik
folk music	folkemusik	folkermoosik
folk song	folkesang	folkersang
instrumental music	instrumentalmusik	instroomehntalmoosik
jazz	jazz	"jazz"
light music	underholdnings- musik	oonerholningsmoosik
orchestral music	orkestermusik	orkehstermoosik
pop music	popmusik	popmoosik

Toys Legetøj

I'd like a toy/game...	Jeg vil gerne have noget legetøj/et spil ...	yigh veel gehrner ha nōāert lighertoi/eht spil
for a boy	til en dreng	til ehn drehng
for a 5-year-old girl	til en pige på 5	til ehn pēēer paw fehm
(beach) ball	en (bade)bold	ehn (bādher)bold
bucket and spade (pail and shovel)	en spand og skovl	ehn span oa sko°°l
building blocks (bricks)	nogle byggeklodser	nōāler bewggerkloser
card game	et kortspil	eht kortspil
chess set	et skakspil	eht skakspil
colouring book	en malebog	ehm mālerboa
doll	en dukke	ehn doogger
electronic game	et elektronisk spil	eht elehktronisk spil
roller skates	et par rulleskøjter	eht par roolerskoiderr
snorkel	en snorkel	ehn "snorkel"
teddy bear	en bamse	ehn bamser
toy car	en legetøjsbil	ehn lighertoisbeel

Your money: banks—currency

At most banks there's sure to be someone who speaks English. You'll find small currency exchange offices (*vekselkontor—* **vɛk**serlkoantoār) in most tourist centres. The exchange rates don't vary much between banks and *vekselkontorer*. Remember to take your passport along with you, as you may need it for identification.

Traveller's cheques and credit cards are widely accepted in tourist-oriented shops, hotels, restaurants, etc. However, if you're exploring the countryside off the beaten track, you'll probably come across stores where they are not taken. The same goes for garages and filling stations—generally, only major agency garages will accept payment in traveller's cheques or by credit card.

Opening hours. With minor variations from town to town, most banks are open from Monday to Friday from 9.30 a.m. to 3 p.m., with late opening on Thursday or Friday from 4 to 6 p.m. In Copenhagen, the exchange office at the Central Railway Station stays open from 7 a.m. to 9 p.m. daily.

Monetary unit. Denmark, Norway and Sweden all use the same name for their currency, but the value differs in each country. The krone (meaning "crown", pronounced **krōā**nern and abbreviated *kr.* or *dkr.*) is divided into 100 øre (**ø**rer).

Coins: 25 and 50 øre, 1, 5, 10 and 20 kroner.
Banknotes: 50, 100, 500 and 1,000 kroner.

Where's the nearest bank?	**Hvor er den nærmeste bank?**	voār ehr dehn **nær**merster bank
Where's the nearest currency exchange office?	**Hvor er det nærmeste vekselkontor?**	voār ehr dɛ **nær**merster **vehk**serlkontoār

At the bank / I banken

I want to change some dollars/pounds.	Jeg ønsker at veksle nogle dollars/pund.	yigh ønsgerr at vehksler noaler "dollars"/poon
I want to cash a traveller's cheque.	Jeg ønsker at indløse en rejsecheck.	yigh ønsgerr at inløser ehn righser"cheque"
What's the exchange rate?	Hvad er vekselkursen?	vadh ehr vehkserlkoorsern
How much commission do you charge?	Hvor meget beregner De i kommission?	voar mighert berrighnerr dee ee koameeshon
Can you cash a personal cheque?	Kan De indløse en personlig check?	kan dee inløser ehn pehrsoanlee "cheque"
Can you telex my bank in London?	Kan De sende et telex til min bank i London?	kan dee sehner eht telex til meen bank ee "london"
I have a/an/some ...	Jeg har ...	yigh har
credit card	kreditkort	krehditkort
Eurocheques	eurochecks	øro"cheques"
letter of credit	et kreditbrev	eht krehditbreh°°
I'm expecting some money from New York. Has it arrived?	Jeg venter nogle penge fra New York. Er de kommet?	yigh vehnder noaler pehnger fra "New York". ehr dɛ komerdh
Please give me ... notes (bills) and some small change.	Vær rar og giv mig ... i sedler og lidt småpenge.	vær rar oa geev migh ... ee sehdhlerr oa leet smawpehnger
Give me ... large notes and the rest in small notes.	Lad mig få ... i store sedler og resten i små sedler.	ladh migh faw ... ee stoarer sehdhlerr oa rehstern ee smaw sehdhlerr

Deposits—Withdrawals / Indskud—Udbetalinger

I want to ...	jeg ønsker at ...	yigh ønsgerr at
open an account	åbne en ny konto	awbner ehn new kontoa
withdraw ... kroner	at få udbetalt ... kroner	at faw oodhbertalt ... kroanerr
Where should I sign?	Hvor skal jeg underskrive?	voar skal yigh oonerskreever

NUMBERS, see page 147

| I'd like to pay this into my account. | **Jeg vil gerne sætte det her ind på min konto.** | yigh veel **gehr**ner **sæd**er DE hehr in paw meen **kont**oa |

Business terms *Forretningsudtryk*

My name is ...	**Mit navn er ...**	meet nown ehr
Here's my card.	**Her er mit kort.**	hehr ehr meet kort
I have an appointment with ...	**Jeg har aftalt et møde med ...**	yigh har **owt**alt eht **mødh**er mehdh
Can you give me an estimate of the cost?	**Kan De give mig et overslag over omkostningerne?**	kan dee **gēē**er migh eht o°°ersla o°°er **om**kostningerner
What's the rate of inflation?	**Hvor høj er inflationen?**	vōar hoi ehr infla**shon**ern
Can you provide me with an interpreter/ a personal computer/ a secretary?	**Kan De skaffe mig en tolk/en PC'er/ sekretær?**	kan dee **skaff**er migh ehn toalk/ehn peh s**Eer**/ s**Ekreh**t**æ**r
Where can I make photocopies?	**Hvor kan jeg tage fotokopier?**	vōar kan yigh ta **fo**tokop**ēē**er

amount	**et beløb**	eht ber**løb**
balance	**en saldo**	ehn **sal**do
capital	**en kapital**	ehn **ka**peetal
cheque	**en check**	en "cheque"
contract	**en kontrakt**	ehn kon**trakt**
discount	**en rabat**	ehn ra**bat**
expenses	**udgifter**	**oodh**geefderr
interest	**en rente**	ehn **rehn**der
investment	**en investering**	ehn inver**stēr**ing
invoice	**en faktura**	ehn fak**too**ra
loss	**et tab**	eht tab
mortgage	**en panteret**	ehn **pan**derreht
payment	**en betaling**	ehn ber**tāl**ing
percentage	**en procentsats**	ehn pro**sent**sats
profit	**et overskud**	eht o°°er**skoodh**
purchase	**et køb**	eht køb
sale	**et salg**	eht sal
share	**en aktie**	ehn **aks**her
transfer	**en overførsel**	ehn o°°er**før**serl
value	**en værdi**	ehn vær**dee**

At the post office

Post offices in Denmark all display a red sign with a crown, bugle and crossed arrows in yellow—and the sign *Kongelig Post og Telegraf*.

Business hours are generally from 9 or 10 a.m. to 5 or 6 p.m. from Mondays to Fridays, and from 9 a.m. to noon on Saturday. In the provinces, hours vary.

Letter (mail) boxes are painted red.

Where's the nearest post office?	**Hvor er det nærmeste posthus?**	vōar ehr dɛ **nær**merster **post**hoos
What time does the post office open/close?	**Hvornår åbner/lukker posthuset?**	vornawr **āwb**nerr/**loog**ger **post**hooserdh
A stamp for this letter/postcard, please.	**Et frimærke til dette brev/postkort.**	eht **free**mærker til **dehd**er breh⁰⁰/**post**kort
A ...øre stamp, please.	**Et ... øres frimærke.**	eht ... **ø**rers **free**mærker
What's the postage for a letter to London?	**Hvad er portoen for et brev til London?**	vadh ehr **port**ōaern for eht breh⁰⁰ til "london"
What's the postage for a postcard to Los Angeles?	**Hvad er portoen for et postkort til Los Angeles?**	vadh ehr **port**ōaern for eht **post**kort til "Los Angeles"
Where's the letter box (mailbox)?	**Hvor er postkassen?**	vōar ehr **post**kassern
I want to send this parcel.	**Jeg ønsker at sende denne pakke.**	yigh **øn**sgerr at **seh**ner **deh**ner **pag**ger

I'd like to send this (by) ...	**Jeg vil gerne sende det her ...**	yigh veel **gehr**ner **sehn**er dE hehr
airmail	**(med) luft**post	(mehdh) **looft**post
express (special delivery)	**expres**	**ehks**prehs
registered mail	**anbefalet**	**an**berfálerdh
At which counter can I cash an international money order?	**Ved hvilken luge kan jeg indløse en international postanvisning?**	vehdh vilkern $\overline{loo}$er kan yigh **inl**øser ehn internashonal **post**anv$\overline{ee}$sning
Where's the poste restante (general delivery)?	**Hvor er poste restanten?**	v$\overline{oa}$r ehr post reh**stangd**en
Is there any post (mail) for me? My name is ...	**Er der noget post til mig? Mit navn er ...**	ehr dehr $\overline{noa}$ert post til migh meet nown ehr

FRIMÆRKER	STAMPS
PAKKER	PARCELS
POSTANVISNINGER	MONEY ORDERS

Telegrams—Telex—Fax *Telegrammer—Telex—Telefax*

All post offices handle telegrams; all larger hotels have fax machines.

I'd like to send a telegram/telex.	**Jeg vil gerne sende et telegram/telex.**	yigh veel **gehr**ner **sehn**er eht tehler**gram**/"telex"
May I have a form, please?	**Må jeg bede om en blanket?**	maw yigh bE om ehn blang**keht**
How much is it per word?	**Hvor meget koster det pr. ord?**	v$\overline{oa}$r **migh**ert **kos**derr dE pehr oar
How long will a cable to Boston take?	**Hvor lang tid vil et telegram tage til Boston?**	v$\overline{oa}$r lang teed veel eht tehler**gram** ta til "boston"
How much will this fax cost?	**Hvor meget vil denne fax koste?**	v$\overline{oa}$r **migh**ert veel **dehn**er faks **kos**der

Telephoning *Telefonering*

International and long-distance calls can be made from phone booths. Within Denmark there are no area codes, just dial the 8-digit number of the subscriber.

Coin boxes, easily recognizable with their green glass, do not return unused coins even if your number is engaged, so insert a minimum at first. Some booths only take cards (a *Telet*), available from kiosks all over town.

Note: Telephone numbers are given in pairs.

Where's the telephone?	**Hvor er telefonen?**	vōar ehr tehler**foan**ern
I'd like a telephone card.	**Jeg vil gerne have et telet.**	yigh veel **gehr**ner ha eht **teh**let
Where's the nearest telephone booth?	**Hvor er den nærmeste telefonboks?**	vōar ehr dehn **nær**merster tehler**foan**boks
May I use your phone?	**Må jeg låne Deres telefon?**	maw yigh **law**ner **deh**rers tehler**foan**
Do you have a telephone directory for Copenhagen?	**Har De en telefonbog for København?**	har dee ehn tehler**foan**bo°° for købern**hown**
I'd like to call ... in England.	**Jeg vil gerne ringe til ... i England.**	yigh veel **gehr**ner **ring**er til ... ee "england"
How do I get the international operator?	**Hvordan kalder jeg rigstelefonen?**	vor**dan** ka**lerr** yigh **rees**tehlerfoanern

Operator *Telefonist*

I'd like Odense 23 45 67.	**Jeg vil gerne have Odense 23 45 67.**	yigh veel **gehr**ner ha **oadhern**ser **treho**tē̄wer **fehm**oforrer **sewvo**trehs
Can you help me get this number?	**Kan De hjælpe mig med at få dette nummer?**	kan dee **yehl**per migh mehdh at faw **dehd**er **noom**merr

NUMBERS, see page 147

| I'd like to place a personal (person-to-person) call. | **Jeg vil gerne bestille en personlig samtale.** | yigh veel **gehr**ner ber**stil**er ehn pehr**soan**lee **sam**täler |
| I'd like to reverse the charges (call collect). | **Jeg vil gerne have, at modtageren betaler.** | yigh veel **gehr**ner ha at **moadh**täerern ber**täl**err |

Speaking *Samtale*

Hello. This is ...	**Hallo. Det er ...**	hal**loa** dE ehr
I'd like to speak to ...	**Jeg vil gerne tale med ...**	yigh veel **gehr**ner **tål**er mehdh
Extension ...	**Lokal**	loa**käl**
Speak louder/more slowly, please.	**Vær rar og tal lidt højere/lidt langsommere.**	vær rar oa tal leet **hoi**erer/leet **lang**soamerer

Bad luck *Uheldig*

Would you try again later, please?	**Vær venlig og prøv igen senere.**	vær **vehn**lee oa prø°° i**gehn seh**nerer
Operator, you gave me the wrong number.	**De gav mig forkert nummer.**	dee gav migh for**kehrd noom**merr
Operator, we were cut off.	**Vi blev afbrudt.**	vee bleh°° **ow**broot

Telephone alphabet *Bogstavering*

A	**Anna**	ana	P	**Peter**	**peht**err
B	**Bernhard**	**behrn**hard	Q	**Quintus**	**kveen**toos
C	**Cecilia**	seh**seel**eea	R	**Rasmus**	**ras**moos
D	**David**	**dä**veedh	S	**Søren**	**sør**ern
E	**Erik**	**ehr**eek	T	**Theodor**	**teho**adoa
F	**Frederik**	**frehdherr**eek	U	**Ulla**	**oo**la
G	**Georg**	**geho**ar	V	**Viggo**	**vig**go
H	**Hans**	hans	W	**William**	**veel**eeam
I	**Ida**	**eed**a	X	**Xerxes**	**sehrk**ses
J	**Johan**	**yoa**han	Y	**Yrsa**	**ewr**sa
K	**Karen**	**kär**ern	Z	**Zacharias**	saka**rée**as
L	**Ludvig**	**loodh**vee	Ø	**Øgir**	**ægg**eer
M	**Marie**	**mar**eeer	Ø	**Øresund**	**ør**ersoorn
N	**Nikolaj**	**neek**oaligh	Å	**Åse**	**aw**ser
O	**Odin**	**oad**een			

Not there *Ikke der*

When will he/she be back?	**Hvornår kommer han/hun tilbage?**	vor**nawr** **koam**err han/hoon tilbåer
Will you tell him/her I called? My name is ...	**Vil De sige til ham/hende, at jeg ringede? Mit navn er ...**	veel dee **sēēe**r til ham/**hehn**er at yigh **ring**erdher? meet nown ehr
Would you ask him/her to call me? My number is ...	**Vil De bede ham/hende ringe til mig? Mit nummer er ...**	veel dee bɛ ham/**hehn**er **ring**er til migh? meet **noom**merr ehr
Would you take a message, please?	**Vil De være rar at tage imod en besked?**	veel dee **vær**er rar ah ta imoadh ehn ber**skehdh**

Charges *Gebyrer*

| What was the cost of that call? | **Hvad kostede den samtale?** | vadh **kos**derdher dehn sam**täl**er |
| I want to pay for the call. | **Jeg ønsker at betale for samtalen.** | yigh **øns**gerr ah ber**täl**er for **sam**tälern |

Der er telefon til Dem.	There's a telephone call for you.
Hvad nummer ringer De?	What number are you calling?
Linien er optaget.	The line's engaged.
Der bliver ikke svaret.	There's no answer.
De har fået forkert nummer.	You've got the wrong number.
Telefonen virker ikke.	The phone is out of order.
Lige et øjeblik.	Just a moment.
Vær rar og vent.	Hold on, please.
Han/Hun er ikke til stede i øjeblikket.	He's/She's out at the moment.

Doctor

In Denmark, treatment and even hospitalization is free for any tourist taken suddenly ill or involved in an accident. For minor treatments, doctors, dentists and chemists will charge on the spot. For EC nationals this money will be partly refunded at the local Danish health service office on production of bills and an E-111 form. You should ensure that your health insurance policy covers the cost of any illness or accident while on holiday.

Can you get me a doctor?	**Kan De få fat på en læge?**	kan dee faw fat paw ehn **læer**
Is there a doctor here?	**Er der en læge her?**	ehr dehr ehn **læer** hehr
I need a doctor, quickly.	**Jeg har brug for en læge, hurtigt.**	yigh har brōō for ehn **læer** **hoor**teet
Where can I find a doctor who speaks English?	**Hvor kan jeg finde en læge, der taler engelsk?**	vōar kan yigh **finner** ehn **læer** dehr **tāler** **ehng**erlsk
Where's the surgery (doctor's office)?	**Hvor har lægen konsultation?**	vōar har **læern** konsoolta**shon**
What are the surgery (office) hours?	**Hvornår er konsultationen åben?**	vor**nawr** ehr konsoolta**shon**ern **āw**bern
Could the doctor come to see me here?	**Kunne lægen komme for at se mig her?**	**koo**ner **læern komer** for at se migh hehr
What time can the doctor come?	**Hvad tid kan lægen komme?**	vadh teed kan **læern komer**
Can you recommend a/an ...?	**Kan De anbefale en ...?**	kan dee **an**berfāler ehn
general practitioner	**praktiserende læge**	praktee**sehr**erner **læer**
children's doctor	**børnelæge**	**bør**nerlæer
eye specialist	**øjenlæge**	**oi**ernlæer
gynaecologist	**gynækolog**	gewnæko**a**loag
Can I have an appointment ...?	**Kan jeg komme ...?**	kan yigh **kom**er
tomorrow	**i morgen**	ee **mōa**ern
as soon as possible	**så snart som muligt**	saw snart som **mool**eet

CHEMIST'S, see page 108

Parts of the body *Legemsdele*

appendix	**blindtarmen**	blintarmern
arm	**armen**	armern
back	**ryggen**	rewggern
bladder	**blæren**	blǣrern
bone	**knoglen**	knoalern
bowel	**tarmen**	tarmern
breast	**brystet**	brewsterdh
chest	**brystkassen**	brewstkassern
ear	**øret**	ȫrerdh
eye(s)	**øjet**	oierdh
face	**ansigtet**	anseegderdh
finger	**fingeren**	feengerern
foot	**foden**	fōadhern
genitals	**kønsdelene**	kȫnsdehlerner
gland	**kirtelen**	keertlern
hand	**hånden**	hawnern
head	**hovedet**	ho°°erdh
heart	**hjertet**	yehrderdh
jaw	**kæben**	kæbern
joint	**leddet**	lehdherdh
kidney	**nyren**	newrern
knee	**knæet**	knǣerdh
leg	**benet**	behnerdh
ligament	**senebåndet**	sɛnerbawnerdh
lip	**læben**	lǣbern
liver	**leveren**	lɛverrern
lung	**lungen**	loongern
mouth	**munden**	moonern
muscle	**muskelen**	moosglern
neck	**halsen/nakken**	halsern/naggern
nerve	**nerven**	nehrvern
nervous system	**nervesystemet**	nehrversewstehmerdh
nose	**næsen**	nǣsern
rib	**ribbenet**	reebehnerdh
shoulder	**skulderen**	skoolerrern
skin	**huden**	hoodhern
spine	**rygraden**	rewgradhern
stomach	**maven**	māvern
tendon	**senen**	sɛnern
thigh	**låret**	lawrerdh
throat	**halsen**	halsern
thumb	**tommelfingeren**	tomerlfeengerrern
toe	**tåen**	tawern
tongue	**tungen**	toongern
tonsils	**mandlerne**	manlerner
vein	**venen**	vehnern

Accident—Injury *Ulykke—Kvæstelse*

There's been an accident.	**Der er sket en ulykke.**	dehr ehr skEt ehn oolewgger
My child has had a fall.	**Mit barn er faldet ned.**	meet bärn ehr **falerdh** nehdh
He/She has hurt his/her head.	**Han/Hun har slået sig i hovedet.**	han/hoon har **slāwerdh** sigh ee **hó**erdh
He's/She's unconscious.	**Han/Hun er bevidstløs.**	han/hoon ehr ber**veest**løs
He's/She's bleeding (heavily).	**Han/Hun bløder (voldsomt).**	han/hoon **blødh**err (**vol**somt)
He's/She's (seriously) injured.	**Han/Hun er kommet (alvorligt) til skade.**	han/hoon ehr **kom**erdh (alvoarleet) til **skādh**er
His/Her arm is broken.	**Armen er brækket.**	**arm**en ehr **brægg**erdh
His/Her ankle is swollen.	**Ankelen er hævet.**	**ankl**ern ehr **hæv**erdh
I've been stung.	**Jeg er blevet stukket.**	yigh ehr **bleh°°**erdh **stoogg**erdh
I've got something in my eye.	**Jeg har fået noget i øjet.**	yigh har **fāw**erdh **nōä**ert ee **oi**erdh
I've got a/an ...	**Jeg har fået ...**	yigh har **fāw**erdh
blister	**en blist**	ehn bleest
boil	**en byld**	ehn bewl
bruise	**et blåt mærke**	eht blawt **mær**ker
burn	**et brandsår**	eht **bran**sāwr
cut	**et snitsår**	eht **sneet**sāwr
graze	**en hudafskrabning**	ehn **hoodh**owskrabning
insect bite	**et insektbid**	eht **in**sehktbeedh
lump	**en bule**	ehn **bool**er
rash	**udslet**	**oodh**sleht
sting	**et stik**	eht steek
swelling	**en hævelse**	ehn **hæv**erlser
wound	**et sår**	eht **sāwr**
Could you have a look at it?	**Kan De se på det?**	kan dee sE paw dE
I can't move my ...	**Jeg kan ikke bevæge ...**	yigh kan **igg**er ber**væ**er
It hurts.	**Det gør ondt.**	dE gør oant

Hvor gør det ondt?	Where does it hurt?
Hvad slags smerte er det?	What kind of pain is it?
dump/skarp/dunkende konstant/kommer og går	dull/sharp/throbbing constant/on and off
Den/Det er...	It's ...
brækket/forstuvet gået ud af led/forvredet	broken/sprained dislocated/torn
Vi må hellere røntgenfotografere det.	I'd like you to have an X-ray.
Vi bliver nødt til at anbringe den/ det i gips.	We'll have to put it in plaster.
Det er betændt.	It's infected.
Er De blevet vaccineret mod stivkrampe?	Have you been vaccinated against tetanus?
Jeg vil give Dem noget smertestillende.	I'll give you a painkiller.

Illness *Sygdomme*

I'm not feeling well.	Jeg føler mig utilpas.	yigh **fö**lerr migh **oo**tilpas
I'm ill.	Jeg er syg.	yigh ehr sew
I feel dizzy.	Jeg er svimmel.	yigh err **svee**mer
I feel ...	Jeg har ...	yigh har
nauseous shivery	kvalme kuldegysninger	**kvalm**er **koo**lergewsningerr
I have a temperature (fever).	Jeg har feber.	yigh har **feh**berr
My temperature is 38 degrees.	Jeg har 38 grader.	yigh har **oad**erotrehdhver **grädh**err
I've been vomiting.	Jeg har kastet op.	yigh har **käs**derdh op
I'm constipated/ I've got diarrhoea.	Jeg har forstoppelse/Jeg har diarré.	yigh har for**stob**erlser/yigh har deear**ε**
My ... hurt(s).	Jeg har ondt i ...	yigh har oant ee

I've got (a/an) ...	Jeg ...	yigh
asthma	**har astma**	har **ast**ma
backache	**har smerter i ryggen**	har **smehr**derr ee **rewg**ern
cold	**er forkølet**	ehr for**kø**lerdh
cough	**har hoste**	har **hoås**der
cramps	**har krampe**	har **kramp**er
earache	**har ondt i ørerne**	har oant ee **ø**rerner
hay fever	**har høfeber**	har **hø**fehberr
headache	**har hovedpine**	har ho°°**erdh**pēēner
nosebleed	**har næseblødning**	har **næ**serblødhning
palpitations	**har hjertebanken**	har **yehr**derbankern
rheumatism	**har reumatisme**	har roima**tees**mer
sore throat	**har ondt i halsen**	har oant ee **hal**sern
stiff neck	**har stiv nakke**	har steev **nag**ger
stomach ache	**har mavepine**	har **mā**verpēēner
sunstroke	**har solstik**	har **soal**steek
I have difficulties breathing.	**Jeg har besvær med at trække vejret.**	yigh har ber**svær** mehd at **trægg**er **vehr**erdh
I have chest pains.	**Jeg har ondt i brystet.**	yigh har oant ee **brews**derdh
I had a heart attack ... years ago.	**Jeg havde et hjerteanfal for ... år siden.**	yigh **hādh**er eht **hyehr**deranfal for ... awr **sēē**dhern
My blood pressure is too high/too low.	**Mit blodtryk er for højt/for lavt.**	meet **bloadh**trewg ehr for hoit/for lavt
I'm allergic to ...	**Jeg kan ikke tåle ...**	yigh kan **igg**er **tāw**ler
I'm diabetic.	**Jeg har sukkersyge.**	yigh har **soogg**ersewer

Women's section *Kvindernes afsnit*

I have period pains.	**Jeg har menstruations-smerter.**	yigh har mehn-strooa**shons**smehrderr
I have a vaginal infection.	**Jeg har underlivs-betændelse.**	yigh har **oon**erleevs-bertænnerlser
I'm on the pill.	**Jeg tager p-piller.**	yigh tar pE-**peel**ler
I haven't had a period for 2 months.	**Jeg har ikke haft menstruation i 2 måneder.**	yigh har **igg**er haft mehnstrooa**shon** ee toa **māw**nerdher
I'm pregnant.	**Jeg er gravid.**	yigh ehr grä**veedh**

Hvor længe har De følt Dem sådan?	How long have you been feeling like this?
Er det første gang, De har haft det sådan?	Is this the first time you've had this?
Jeg tager temperaturen/måler blodtrykket.	I'll take your temperature/blood pressure.
Vær rar og rul ærmet op.	Roll up your sleeve, please.
Vær rar og tag tøjet af (på overkroppen).	Please undress (down to the waist).
Vær rar og læg Dem her.	Please lie down over here.
Luk munden op.	Open your mouth.
Dyb indånding.	Breathe deeply.
Host lidt.	Cough, please.
Hvor gør det ondt?	Where does it hurt?
De har ...	You've got (a/an) ...
blindtarmsbetændelse	appendicitis
blærebetændelse	cystitis
mavekatar	gastritis
influenza	flu
madforgiftning	food poisoning
betændelse i ...	inflammation of ...
gulsot	jaundice
en kønssygdom	venereal disease
lungebetændelse	pneumonia
mæslinger	measles
Det er (ikke) smitsomt.	It's (not) contagious.
Det er en allergi.	It's an allergy.
Jeg vil give Dem en indsprøjtning.	I'll give you an injection.
Jeg vil have en blodprøve/afføringsprøve/urinprøve.	I want a specimen of your blood/stools/urine.
De skal holde sengen i ... dage.	You must stay in bed for ... days.
De bør undersøges af en speciallæge.	I want you to see a specialist.
De skal indlægges på hospitalet til undersøgelse.	I want you to go to the hospital for a general check-up.

Prescription—Treatment *Recept—Behandling*

This is my usual medicine.	**Det her er min sædvanlige medicin.**	dɛ hehr ehr meen sædhvan**leeer** mehdee**seen**
Can you give me a prescription for this?	**Kan jeg få en recept på det?**	kan yigh faw ehn reh**sehpt** paw dɛ
Can you prescribe a/an/some ...?	**Kan De skrive recept på ...?**	kan dee **skreever** reh**sehpt** paw
antidepressant	**et middel mod depression**	eht **meedherl** moadh dehpreh**shon**
sleeping pills	**nogle sovetabletter**	**noaler** so°°ertablehderr
tranquillizer	**et beroligende middel**	eht beh**roaleeerner meedherl**
I'm allergic to certain antibiotics/penicillin.	**Jeg kan ikke tåle visse antibiotika/ penicillin.**	yigh kan **igger** tawler **visser** antibi**oa**tika/ peni**cillin**
I don't want anything too strong.	**Jeg vil ikke have noget, der er for stærkt.**	yigh veel **igger** ha **noaert** dehr ehr for stærkt
How many times a day should I take it?	**Hvor mange gange om dagen skal jeg tage det?**	voar **manger ganger** om **daern** skal yigh ta dɛ
Must I swallow them whole?	**Skal jeg sluge dem hele?**	skal yigh **slooer** dehm **hehler**

Hvad slags behandling får De?	What treatment are you having?
Hvad medicin tager De?	What medicine are you taking?
Ved indsprøjtning eller gennem munden?	By injection or orally?
Tag ... teskeer af denne medicin ...	Take ... teaspoons of this medicine ...
Tag en pille med et glas vand ...	Take one pill with a glass of water...
hver ... time	every ... hours
... gange om dagen	... times a day
før/efter hvert måltid	before/after each meal
om morgenen/om aftenen	in the morning/at night
hvis De har smerter	if there is any pain
i ... dage	for ... days

CHEMIST'S, see page 107

Fee *Honorar*

How much do I owe you?	**Hvor meget bliver det?**	vōar **might**ert **blee**er dɛ
May I have a receipt for my health insurance?	**Må jeg få en kvittering til min sygeforsikring?**	maw yigh faw ehn kveett**er**ing til meen **sew**erforsikring
Can I have a medical certificate?	**Kan jeg få en lægeeattest?**	kan yigh faw ehn l**æ**erattehst
Would you fill in this health insurance form, please?	**Vil De være venlig at udfylde denne blanket til sygeforsikringen?**	veel dee v**æ**rer **vehn**lee at **oodh**fewller **dehn**er blang**keht** til **sew**erforsikringern

Hospital *Hospital*

Please notify my family.	**Vær venlig og underret min familie.**	vær **vehn**lee oa **oon**erreht meen fa**mee**lyer
What are the visiting hours?	**Hvornår er der besøgstid?**	vor**nawr** ehr dehr ber**sö**steed
When can I get up?	**Hvornår kan jeg stå op?**	vor**nawr** kan yigh stå op
When will the doctor come?	**Hvornår kommer lægen?**	vor**nawr** komer l**æ**ern
I'm in pain.	**Jeg har smerter.**	yigh har **smehr**derr
I can't eat/sleep.	**Jeg kan ikke spise/sove.**	yigh kan **igg**er sp**ee**ser/so°°er
Where is the bell?	**Hvor er ringeklokken?**	vōar ehr **ring**erkloggern

nurse	**en sygeplejerske**	ehn s**ew**erplighersger
patient	**en patient**	ehn pa**shehnt**
anaesthetic	**en narkose**	ehn nar**kōā**ser
blood transfusion	**en blodtransfusion**	ehn **blōadh**-transfooshon
injection	**en indsprøjtning**	ehn **in**sproitning
operation	**en operation**	ehn opeh**ra**shon
bed	**en seng**	ehn sehng
bedpan	**et bækken**	eht **bæg**gern
thermometer	**et termometer**	eht termoa**mehd**err

Dentist *Tandlæge*

Can you recommend a good dentist?	**Kan De anbefale en god tandlæge?**	kan dee anberfåler ehn goadh tanlæer
Can I make an (urgent) appointment to see Dr ...?	**Kan jeg få en tid med tandlægen ... (så hurtigt som muligt)?**	kan yigh faw ehn teedh mehdh tanlæern ... (saw hoorteet som mooleet)
Couldn't you make it earlier?	**Kan jeg ikke komme tidligere?**	kan yigh igger komer teedhleeerer
I have a broken tooth.	**Jeg har brækket en tand.**	yigh har bræggerdh ehn tan
I have toothache.	**Jeg har tandpine.**	yigh har tanpeener
I have an abscess.	**Jeg har en byld.**	yigh har ehn bewl
This tooth hurts.	**Det gør ondt i denne tand.**	dɛ gør oant ee dehner tan
at the top	**foroven**	foro°°ern
at the bottom	**forneden**	fornehdhern
at the front	**foran**	foran
at the back	**bagved**	bavehdh
Can you fix it temporarily?	**Kan De behandle den midlertidigt?**	kan dee berhanler dehn meedhlerteedheet
I don't want it pulled out.	**Jeg vil ikke have den trukket ud.**	yigh veel igger ha dehn trooggerdh oodh
Could you give me an anaesthetic?	**Kunne jeg få en bedøvelse?**	kooner yigh faw ehn berdöverlser
I've lost a filling.	**Jeg har tabt en plombe.**	yigh har tabt ehn ploamber
My gums ...	**Tandkødet ...**	tankødherdh
are very sore	**er meget ømt**	ehr mighert ømt
are bleeding	**bløder**	blødherr
I've broken my dentures.	**Jeg har brækket min protese.**	yigh har bræggerdh meen proatehser
Can you repair my dentures?	**Kan De reparere min protese?**	kan dee rehparĒrerr meen proatehser
When will they be ready?	**Hvornår vil den være færdig?**	vornawr veel den værer færdee

Reference section

Where do you come from? *Hvor kommer De fra?*

Africa	**Afrika**	afrika
Asia	**Asien**	aseeern
Australia	**Australien**	owstraleeern
Europe	**Europa**	øroapa
North America	**Nordamerika**	noaramehrika
South America	**Sydamerika**	sewdhamehrika

Countries *Lande*

Austria	**Østrig**	øsdree
Belgium	**Belgien**	behlgeeern
Canada	**Canada**	kanada
China	**Kina**	keena
Czech Republic	**Tjekkiet**	chehkkeeerdh
Denmark	**Danmark**	danmark
England	**England**	ehnglan
Estonia	**Estland**	ehstlan
Finland	**Finland**	finlan
France	**Frankrig**	frankree
Germany	**Tyskland**	tewsklan
Great Britain	**Storbritannien**	stoarbritanyern
Greece	**Grækenland**	grækernlan
India	**Indien**	indeeern
Ireland	**Irland**	irlan
Israel	**Israel**	israehl
Italy	**Italien**	italeeern
Japan	**Japan**	yapan
Latvia	**Letland**	letlan
Lithuania	**Litauen**	litouern
Luxembourg	**Luxembourg**	looksehmboor
Netherlands	**Nederlandene**	nehdherlanerner
Norway	**Norge**	noarer
Portugal	**Portugal**	portoogal
Russia	**Rusland**	rooslan
Scotland	**Skotland**	skotlan
Slovakia	**Slovakiet**	sloavakeeerdh
South Africa	**Sydafrika**	sewdhafrika
Spain	**Spanien**	spaneeern
Sweden	**Sverige**	svehreeer
Switzerland	**Schweiz**	shvights
Turkey	**Tyrkiet**	tewrkeeerdh
Ukraine	**Ukraine**	ookrighner
United States	**USA**	oo ehs ah
Wales	**Wales**	"wales"

Numbers *Tal*

0	**nul**	nool
1	**en**	ehn
2	**to**	toa
3	**tre**	treh
4	**fire**	feerer
5	**fem**	fehm
6	**seks**	sehks
7	**syv**	sewv
8	**otte**	oader
9	**ni**	nee
10	**ti**	tee
11	**elleve**	ehlver
12	**tolv**	toal
13	**tretten**	trehdern
14	**fjorten**	fyoardern
15	**femten**	fehmdern
16	**seksten**	sighsdern
17	**sytten**	sewdern
18	**atten**	addern
19	**nitten**	needdern
20	**tyve**	tewver
21	**enogtyve**	ehnotewver
22	**tooggyve**	toaotewver
23	**treogtyve**	trehotewver
24	**fireogtyve**	feerotewver
25	**femogtyve**	fehmotewver
26	**seksogtyve**	sehksotewver
27	**syvogtyve**	sewvotewver
28	**otteogtyve**	oaderotewver
29	**niogtyve**	neeotewver
30	**tredive**	trehdhver
31	**enogtredive**	ehnotrehdhver
32	**toogtredive**	toaotrehdhver
33	**treogtredive**	trehotrehdhver
40	**fyrre**	førrer
41	**enogfyrre**	ehnoførrer
42	**toogfyrre**	toaoførrer
43	**treogfyrre**	trehoførrer
50	**halvtreds**	haltrehs
51	**enoghalvtreds**	ehnohaltrehs
52	**tooghalvtreds**	toaohaltrehs
53	**treoghalvtreds**	trehohaltrehs
60	**tres**	trehs
61	**enogtres**	ehnotrehs
62	**toogtres**	toaotrehs

63	**treogtres**	**treh**otrehs
70	**halvfjerds**	**hal**fyehrs
71	**enoghalvfjerds**	**ehn**ohalfyehrs
72	**tooghalvfjerds**	**toa**ohalfyehrs
73	**treoghalvfjerds**	**treh**ohalfyehrs
80	**firs**	feers
81	**enogfirs**	**ehn**ofeers
82	**toogfirs**	**toa**ofeers
83	**treogfirs**	**treh**ofeers
90	**halvfems**	half**ehms**
91	**enoghalvfems**	**ehn**ohalfehms
92	**tooghalvfems**	**toa**ohalfehms
93	**treoghalvfems**	**treh**ohalfehms
100	**hundrede**	**hoon**rerdher
101	**hundrede og et**	**hoon**rerdher oa eht
102	**hundrede og to**	**hoon**rerdher oa toa
110	**hundrede og ti**	**hoon**rerdher oa tee
120	**hundrede og tyve**	**hoon**rerdher oa **tew**ver
130	**hundrede og tredive**	**hoon**rerdher oa **trehdh**ver
140	**hundrede og fyrre**	**hoon**rerdher oa **før**rer
150	**hundrede og halvtreds**	**hoon**rerdher oa hal**trehs**
160	**hundrede og tres**	**hoon**rerdher oa trehs
170	**hundrede og halvfjerds**	**hoon**rerdher oa half**fyehrs**
180	**hundrede og firs**	**hoon**rerdher oa feers
190	**hundrede og halvfems**	**hoon**rerdher oa half**ehms**
200	**to hundrede**	toa **hoon**rerdher
300	**tre hundrede**	treh **hoon**rerdher
400	**fire hundrede**	**fee**rer **hoon**rerdher
500	**fem hundrede**	fehm **hoon**rerdher
600	**seks hundrede**	sehks **hoon**rerdher
700	**syv hundrede**	sewv **hoon**rerdher
800	**otte hundrede**	**oad**er **hoon**rerdher
900	**ni hundrede**	nee **hoon**rerdher
1000	**tusind**	**too**sin
1100	**elleve hundrede**	**ehl**ver **hoon**rerdher
1200	**tolv hundrede**	toal **hoon**rerdher
2000	**to tusind**	toa **too**sin
5000	**fem tusind**	fehm **too**sin
10,000	**ti tusind**	tee **too**sin
50,000	**halvtreds tusind**	hal**trehs too**sin
100,000	**hundrede tusind**	**hoon**rerdher **too**sin
1,000,000	**en million**	ehn meel**yoan**
1,000,000,000	**en milliard**	ehn meel**yard**

first	**første**	**før**sder
second	**anden/andet**	**a**nern/**a**nerdh
third	**tredje**	**trehdh**yer
fourth	**fjerde**	**fyeh**rer
fifth	**femte**	**fehm**der
sixth	**sjette**	**sheh**dder
seventh	**syvende**	s͞ew͞verner
eighth	**ottende**	**oa**derner
ninth	**niende**	n͞e͞eerner
tenth	**tiende**	t͞e͞eerner
once/twice	**en gang/to gange**	ehn gang/toa **gang**er
three times	**tre gange**	treh **gang**er
a half	**en halv/et halvt**	ehn hal/ eht halt
half a ...	**en halv .../et halvt ...**	ehn hal/eht halt
half of ...	**halvdelen af ...**	**hal**dehlern ah
half (adj.)	**halv/halvt**	hal/halt
a quarter/one third	**en kvart/en tredjedel**	ehn kvart/ehn **trehdh**yerdehl
a pair of	**et par**	eht par
a dozen	**et dusin**	eht doos**in**
one per cent	**en procent**	ehn pros**ent**
3.4%	**3,4%**	treh **komma feer**er pros**ent**

Date and time *Dato og tid*

1981	**nitten hundrede og enogfirs**	n͞eeddern **hoon**rerdher oa **ehn**of͞eers
1993	**nitten hundrede og treoghalvfems**	n͞eeddern **hoon**rerdher oa **treh**ohalfehms
2005	**to tusind og fem**	toa t͞oo͞sin oa fehm

Year and age *År og alder*

year	**et år**	eht awr
leap year	**et skudår**	eht **skoodh**awr
decade	**et tiår**	eht **tee**awr
century	**et århundrede**	eht **awrhoon**rerdher
this year	**i år**	ee awr
last year	**i fjor**	ee fyoar
next year	**næste år**	**næs**der awr
each year	**hvert år**	vehrt awr
2 years ago	**for to år siden**	for toa awr s͞e͞edhern
in one year	**om et år**	om eht awr
in the eighties	**i firserne**	ee **feer**serner
the 16th century	**1500-tallet/ sekstende århundrede**	**fehm**dern **hoon**rerdh **tal**erdh/**sighs**terner **awrhoon**rerdher

in the 20th century	**i det tyvende århundrede**	ee deht **tew**vernder awr**hoon**rerdher
How old are you?	**Hvor gammel er De?**	voar **gam**erl ehr dee
I'm 30 years old.	**Jeg er 30 år.**	yigh ehr **trehdh**ver awr
He/She was born in 1960.	**Han/Hun er født i 1960.**	han/hoon ehr føt ee **needd**ern **hoon**rerdh oa trehs
What is his/her age?	**Hvad er hans/hendes alder?**	vadh er hans/**heh**ners **al**err
Children under 16 are not admitted.	**Ingen adgang for børn under 16.**	**ing**ern **adh**gang for børn **oon**er **sigh**stern

Seasons *Årstider*

spring/summer	**forår/sommer**	fo**rawr**/**som**err
autumn/winter	**efterår/vinter**	**ehf**derawr/**vind**err
in spring	**om foråret**	om fo**rawr**edh
during the summer	**i løbet af sommeren**	ee **løb**erdh ah **som**erern
in autumn	**om efteråret**	om **ehf**derawrerdh
during the winter	**i løbet af vinteren**	ee **løb**erdh ah **vind**erern
high season	**højsæson**	**hois**æsong
low season	**lavsæson**	**lows**æsong

Months *Måneder*

January	**januar**	**yan**ooar
February	**februar**	**fehb**rooar
March	**marts**	marts
April	**april**	a**preel**
May	**maj**	migh
June	**juni**	**yoo**nee
July	**juli**	**yoo**lee
August	**august**	ow**goost**
September	**september**	sehp**tehm**berr
October	**oktober**	ok**toa**ber
November	**november**	noa**vehm**berr
December	**december**	deh**sehm**berr
in September	**i september**	ee sehp**tehm**berr
since October	**siden oktober**	**seed**hern ok**toa**berr
the beginning of January	**begyndelsen af januar**	ber**gewn**erlsern ah **yan**ooar
the middle of February	**midten af februar**	**midd**ern ah **fehb**rooar
the end of March	**slutningen af marts**	**sloot**ningern ah marts

Days and date *Dage og dato*

What day is it today?	**Hvad dag er det i dag?**	vadh dai ehr dɛ ee dai
Sunday	**søndag**	**søn**dai
Monday	**mandag**	**man**dai
Tuesday	**tirsdag**	**teers**dai
Wednesday	**onsdag**	**oans**dai
Thursday	**torsdag**	**toars**dai
Friday	**fredag**	**freh**dai
Saturday	**lørdag**	**lør**dai
It's ...	**Det er ...**	dɛ ehr
July 1	**den 1./første juli**	dehn **førs**der **yoo**lee
March 10	**den 10./tiende marts**	dehn **teeer**ner marts
in the morning	**om morgenen/om formiddagen**	om **moa**ernern/om for**mid**daern
during the day	**i løbet af dagen**	ee **lø**berdh ah **da**ern
in the afternoon	**om eftermiddagen**	om **ehf**dermiddaern
in the evening	**om aftenen**	om **af**dernern
at night	**om natten/om aftenen**	om **nad**dern/om **af**dernern
the day before yesterday	**i forgårs**	ee **for**gawrs
yesterday	**i går**	ee gawr
today	**i dag**	ee dai
tomorrow	**i morgen**	ee **moa**ern
the day after tomorrow	**i overmorgen**	ee o°°er**moa**ern
the day before	**dagen før**	**da**ern før
the next day	**næste dag**	**næs**der dai
two days ago	**for to dage siden**	for toa **da**er **seedh**ern
in three days' time	**om tre dage**	om treh **da**er
last week	**sidste uge**	**sees**der **oo**er
next week	**næste uge**	**næs**der **oo**er
for a fortnight (two weeks)	**i fjorten dage (to uger)**	ee **fyoar**dern **da**er (toa **oo**err)
birthday	**fødselsdag**	**fø**selsdai
day off	**fridag**	**free**dai
holiday	**helligdag**	**hehl**eedai
holidays/vacation	**ferie**	**fehr**yer
week	**uge**	**oo**er
weekend	**weekend**	"weekend"
working day	**hverdag/ arbejdsdag**	**vehr**dai/**ar**bighdsdai

Public holidays *Offentlige helligdage*

Though Denmark's banks, offices and major shops close on public holidays, museums, tourist attractions and cafés will be open.

January 1	**Nytår**	New Year's Day
June 5	**Grundlovsdag**	Constitution Day (afternoon only)
December 24	**Juleaften**	Christmas Eve
December 25	**Juledag**	Christmas Day
December 26	**2. juledag**	Boxing Day
Moveable Dates:	**Skærtorsdag**	Maundy Thursday
	Langfredag	Good Friday
	2. påskedag	Easter Monday
	St. Bededag	Prayer Day
	Kristi himmelfart	Ascension Day
	2. pinsedag	Whit Monday

Greetings and wishes *Hilsner og ønsker*

Merry Christmas!	**Glædelig jul!**	glæ̃dherlee yōōl
Happy New Year!	**Godt nytår!**	god **newd**awr
Happy Easter!	**God påske!**	goadh **pāws**ger
Happy birthday!	**Til lykke med fødselsdagen!**	til **lew**ger mehdh **fø**selsdaern
Best wishes!	**Bedste ønsker!**	**behs**der **ōns**gerr
Congratulations!	**Til lykke!**	til **lew**gger
Good luck!	**Held og lykke!**	hehl oa **lewg**ger
All the best!	**Alt godt!**	alt god
Have a good trip!	**God tur!**	goadh tōōr
Have a good holiday!	**God ferie!**	goadh **feh**ryer
Best regards from ...	**Bedste hilsner fra .../Jeg skal hilse fra ...**	**behs**der **heels**nerr fra/ yigh skal **heels**er fra
My regards to ...	**Hils ...**	heels

What time is it? *Hvad er klokken?*

Excuse me. Can you tell me the time?	Undskyld. Kan De sige mig, hvad klokken er?	oonskewl. kan dee seeer migh vadh kloggern ehr
It's ...	Den er ...	dehn ehr
five past one	fem minutter over et	fehm minooderr o°°er eht
ten past two	ti minutter over to	tee minooderr o°°er toa
a quarter past three	kvart over tre	kvart o°°er treh
twenty past four	tyve minutter over fire	tewver minooderr o°°erfeeer
twenty-five past five	fem minutter i halvseks	fehm minooderr ee halsehks
half past six	halvsyv	halsewv
twenty-five to seven	fem minutter over halvsyv	fehm minooderr o°°er halsewv
twenty to eight	tyve minutter i otte	tewver minooderr ee oader
a quarter to nine	kvart i ni	kvart ee nee
ten to ten	ti minutter i ti	tee minooderr ee tee
five to eleven	fem minutter i elleve	fehm minooderr ee ehlver
twelve o'clock (noon/ midnight)	tolv/fireogtyve	toal/feereroatewver
in the morning	om morgenen	om moaernern
in the afternoon	om eftermiddagen	om ehfdermidaern
in the evening	om aftenen	om afdernern
The train leaves at ...	Toget går klokken ...	toaerdh gawr kloggern ...
13.04 (1.04 p.m.)	13.04	trehdern nool feerer
0.40 (0.40 a.m.)	0.40	nool førrer
in five minutes	om fem minutter	om fehm minooderr
in a quarter of an hour	om et kvarter	om eht kvartehr
half an hour ago	for en halv time siden	for ehn hal teemer seedern
about two hours	ca. to timer	seerka toa teemerr
more than 10 minutes	mere end ti minutter	mehrer ehn tee minooderr
less than 30 seconds	mindre end 30 sekunder	mindrer ehn trehdhver sekoonder
The clock is fast/ slow.	Uret går for hurtigt/langsomt.	oorerdh gawr for hoorteet/ langsomt

* In everyday conversation, time is expressed as shown here. However, official time uses a 24-hour clock, so that afternoon hours are counted from 13 to 24.

Common abbreviations *Almindelige forkortelser*

adr.	addresse	address
afs.	afsender	from (on a letter)
A/S	aktieselskab	Ltd.
bem.	bemærk	please note
bl.a.	blandt andet	among other things
co.	kompagni	company
D	Damer	Ladies
DFDS	De Forenede Dampskibs-selskaber	United Danish Shipping Companies
DK	Danmark	Denmark
DSB	De Danske Statsbaner	Danish State Railways
d.v.s.	det vil sige	that is
EF	Det Europæiske Fællesskab	European Community
FDM	De Forenede Danske Motorejere	Danish Automobile Club
f.eks.	for eksempel	for example
FN	De Forenede Nationer	United Nations
frk.	frøken	Miss
f.t.	for tiden	now
H	Herrer	Gentlemen
hk	hestekræfter	horsepower
hr.	herre	Mr.
ing.	ingeniør	engineer
i.st.f.	i stedt for	instead of
jfr.	jævnfør	see
kr.	kroner	crowns
L.	lille	small (of towns)
maks.	maksimum	maximum
min.	minimum	minimum
m.m.	med mere	and so on
nr.	nummer	number
o.s.v.	og så videre	and so on
p.gr.af	på grund af	because of
s.	sal	floor
St.	Store	big (of towns)
skt.	Sankt	Saint
sml.	sammenlign	compare
t.h.	til højre	on the right
t.v.	til venstre	on the left
v.s.a.	ved siden af	beside

Signs and notices *Skilte og opslag*

Adgang vorbudt for uvedkommende	Trespassers will be prosecuted
Alt optaget	No vacancies
Damer	Ladies
Det er forbudt at henkaste affald	No littering
Døren er åben	Enter without knocking
Elevator	Lift
Fare (Livsfare)	Danger (of death)
... forbudt	... forbidden
Forsigtig	Caution
Gratis adgang	Free admittance
Herrer	Gentlemen
Indgang	Entrance
Indgangen må ikke spærres	Do not block entrance
Information	Information
Ingen adgang/Adgang forbudt	No admittance
I uorden	Out of order
Kasse	Cash desk
Koldt	Cold
Ledig	Vacant
Må ikke berøres	Do not touch
Ned	Down
Nødudgang	Emergency exit
Nymalet	Wet paint
Op	Up
Optaget	Occupied
Pas på! Hunden bider!	Beware of the dog
Privat vej	Private road
Reserveret	Reserved
Ring	Please ring
Rygning forbudt	No smoking
Skub	Push
Til leje	For hire
Til leje	To let
Til salg	For sale
Træk	Pull
Udgang	Exit
Udsalg	Sale
Udsolgt	Sold out
Varmt	Hot
Vent	Please wait
Vil ikke forstyrres	Do not disturb
Åben	Open

REFERENCE SECTION

Emergency *Nødstilfælde*

Call the police	**Tilkald politiet**	tilkal politierdh
Consulate	**Konsulat**	konsoolat
DANGER	**FARE**	fārer
Embassy	**Ambassade**	ambassadher
FIRE	**BRAND**	bran
Gas	**Gas**	gas
Get a doctor	**Tilkald læge**	tilkal læær
Go away	**Gå væk**	gaw vehk
HELP	**HJÆLP**	yehlp
Get help quickly	**Tilkald hjælp— hurtigt**	tilkal yehlp **hoort**eet
I'm ill	**Jeg er syg**	yigh ehr sew
I'm lost	**Jeg er faret vild**	yigh ehr fārerdh veel
Leave me alone	**Lad mig være i fred**	ladh migh væærer ee frehdh
LOOK OUT	**GIV AGT**	giv agt
Poison	**Gift**	gift
POLICE	**POLITI**	politi
Stop that man/ woman	**Stands den mand/ kvinde**	stans dehn man/**kveen**er
STOP THIEF	**STOP TYVEN**	stop **tewv**ern

Emergency telephone numbers *Nødnumre*

The all-purpose emergency number is 000, and called from public phone boxes it's free. Speak distinctly (English will be understood) and state your number and location.

Lost property—Theft *Hittegods — Tyveri*

Where's the ...?	**Hvor er ...?**	voar ehr
lost property (lost and found) office	**hittegodskontoret**	heedergoaskontoarerdh
police station	**politistationen**	politistashonern
I want to report a theft.	**Jeg vil anmelde et tyveri.**	yigh veel anmehler eht tewverree
My ... has been stolen.	**Min/Mit ... er blevet stjålet**	meen/meet ... ehr bleh°°erdh styawlerdh
I've lost my ...	**Jeg har tabt ...**	yigh har tabt
handbag	**min håndtaske**	meen hawntasger
passport	**mit pas**	meet pas
wallet	**min tegnebog**	meen tighnerboa

CAR ACCIDENTS, see page 78

Diverse

Conversion tables

Centimetres and inches

To change centimetres into inches, multiply by .39.

To change inches into centimetres, multiply by 2.54.

	in.	feet	yards
1 mm	0.039	0.003	0.001
1 cm	0.39	0.03	0.01
1 dm	3.94	0.32	0.10
1 m	39.40	3.28	1.09

	mm	cm	m
1 in.	25.4	2.54	0.025
1 ft.	304.8	30.48	0.304
1 yd.	914.4	91.44	0.914

(32 metres = 35 yards)

Temperature

To convert centigrade into degrees Fahrenheit, multiply centigrade by 1.8 and add 32.

To convert degrees Fahrenheit into centigrade, subtract 32 from Fahrenheit and divide by 1.8.

Kilometres into miles

1 kilometre (km.) = 0.62 miles

km.	10	20	30	40	50	60	70	80	90	100	110	120	130
miles	6	12	19	25	31	37	44	50	56	62	68	75	81

Miles into kilometres

1 mile = 1.609 kilometres (km.)

miles	10	20	30	40	50	60	70	80	90	100
km.	16	32	48	64	80	97	113	129	145	161

Fluid measures

1 litre (l.) = 0.88 imp. quart or 1.06 U.S. quart
1 imp. quart = 1.14 l.   1 U.S. quart = 0.95 l.
1 imp. gallon = 4.55 l.   1 U.S. gallon = 3.8 l.

litres	5	10	15	20	25	30	35	40	45	50
imp. gal.	1.1	2.2	3.3	4.4	5.5	6.6	7.7	8.8	9.9	11.0
U.S. gal.	1.3	2.6	3.9	5.2	6.5	7.8	9.1	10.4	11.7	13.0

Weights and measures

1 kilogram or kilo (kg.) = 1000 grams (g.)

100 g. = 3.5 oz.	½ kg. = 1.1 lb.
200 g. = 7.0 oz.	1 kg. = 2.2 lb.

1 oz. =   28.35 g.
1 lb. = 453.60 g.

CLOTHING SIZES, see page 114/YARDS AND INCHES, see page 112

Diverse

Basic grammar

The Danish and English languages are historically closely related. This can be seen most clearly in the vocabulary, e.g. *arm*, arm, *under*, under, *land*, country, *frost*, frost, etc. Danish is comfortingly like English in having few grammatical inflections. If the existence of two genders seems to complicate matters, remember that most nouns are of common gender, and a mistake here will rarely lead to misunderstanding.

A relatively simple grammatical structure, combined with a somewhat familiar vocabulary, makes it possible for an English-speaker to acquire a working knowledge of Danish without too much difficulty.

Here is the briefest possible outline of the essential features of Danish grammar.

Noun and articles

All nouns in Danish are either common or neuter in gender. (Most nouns are of common gender, but because many very frequent nouns are of neuter gender, it's best to learn each together with its article.)

1. Indefinite article (a/an)

A/an is expressed by **en** with common nouns and by **et** with neuter nouns.

Indefinite plurals are formed by adding **-e** or **-er** to the singular.

	singular		plural	
common gender neuter gender	*en* bil *et* hus	a car a house	bil*er* hus*e*	cars houses

Some nouns remain unchanged in the plural.

singular: *et* **rum**   a room   plural: **rum**   rooms

2. Definite article (the)

Where we in English say ''the car'', the Danes say the equivalent of ''car-the'', i.e. they tag the definite article onto the end of the noun.

In the singular, common nouns take an **-en** ending, neuter nouns an **-et** ending. In the plural, both take an **-(e)ne** or **-(er)ne** ending.

	singular		plural	
common gender neuter gender	**bil**en **tog**et	the car the train	**bil**erne **tog**ene	the cars the trains

3. Possessives

The possessive form is shown by adding **-s**.

> **katten**s **hale**   the cat's tail
> **Jørgen**s **bror**   George's brother

Adjectives

1. Adjectives usually precede the noun.
2. In certain circumstances, the adjective takes an ending.

Indefinite form:

singular { common nouns: adjective remains unchanged;

plural { with both common and neuter nouns, the adjective takes an **-e** ending

	singular		plural	
common neuter	**en stor bil** a big car **et stort hus** a big house		**stor**e **bil**er big cars **stor**e **hus**e big houses	

Definite form:

The adjective takes an **-e** ending everywhere, with both common and neuter nouns, in both singular and plural. However, in this definite usage, **den** must be placed in front of the adjective in the case of common nouns in the singular, **det** in the case of singular neuter nouns and **de** with any plural.

	singular		plural	
common	*den* **stor**e **bil**	the big car	*de* **stor**e **bil**er	the big cars
neuter	*det* **stor**e **hus**	the big house	*de* **stor**e **hus**e	the big houses

Demonstrative adjectives

	common	neuter	plural
this/these	**denne**	**dette**	**disse**
that/those	**den**	**det**	**de**

denne **bil**   this car   *dette* **hus**   this house

Possessive adjectives

	common	neuter	plural
my	**min**	**mit**	**mine**
your (familiar; see page 162)	**din**	**dit**	**dine**
our*	**vor**	**vort**	**vore**
his		**hans**	
hers		**hendes**	
its		**dens/dets****	
their		**deres**	
your (familiar; see page 162)		**jeres**	
your (formal; see page 162)		**Deres**	

*You will also hear **vores** used in place of each of these more formally correct terms.
Use **dens if "it" is of common gender, and **dets** if "it" is neuter.

Personal pronouns

	subject	object
I	**jeg**	**mig**
you (familiar; see note below)	**du**	**dig**
he	**han**	**ham**
she	**hun**	**hende**
it	**den/det***	***den/det**
we	**vi**	**os**
you (familiar; see note below)	**I**	**jer**
you (formal; see note below)	**De**	**Dem**
they	**de**	**dem**

Note: Like many other languages, Danish has two forms for "you" and "your". The personal pronoun **du** (plural **I**) and its corresponding possessive adjectives **din**, **dit**, **dine** (plural **jeres**) are used when talking to relatives, close friends and children and between young people. The personal pronoun **De** (plural **Dem**) and its corresponding possessive adjective **Deres** is used in all other cases.

Verbs

Here we are concerned only with the infinitive, present tense and imperative.

The infinitive of Danish verbs generally ends in **-e**, **-o**, **-ø** or **-å**, and is preceded by **at** (corresponding to English "to").

at rejse	to travel	**at gå**	to walk
at tro	to believe	**at spise**	to eat

The present tense drops the **at** and adds **-r** to the infinitive. This form remains unchanged for all persons.

jeg rejser	I travel	**jeg går**	I walk
jeg tror	I believe	**jeg spiser**	I eat

The imperative is exactly the same form as the stem of the verb.

rejs!	travel!	**gå!**	walk!
tro!	believe!	**spis!**	eat!

---

*Use **den** if "it" is of common gender, and **det** if "it" is neuter.

Here are three useful auxiliary verbs:

	to be	to have	to be able to, can
infinitive	**at være**	**at have**	**at kunne**
present tense (same forms for all persons)	**jeg er**, etc.	**jeg har**, etc.	**jeg kan**, etc.
imperative	**vær!**	**hav!**	—

Adverbs

Adverbs are generally formed by adding **-t** to the corresponding adjective.

> **Hun går hurtigt.** She walks quickly.

Negatives

Negatives are formed by inserting the word **ikke** after the verb:

> **Jeg taler dansk.** I speak Danish.
> **Jeg taler *ikke* dansk.** I do not speak Danish.

Questions

Questions are formed by reversing the order of the subject and verb:

> **Du ser bilen.** You see the car.
> **Ser du bilen?** Do you see the car?

There is/there are

Der er is employed for both ''there is'' and ''there are''.

> ***Der er* mange turister.** There are many tourists.

It is

> ***Det er* varmt i dag.** It is warm today.

Dictionary
and alphabetical index

English–Danish

c common	nt neuter	pl plural

A
a en c, et nt 159
abbey munkekloster nt 81
abbreviation forkortelse c 154
able, to be kunne 163
about *(approximately)* ca. 153
above ovenpå 15, ovenover 63
abscess byld c 145
absent ikke til stede 136
absorbent cotton vat c 108
accept, to tage imod 62
accessories tilbehør nt 115, 125
accident ulykke c 79, 139
account konto c 130, 131
ache smerte c 141
adaptor adapter nt 118
address adresse c 21, 31, 76, 79, 102
address book adressebog c 104
adhesive selvklæbende 105
adhesive tape tape nt 104
admission adgang c 82, 89, 155
admitted adgang for 150
Africa Afrika 146
after efter 15
after-shave lotion barberlotion c 109
afternoon, in the om eftermiddagen 151, 153
again igen 96, 135
against mod 140
age alder c 149, 150
ago for ... siden 149, 151
air bed luftmadras c 106
air conditioning klimaanlæg nt 23, 28
air mattress luftmadras c 106
airmail luftpost c 133
airplane fly nt 65
airport lufthavn c 16, 21, 65
aisle seat plads cved midtergangen 65
alarm clock vækkeur nt 121
alcohol alkohol c 37, 59
alcoholic alkoholisk c 59

allergic kan ikke tåle 141, 143
almond mandel c 55
alphabet alfabet nt 9
also også 15
alter, to *(garment)* ændre 115
altitude sickness bjergsyge c 107
amazing forbløffende 84
amber rav nt 122
ambulance ambulance c 79
American amerikaner c 93
American plan helpension c 24
amethyst ametyst c 122
amount beløb nt 62
amplifier forstærker c 118
anaesthetic narkose c 144, 145
analgesic smertestillende middel nt 108
anchovy ansjos c 45
and og 15
animal dyr nt 85
aniseed anisfrø pl 53
ankle ankel c 139
another en ... til 58
answer svar nt 136
antibiotic antibiotikum nt 143
antidepressant middel nt mod depression c 143
antique shop antikvitetsforretning c 98
antiques antikviteter pl 83
antiseptic cream antiseptisk creme c 108
any nogen 14
anyone nogen 12, 16
anything noget 17, 24, 25, 101, 112
anywhere et eller andet sted 89
apartment lejlighed c 22
aperitif aperitif c 59
appendicitis blindtarmsbetændelse c 142
appendix blindtarm c 138
appetizer forret c 41

apple æble *nt* 55, 63, 119
apple juice æblesaft *c* 60
appliance udstyr *nt* 118
appointment aftalt møde *nt* 131, 137, 145
apricot abrikos *c* 55
April april 150
archaeology arkæologi *c* 83
architect arkitekt *c* 83
arm arm *c* 138, 139
around *(approximately)* ved 31
arrangement *(set price)* tilbud *c* 20
arrival ankomst *c* 16, 65
arrive, to ankomme 65, 68, 70, 146
art kunst *c* 83
art gallery kunstgalleri *nt* 81, 98
artichoke artiskok *c* 51
article vare *c* 101
artificial light indendørs optagelse *c* 124
artist kunstner *c* 81, 83
Asia Asien 146
ask for, to bede om 25, 61, 136
asparagus asparges *c* 51
aspirin aspirin *c* 108
assorted blandet 41
asthma astma *c* 141
astringent ansigtstonic *c* 109
at ved 15
at least mindst 24
at once med det samme 31
aubergine aubergine *c* 51
August august 150
aunt tante *c* 93
Australia Australien 146
Austria Østrig 146
automatic automatisk 20, 122, 124
autumn efterår *nt* 150
average middelgod 91
awful forfærdeligt 84, 94

B
baby baby *c* 24, 110
baby food babymad *c* 110
babysitter babysitter *c* 27
back ryg *c* 138
back, to be/to get komme tilbage 21, 80, 136
backache smerter *pl* i ryggen 141
backpack rygsæk *c* 106
bacon bacon *nt* 40
bacon and eggs æg og bacon 40

bad dårlig 14, 95
bag taske *c* 18, 103
baggage bagage *c* 18, 26, 31, 71
baggage cart bagagevogn *c* 18, 71
baggage check bagageopbevaring *c* 67, 71
baggage locker bagageboks *c* 18, 67, 71
baked bagt 46, 48
baker's bager *c* 98
balance *(finance)* saldo *c* 131
balcony altan *c* 23
ball-point pen kuglepen *c* 104
ballet ballet *c* 88
banana banan *c* 55, 63
Band-Aid plaster *nt* 108
bandage bandage *c* 108
bangle armring *c* 121
bangs pandehår *nt* 30
bank *(finance)* bank *c* 98, 129, 130
banknote seddel *c* 130
bar *(room)* bar *c* 33, 67
barber's herrefrisør *c* 30, 98
basil basilikum *pl* 53
basketball basketball *c* 89
bath bad *nt* 23, 25, 27
bath salts badesalt *nt* 109
bath towel badehåndklæde *nt* 27
bathing hut badehus *nt* 91
bathing suit badedragt *c* 115
bathrobe badekåbe *c* 115
bathroom badeværelse *nt* 27
battery batteri *nt* 75, 78, 118, 121, 125
be, to være 163
beach strand *c* 90
beach ball badebold *c* 128
bean bønne *c* 51
beard skæg *nt* 31
beautiful smuk 14, 84
beauty salon skønhedssalon *c* 30, 98
bed seng *c* 24, 28, 142, 144
bed and breakfast værelse *nt* og morgenmad *c* 24
bedpan bækken *nt* 144
beef oksekød *nt* 46
beer øl *nt* 57, 63
beet(root) rødbeder *pl* 51
before *(time)* før 15
begin, to begynde 80, 87
beginner begynder *c* 91
beginning begyndelse *c* 150
behind bagved 15, 77
beige beige 112
Belgium Belgien 146
bell *(electric)* ringeklokke 144

below nedenunder 15
belt bælte *nt* 116
berth køje *c* 69, 70
better bedre 14, 25, 101
between mellem 15
bicycle cykel *c* 74
big stor 14, 101
bilberry blåbær *nt* 55
bill regning *c* 28, 31, 62, 102
bill *(banknote)* seddel *c* 130
billion *(Am.)* milliard *c* 148
binoculars kikkert *c* 123
bird fugl *c* 85
birth fødsel *c* 25
birthday fødselsdag *c* 152
biscuit *(Br.)* kiks *c* 63
black sort 112
black and white *(film)* sort/hvid (film) *c* 124, 125
black coffee sort kaffe *c* 40, 60
blackcurrant solbær *nt* 55
bladder blære *c* 138
blade barberblad *nt* 109
blanket tæppe *nt* 27
bleach blegning *c* 30
bleed, to bløde 139, 145
blind *(window shade)* rullegardin *nt* 29
blister blist *c* 139
blocked stoppet 28
blood blod *nt* 142
blood pressure blodtryk *nt* 141
blood transfusion blodtransfusion *c* 144
blouse bluse *c* 115
blow-dry føntørret 30
blue blå 112
blueberry blåbær *nt* 55
blusher blusher *c* 109
boar vildsvin *nt* 49
boat båd *c* 74
bobby pin hårklemme *c* 110
body legeme *nt* 138
boil byld 139
boiled kogt 48, 52
boiled egg kogt æg *nt* 40
bone knogle *c* 138
book bog *c* 12, 104
booking office billetkontor *nt* 19; pladsreservering *c* 67
booklet *(of tickets)* rabatkort *nt* 73
bookshop boghandel *c* 98, 104
boot støvle *c* 117
born født 150
botanical gardens botanisk have *c* 81

botany botanik *c* 83
bottle flaske *c* 17, 59
bottle-opener oplukker *c* 120
bottom forneden 145
bow tie butterfly *c* 115
bowel tarm *c* 138
box æske *c* 119
boxing boksning *c* 89
boy dreng *c* 111, 128
boyfriend kæreste *c* 93
bra bh *c* 115
bracelet armbånd 121
braces *(suspenders)* seler *pl* 115
braised grydestegt 48
brake bremse *c* 78
brake fluid bremsevæske *c* 75
brandy brandy *c* 59
bread brød *nt* 36, 40, 63
break down, to få motorstop *nt* 78
break, to være i uorden 29; gå i stykke 118
breakdown motorstop *nt* 78
breakdown van kranbil *c* 78
breakfast morgenmad *c* 24, 34, 38, 40
breast bryst *nt* 138
breathe, to trække vejret 141, 142
bridge bro *c* 85
bring down, to få ned 31
bring, to lade få 13, bringe 58
British brite *c* 93
broken i stykker 119, 123
brooch broche *c* 121
brother bror *c* 93
brown brun 112
bruise blåt mærke 139
brush børste *c* 110
Brussels sprouts rosenkål *pl* 51
bubble bath skumbad *nt* 109
bucket spand *c* 128, 120
buckle spænde *c* 116
build, to bygge 83
building bygning *c* 81, 83
building blocks/bricks byggeklodser *pl* 128
bulb *(light)* pære *c* 28, 75, 119
bump *(lump)* klump *c* 139
burn brandsår *nt* 139
burn out, to *(bulb)* være gået 28
bus bus *c* 18, 19, 65, 72, 80
bus stop busholdeplads *c* 73
business forretninger *pl* 16
business class business class *c* 65
business district forretningskvarter *nt* 81
business trip forretningsrejse *c* 93

busy optaget 96
but men 15
butane gas flaskegas c 32, 106
butcher's slagter c 98
butter smør 36, 40, 63
button knap c 29, 116
buy, to købe 82, 100, 104, 123

C

cabana badehus nt 91
cabbage kål c 51
cabin (ship) kahyt c 74
cable telegram nt 133
cable release trådudløser c 125
cake kage c 37, 56, 63, 64
calculator -regner c 105
calendar kalender c 104
call (phone) (telefon)samtale c 135, 136
call collect, to modtageren betaler 135
call, to ringe 136
call, to (give name) kalde 11
call, to (phone) ringe 134, 136
call, to (summon) ringe efter/tilkalde 79, 156
calm rolig 90
camel-hair kamelhår 113
camera kamera nt 124, 125
camera case fototaske nt 125
camera shop fotoforretning c 98
camp site campingplads c 32
camp, to kampere 32
campbed campingseng c 106
camping camping c 32
camping equipment campingudstyr nt 106
can (be able to) kan 12, 13, 162
can (container) dåse c 119
Canada Canada 146
Canadian canadier c 93
cancel, to annullere 65
candle stearinlys nt 120
candy slik nt 126
candy store chokoladeforretning c 98
cap kasket c 115
capers kapers pl 54
capital (finance) kapital c 131
car bil c 19, 20, 26, 32, 75,
car hire biludlejning c 20
car mechanic bilmekaniker c 78
car park parkeringsplads c 77
car racing bilvæddeløb nt 89
car radio bilradio c 118

car rental biludlejning c 20
carafe karaffel c 58
carat karat c 121
caravan campingvogn c 32
carbon paper karbonpapir nt 104
carbonated water dansk vand nt 60
carburettor karburetor c 78
card kort 93, 131
card game kortspil nt 128
cardigan cardigan c 115
carp karpe c 45
carrot gulerod c 51
carry, to bære 21
cart vognen c 18
carton (of cigarettes) karton (cigaretter) nt 17
cartridge (camera) kassette c 124
case taske, kuffert, etui nt 125
cash desk kasse c 103, 155
cash, to indløse 130, 133
cassette kassette c 118, 127
cassette recorder kassettebåndoptager c 118
castle borg c 81
catacombs katakombe c 81
catalogue katalog nt 82
cathedral domkirke c 81
Catholic katolsk c 84
cauliflower blomkål c 51
caution forsigtig 155
celery selleri nt 51
cemetery kirkegård c 81
centimetre centimeter c 111
centre centrum nt 19, 21, 76, 81
century århundrede nt 149
ceramics keramik c 83, 127
cereal cornflakes pl 40
certain vis 143
certificate attest c 144
chain (jewellery) kæde c 121
chain bracelet armlænke c 121
chair stol c 106
chamber music kammermusik c 128
change (money) byttepenge pl 62, 77, 130
change, to bytte 61; ændre 65; skifte 68, 73, 75, 123
change, to (money) veksle 18, 130
chapel kapel nt 81
charcoal trækul nt 106
charge gebyr nt 20, 32, 77, 89, 136
charge, to koste 24, 130
charm (trinket) charm c 121
charm bracelet armbånd med vedhæng c 121

cheap billig 14, 24, 25, 101
check check c 130, 131
check-up *(medical)* undersøgelse c 142
check *(restaurant)* regning c 62
check in, to *(airport)* checke ind 61
check out, to rejse 31
check, to kontrollere 75; checke 123
check, to *(luggage)* indskrive 71
cheese ost c 54, 64
chef køkkenchef c 39
chemist's apotek nt 98, 107
cheque check c 130, 131
cherry kirsebær nt 55
chess skak c 93
chess set skakspil nt 128
chest brystkasse c 138, 141
chestnut kastanje c 55
chewing gum tyggegummi nt 126
chewing tobacco skrå c 126
chicken kylling c 49
chicken breast kyllingebryst nt 49
chicory julesalat c 51
chiffon chiffon nt 113
child barn c 24, 61, 82, 93, 139, 150
children's doctor børnelæge c 137
China Kina 146
chips pommes frites pl 50, 63
chives purløg pl 54
chocolate chokolade c 64, 119, 126
chocolate *(hot)* (varm) chokolade c 40, 60
chocolate bar plade chokolade c 64
choice vælg nt 39
chop *(meat)* kotelet c 47
Christmas jul c 152
chromium krom nt 122
church kirke c 81, 84
cigar cigar c 126
cigarette case cigaretetui nt 121, 126
cigarette cigaret c 17, 95, 126
cigarette holder cigaretrør nt 126
cigarette lighter cigarettlighter c 121, 126
cine camera filmkamerær nt 124
cinema biograf c 86, 96
cinnamon kanel nt 54
circle *(theatre)* balkon c 87
city centre byens centrum c 81
classical klassisk 128
clean ren 61
clean, to gøre rent 29, 76
cleansing cream rensecreme c 109
cliff klippe c 85
clip clips c 121

cloakroom garderobe c 87
clock ur nt 121, 153
clock-radio radiovækkeur c 118
close, to lukker 11, 82, 107, 132
closed lukket 155
cloth stof nt 117
clothes klæder, tøj pl 29, 115
clothing klæder c 111
cloud sky c 94
clove kryddernellike c 54
coach *(bus)* rutebil c 72
coat frakke c 115
coconut kokosnød c 55
cod torsk c 45
coffee kaffe c 40, 60, 64
coin mønt c 83
cold *(illness)* forkølelse c 107, 141
cold cuts afskåret pålæg nt 64
cold koldt 14, 25, 40, 61, 94, 155
collar flip c 116
colour farve c 103, 111, 124, 125
colour chart farvekort nt 30
colour rinse farveskylning c 30
colour shampoo farveshampoo c 110
colour slide diapositiv nt 124
colourfast farveægte 113
comb kam c 110
come, to komme 36, 95, 137, 144, 146
comedy lystspil c 86
commission *(fee)* kommission c 130
common *(frequent)* almindelig 154
compact disc CD c 127
compartment *(train)* kupe c 70
compass kompas nt 106
complaint klage c 61
concert koncert c 88
concert hall koncertsal c 81, 88
condom kondom c 108
conductor *(orchestra)* dirigent c 88
confectioner's konditori 98
conference room mødelokale nt 23
confirm, to bekræfte 65
confirmation bekræftelsen c 23
congratulations til lykke c 152
connection *(transport)* forbindelse c 68
constipation forstoppelse c 140
consulate konsulat c 156
contact lens kontaktlinse c 123
contagious smitsom 142
contain, to indeholde 37
contraceptive præventivmiddel nt 108
contract kontrakt c 131
control kontrol c 16
cookie småkage c 64

cool box køleboks *c* 106
copper kobber *nt* 122
coral koral *c* 122
corduroy jernbanefløjl *nt* 113
corn *(Am.)* majs *c* 51
corn *(foot)* ligtorn *c* 108
corn plaster ligtorneplaster *nt* 108
corner hjørne *nt* 21, 36, 77
cost omkostning *c* 131, 136
cost, to koste 11, 80, 133
cot barneseng *c* 24
cotton bomuld *c* 113
cotton wool vat *nt* 108
cough hoste *c* 107, 141
cough drops hostesaft *c* 108
cough, to hoste 142
counter luge *c* 133
country land *c* 92, 146
countryside, in the på landet *nt* 85
courgette courgette *c* 51
courgette courgette 51
court house retsbygning *c* 81
cousin fætter (m) *c* 93; kusine (f) *c* 93
cover charge beregning *c* for kuvert *c* 62
crab krebs *c* 45
cramp krampe *c* 141
crayon farveblyant *c* 104
cream fløde *c* 56, 60
cream *(toiletry)* creme *c* 109
crease resistant krølfrit 113
credit kredit *c* 130
credit card kreditkort *nt* 20, 31, 62, 102, 130
crepe crepe *c* 114
crisps franske kartofler *pl* 64
crockery spisestel *nt* 120
cross kors *nt* 121
cross-country skiing langrend *nt* 91
crossing *(maritime)* overfart *c* 74
crossroads vejkryds *nt* 77
crown *(currency)* krone *c* 19
crystal krystal *nt* 122
cucumber agurk *c* 42, 51
cuff link manchetknap *c* 121
cuisine køkken *nt* 34
cumin kommen *c* 54
cup kop *c* 36, 60, 120
curler curler *c* 110
currency valuta *c* 129
currency exchange office valutakontor *nt* 18, 67
current strøm *c* 90
curtain gardin *nt* 28
customs told *c* 16, 102

cut *(wound)* snitsår *nt* 139
cut glass slebet glas *nt* 122
cut off, to *(interrupt)* afbryde 135
cut, to *(with scissors)* klippe 30
cuticle remover neglebåndsfjerner *c* 109
cutlery spisebestik *nt* 120
cutlet kotelet *c* 47
cycling cykling *c* 89
cystitis blærebetændelse *c* 142

D

dairy mejeri *nt* 98
dance dans *c* 96
dance, to danse 88, 96
danger fare *c* 155, 156
dangerous farlig 90
Danish dansk 11, 12, 19, 95, 113
dark mørk 25, 101, 111, 112
date *(appointment)* stævnemøde *nt* 95
date *(day)* dato *c* 25, 151;
date *(fruit)* daddel *c* 55
daughter datter *c* 93
day dag *c* 20, 24, 32, 80, 94, 151
day off fridag *c* 151
decade tiår *nt* 149
decaffeinated koffeinfri 40, 60
December december 150
decision beslutning *c* 25
deck *(ship)* dæk *nt* 74
deck chair liggestol *c* 91, 106
declare, to *(customs)* fortolde 17
deep dyb 142
degree *(temperature)* grad *c* 140
delay forsinket 69
delicatessen viktualieforretning *c* 98
delicious dejlig 62
deliver, to levere 102
delivery levering *c* 102
denim denim *c* 113
Denmark Danmark 146
dentist tandlæge *c* 98, 145
denture protese *c* 145
deodorant deodorant *c* 109
department *(museum)* afdeling *c* 83
department *(shop)* afdeling *c* 100
department store stormagasin *nt* 98
departure afgang *c* 16
deposit *(bank)* indskud *c* 130
deposit *(down payment)* depositum *nt* 20
dessert dessert *c* 37, 56

detour *(traffic)* omkørsel *c* 79
diabetic diabetiker *c* 37
diamond diamant *c* 122
diaper ble *c* 110
diarrhoea diarré *c* 140
dictionary ordbog *c* 104
diesel diesel *c* 75
diet diæt *c* 37
difficult svær 14
difficulty vanskelighed *c* 28
digital digital 122
dill dild *c* 53
dine, to spise middag 94
dining car spisevogn *c* 68, 71
dining room spisesalen *c* 27
dinner middag *c* 34, 94
direct direkte 65
direct, to vise vej til 13
direction vejangivelse *c* 76
director *(theatre)* instruktør *c* 86
directory *(phone)* telefonbog *c* 134
disabled handicappede *pl* 82
disc *(parking)* (parkerings)skive *c* 77
discotheque diskotek *nt* 88, 96
discount rabat *c* 131
disease sygdom *c* 142
dish ret *c* 36, 39
dishwashing detergent
  opvaskemiddel *nt* 120
disinfectant desinficeringsmiddel *nt* 108
dislocated gået ud af led 140
dissatisfied misfornøjet 103
district *(of town)* kvarter *nt* 81
disturb, to forstyrre 155
diversion *(traffic)* omkørsel *c* 79
dizzy svimmel 140
doctor læge *c* 79, 137, 144, 156
doctor's office konsultation *c* 137
dog hund *c* 155
doll dukke *c* 128
dollar dollar *c* 18, 102, 130
double bed dobbeltseng *c* 23
double room dobbeltværelse *nt* 19, 23
down ned 15
downhill skiing styrtløb *nt* 91
downtown indre by 81
dozen dusin *nt* 149
drawing paper tegnepapir *nt* 104
drawing pins tegnestift *nt* 104
dress kjole *c* 115
dressing gown slåbrok *c* 115
drink drikkevare *c* 57, 59, 60, 61; drink *c* 95
drink, to drikke 35, 36, 37

drinking water drikkevand *nt* 32
drip, to dryppe 28
drive, to køre 21, 76
driving licence kørekort *nt* 20, 79
drop *(liquid)* dråbe *c* 108
drugstore apotek *nt* 98, 107
dry tør 30, 59, 110
dry cleaner's kemisk rensning *c* 29
dry shampoo tørshampoo *c* 110
duck and *c* 49
dummy *(baby's)* sut *c* 110
during i løbet af 15, 150, 151
duty-free shop toldfri butik *c* 19
duty *(customs)* told *c* 16
dye farvning *c* 30

E
each hver 149
ear øre *nt* 138
ear drops øredråber *pl* 108
earache ondt i ørerne 141
early tidligt 14, 31
earring ørenring *c* 121
east øst 77
Easter påske *c* 152
easy nem 14
eat, to spise 36, 37, 144
eel ål *c* 45
egg æg *nt* 40, 43, 64
eggplant aubergine *c* 51
eight otte 147
eighteen atten 147
eighth ottende 149
eighty firs 148
elastic elastik *c* 108
elastic bandage elastikbind *nt* 108
electric(al) elektrisk 118
electrical appliance elektrisk udstyr *nt* 118
electrical goods shop
  elektricitetsforretning *c* 98
electricity elektricitet *c* 24, 32
electronic elektronisk 128
elevator elevator *c* 27, 100
eleven elleve 147
embarkation point kaj *c* 74
embassy ambassade *c* 156
embroidery broderi *nt* 127
emerald smaragd *c* 122
emergency nødstilfælde *nt* 156
emergency exit nødudgang *c* 27, 99, 155

emery board sandfil til neglene *c* 109
empty tom 14
enamel emalje *c* 122
end slutning *c* 150
engaged *(phone)* optaget 136
engagement ring forlovelsesring *c* 122
engine *(car)* motor *c* 78
England England 134, 146
English englænder *c* 93
English engelsk 12, 16, 80, 82, 84, 104, 105, 126
enjoy oneself, to more sig 96
enjoyable nyd 31
enlarge, to forstørre 125
enough nok 14, 68
entrance indgang *c* 67, 99, 155
entrance fee entré *c* 82
envelope konvolut *c* 27, 104
equipment udstyr *c* 91, 106
eraser viskelæder *nt* 104
escalator rulletrappe *c* 100
estimate overslag *nt* 131
estimate *(cost)* tilbud *nt* 78
Eurocheque eurocheck *c* 130
Europe Europa 146
European Community Europæiske Fællesskab 154
evening aften 95, 96
evening dress selskabstøj, være selskabsklædt *c* 88
evening dress aftenkjole *c* 115
evening dress *(woman's)* aftenkjole *c* 115
evening, in the om aftenen 151, 153
every hver 143
everything alt 31
exchange rate vekselkursen *c* 19, 130
exchange, to bytte 103
excursion udflugt *c* 80
excuse, to undskylde 11
exercise book kladdehæfte *nt* 104
exhaust pipe udstødningsrør *nt* 78
exhibition udstilling *c* 81
exit udgang *c* 67, 99, 155
expect, to vente 130
expenses udgifter *pl* 131
expensive dyr 14, 19, 24, 101
exposure *(photography)* billede *nt* 124
exposure counter tæller *c* 125
express ekspres 133
expression udtryk *nt* 10, 100
expressway motorvej *c* 76
extension *(phone)* lokal 135
extension cord/lead forlængerledning *c* 118

extra ekstra 27
eye øje *nt* 138, 139
eye drops øjendråber *pl* 108
eye shadow øjenskygge *c* 109
eye specialist øjenlæge *c* 137
eyebrow pencil øjenbrynsstift *c* 109
eyesight syn *nt* 123

F

fabric *(cloth)* tøjstof *nt* 112
face ansigt *nt* 138
face pack ansigtsmaske *c* 30
face powder pudder *nt* 109
factory fabrik *c* 81
fair messe *c* 81
fall *(autumn)* efterår *c* 150
fall, to falde 139
family familie *c* 93, 144
fan ventilator *c* 28
fan belt ventilatorrem *c* 75
far langt væk 14, 100
fare *(ticket)* billet *c* 68, 73
farm bondegård *c* 85
fast hurtig 124
fat *(meat)* fedt *(stoffer)* 37
father far *c* 93
faucet vandhane *c* 28
fax fax *nt* 133
February februar 150
fee *(doctor's)* honorar *nt* 144
feeding bottle sutteflaske *c* 110
feel, to *(physical state)* føle 140, 142
felt filt *c* 113
felt-tip pen filtpen *c* 104
ferry færge *c* 74
fever feber *c* 140
few få 14
few *(a few)* et par stykker 14
field mark *c* 85
fifteen femten 147
fifth femte 149
fifty halvtreds 147
fig figen *c* 55
file *(tool)* fil *c* 109
fill in, to udfylde 26, 144
filling *(tooth)* plombe *c* 145
filling station benzinstation *c* 75
film film *c* 86, 124, 125
film winder fremtrækker *c* 125
filter filter *nt* 125
filter-tipped med filter *nt* 126
find, to finde 11, 12, 76, 84, 100

fine *(OK)* godt 10, 25, 92
fine arts kunst c 83
finger finger c 138
Finland Finland 146
fire brand 156
first første 67, 73, 77, 149
first-aid kit nødhjælpskasse c 108
first class første klasse c 69
first course forret c 41
first name fornavn 25
fish fisk c 45
fishing fiskeri nt 90
fishing permit fiskekort nt 90
fishing tackle fiskegrejer pl 106
fishmonger's fiskehandler c 98
fit, to passe 114
fitting room prøverum nt 114
five fem 147
fix, to behandle 75, 145
fizzy *(mineral water)* dansk vand nt 60
flannel flonel 113
flash *(photography)* flash c 125
flashlight lommelygte c 106
flat *(apartment)* lejlighed c 22
flat *(shoe)* flade pl 117
flat tyre punktering c 75, 78
flea market loppemarked nt 81
flight fly nt 65
floor etage nt 27
floor show show nt 88
florist's blomsterhandler c 98
flour mel c 37
flower blomst c 85
flu influenza c 142
fluid væske c 75, 123
foam rubber mattress skumgummimadras c 106
fog tåge c 94
folding chair klapstol c 106
folding table klapbord nt 106
folk music folkemusik c 128
follow, to følge 77
food mad 37, 61, 110
food poisoning madforgiftning 142
foot fod c 138
foot cream fodcreme c 109
football fodbold c 89
footpath gangsti c 85
for for 15
forbidden forbudt 155
forecast vejrudsigt c 94
foreign udenlandsk 56
forest skov c 85
forget, to glemme 61
fork gaffel c 36, 61, 120

form *(document)* blanket c 25, 26, 133, 144
fortnight to uger/fjorten dage pl 151
fortress fort nt 81
forty fyrre 147
foundation cream underlagscreme c 109
fountain springvand nt 81
fountain pen fyldepen c 104
four fire 147
fourteen fjorten 147
fourth fjerde 149
frame *(glasses)* stel nt 123
France Frankrig 146
free ledigt 14, 70, 80
French fransk 11
French bean grønne bønner 51
French fries pommes frites pl 50, 63
fresh frisk 54, 61
Friday fredag 151
fried stegt 46, 48
fried egg spejlæg nt 40
friend ven c 95
fringe pandehår nt 30
from fra 15
frost frostvejr nt 94
fruit frugt c 55
fruit cocktail frugtsalat c 55
fruit juice frugtsaft, juice c 40, 60
fruit salad frugtsalat c 55
frying pan stegepande c 120
full fuld 14
full board helpension c 24
full insurance fuld forsikring c 20
furniture møbel nt 83, 127
furrier's buntmager c 98

G

gabardine gabardine nt 113
gallery galleri nt 81, 98
game spil nt 128
game *(food)* vildt nt 48
garage garage c 26, 78
garden have c 85
gardens haverne pl 81
garlic hvidløg nt 54
gas gas c 156
gasoline benzin c 75, 78
gastritis mavekatar c 142
gauze gaze c 108
gem ædelsten c 121
general almindelig 27, 100, 137

general delivery poste restante c 133
general practitioner praktiserende
læge c 137
genitals kønsdele pl 138
gentleman herre c 154
genuine ægte 117
geology geologi c 83
Germany Tyskland 146
get off, to stige af 73
get past, to komme forbi 69
get to, to komme til 19, 76
get up, to stå op 144
get, to (find) komme til 11, 19
gherkin sylteagurk c 54, 64
gift gave c 17
gin gin c 59
gin and tonic gin og tonic 59
ginger ingefær c 54
girdle hofteholder c 115
girl pige c 111, 128
girlfriend kæreste c 93
give, to give 13; lade få 63, 75, 123, 126
gland kirtel c 138
glass glas nt 36, 58, 59, 61, 143
glasses brille pl 123
gloomy trist 84
glove handske c 115
glue lim nt 104
go away! gå væk! 156
go back, to køre tilbage 77
go out, to gå ud 96
gold guld nt 121, 122
gold plated forgyldning c 122
golden gylden 112
golf golf c 89
golf course golfbane c 89
good god 14
good afternoon god dag 10
good evening god aften 10
good morning god morgen 10
good night god nat 10
goodbye farvel 10
goose gås c 49
gooseberry stikkelsbær nt 55
gram gram nt 119
grammar grammatik c 159
grammar book grammatik c 105
grape vindrue c 55
grapefruit grapefrugt c 55
grapefruit juice grapefrugtsaft c 40, 60
gray grå 112
graze hudafskrabning c 139
greasy fedtet 30, 110
great (excellent) vældig hyggeligt 95
Great Britain Storbritannien 146

Greece Grækenland 146
green grøn 112
green bean grønne bønner c 51
greengrocer's grønthandler c 98
greeting hilsen 10, 152
grey grå 112
grilled grillet 46, 48
grocer's købmand c 98; madvarer c 120
groundsheet teltunderlag nt 106
group gruppe c 82
guesthouse pensionat c 19, 22
guide guide c 80
guidebook brochure c 82; rejsefører c 104, 105
guinea fowl perlehøne c 49
gum (teeth) tandkød nt 145
gymnasium gymnastiksal c 23
gynaecologist gynækolog c 137

H
hair hår nt 30, 110
hair dryer hårtørrer c 118
hair gel hårgele c 30, 110
hair lotion hårvand nt 110
hair spray hårlak c 30, 110
hairbrush hårbørste c 110
haircut have håret klippet 30
hairdresser damefrisør c 30, 98
hairgrip hårklemme c 110
hairpin hårnål c 110
half halv 149
half halvdel c 149
half an hour en halv time c 153
half board halvpension c 24
half price halv pris c 68
hall (large room) sal c 81, 88
hall porter portier c 26
ham skinke c 40, 42, 64
ham and eggs skinke og æg 40
hammer hammer c 120
hammock hængekøje c 106
hand hånd c 138
hand cream håndcreme c 109
hand washable vaske i hånden 113
handbag håndtaske c 115, 156
handicrafts kunsthåndværk nt 83
handkerchief lommetørklæde nt 115
handmade håndlavet 112
hanger bøjle c 27
happy god 152
harbour havn c 74, 81

hard hård 123
hard-boiled *(egg)* hårdkogt *(æg)* nt 40
hardware store isenkræmmer c 99
hare hare c 49
hat hat c 115
have to, to *(must)* skulle 17, 68, 69; måtte 95
have, to have 163
hay fever høfeber c 107, 141
hazelnut hasselnød c 55
he han 162
head hoved nt 138, 139
head waiter overtjener c 61
headache hovedpine c 141
headlight billygte c 79
headphones hovedtelefon c 118
health food shop helsekostforretning c 99
health insurance sygeforsikring c 144
health insurance form blanket til sygeforsikring c 144
heart hjerte nt 138
heart attack hjerteanfald nt 141
heat, to opvarme 90
heating varme c 28, 23
heavy tung 14
heel hæl c 117
hello hej 10; hello 135
help hjælp c 156
help! hjælp! 156
help, to hjælpe 13, 21, 71, 100, 134
help, to *(oneself)* tage selv 119
her hende, hendes, sin, sit 161
herb tea urtete c 60
herbs urter pl 53
here her 14
herring sild c 45
hi hej 10
high høj 141
high højde c 85
high season højsæson c 150
high tide flod c 90
hill bakke c 85
hire udlejning c 20, 74
hire, to leje 19, 20, 74, 90, 91, 118, 155
his hans, sin, sit 161
history historie c 83
hold on! *(phone)* vent! 136
hole hul nt 29
holiday helligdag c 151, 152
holidays ferie c 16, 151
home hjem nt 96
home address hjemmeadresse c 31
home town by nt 25
honey honning c 40

hope, to håbe 96
hors d'oeuvre forret, hors d'oeuvre c 41
horse racing hestevæddeløb nt 89
horseback riding ridning c 89
horseradish peberrod c 54
hospital hospital nt 99, 142, 144
hot-water bottle varmedunk c 27
hot *(warm)* varm 25, 94
hot water varmt vand nt 23, 28, 40
hotel hotel nt 19, 21, 22, 26, 80, 96, 102
hotel directory/guide hotelfortegnelse c 19
hotel reservation værelsesbestilling c 19
hour time c 80, 143; hvad klokkener 153
house hus nt 83, 85
household article husholdningsartikel c 120
how hvordan 11
how far hvor langt 11, 76, 85
how long hvor længe 11, 24
how many hvor mange 11
how much hvor meget 11, 24
hundred hundrede nt 148
hungry sulten 13, 35
hunting jagt c 90
hurry, to be in a have det travlt 21, 36
hurt, to gøre ondt 139, 140, 142, 145
husband mand c 93

I
I jeg 162
ice is c 94
ice cream is c 56
ice cube isterning c 27
ice pack ispose c 106
iced tea isafkølet te c 60
if hvis 143
ill syg 140, 156
illness sygdom c 140
important vigtig 13
imported importeret 112
impressive imponerende 84
in i 15
include, to iberegne/inkludere 24, 31
included inkluderet/medregnet 20, 63
India Indien 146
indoor indendørs 90
inexpensive billige 35, ikke for dyrt 124

infected betændt 140
infection betændelse c 141
inflammation betændelse c 142
inflation inflation c 131
inflation rate prisstigning c 131
influenza influenza c 142
information information c 67, 155
injection indsprøjtning c 142,143, 144
injure, to komme til skade 139
injured kommet til skade 79
injury kvæstelse c 139
ink blæk nt 105
inn kro c 33
inquiry forespørgsel c 67
insect bite insektbid nt 107, 139
insect repellent insekt-spray nt 108
insect spray insekt-spray nt 106
inside indenfor 14
instead of i stedet for 37
instrumental music
   instrumentalmusik c 128
insurance forsikring c 20, 144
insurance company forsikringsselskab
   79
interest (finance) rente c 131
interested, to be være interessseret i
   83, 96
interesting interessant 84
international international 133, 134
interpreter tolk c 131
intersection vejkryds nt 77
introduce, to præsentere 92
introduction (social) præsentation c
   92
investment investering c 131
invitation indbydelse c 94
invite, to indbyde 94
invoice faktura c 131
iodine jod c 108
Ireland Irland 146
Irish irlænder c 93
iron (for laundry) strygejern nt 118
iron, to stryge 29
ironmonger's isenkræmmer c 99
Israel Israel 146
it den, det 162
Italy Italien 146
its dens, dets, sin, sit 161
ivory elfenben nt 122

J
jacket jakke c 115

jade jade c 122
jam (preserves) syltetøj n 40, 63
jam, to kunne ikke åbnes 28
January januar 150
Japan Japan 146
jar (container) glas nt 119
jaundice gulsot c 142
jaw kæbe c 138
jazz jazz c 128
jeans cowboybukser pl 115
jersey ulden trøje c 115
jewel box smykkeskrin nt 121
jeweller's guldsmed c 99, 121
joint led nt 138
journey rejse c 72
juice saft, juice c 37, 40, 60
July juli 150
jumper jumper c 115
June juni 150
just (only) bare 12, 100

K
keep, to beholde 62
kerosene petroleum nt 106
key nøgle c 27
kidney nyre c 138
kilo(gram) kilo(gram) nt 119
kilometre kilometer 20, 78
kind pænt 95
kind (type) slags c 85, 140
knee knæ nt 138
kneesocks knæstrømper pl 115
knife kniv c 36, 61, 120
knock, to banke på 155
know, to vide 16, 24, 96

L
label etiket c 105
lace knipling nt 114
lady dame c 155
lake sø c 85
lamb (meat) lammekød nt 47
lamp lampe 29, 106, 118
landscape landskab nt 92
language sprog nt 104
lantern lygte c 106
large stor 20, 101, 130
last sidst 14, 67, 73, 149, 151
late sent 14

later senere 135
laugh, to le 95
launderette møntvaskeri *nt* 99
laundry *(clothes)* vask *c* 29
laundry *(place)* vaskeri 29, 99
laundry service tøjvask *c* 23
laxative afføringsmiddel *nt* 108
lead *(metal)* bly *nt* 75
lead *(theatre)* hovedrolle *c* 86
leap year skudår *nt* 149
leather læder *nt* 113, 117
leave, to tage afsted 31; afgår 68
leave, to *(leave behind)* efterlade 71
leeks porrer *pl* 51
left til venstre 21, 69, 77
left-luggage office bagageopbevaring
  c 67, 71
leg ben *nt* 138
lemon citron *c* 37, 40, 55, 60
lemonade limonade *c* 60
lens *(camera)* objektiv *nt* 125
lens *(glasses)* linse *c* 123
lentils linser *pl* 51
less mindre 14
lesson undervisning *c* 91
let, to *(hire out)* leje 155
letter brev *nt* 28, 132
letter box postkasse *c* 132
letter of credit kreditbrev *nt* 130
lettuce salat *pl* 51
library bibliotek *nt* 81, 99
licence *(driving)* kørekort *nt* 20, 79
lie down, to lægge sig 142
life belt redningsbælte *nt* 74
life boat redningsbåd *c* 74
life guard *(beach)* livredder *c* 90
lift *(elevator)* elevator *c* 27, 100
light let 14, 56, 101
light lys *nt* 28, 79, 124
light *(colour)* lys 101, 111, 112
light meter lysmåler *c* 125
lighter lighter *c* 126
lighter fluid/gas lightervæske *c* 126
lightning lyn *nt* 94
like vil gerne have 111
like, to vil gerne 13, 20, 23
like, to *(please)* kan lide 25, 92, 102
linen *(cloth)* lærred *nt* 113
lip læbe *c* 138
lipsalve læbepomade *c* 109
lipstick læbestift *c* 109
liqueur likør *c* 59
listen, to høre på 128
litre liter 75, 119
little *(a little)* en smule 14

live, to bo 83
liver lever *c* 138
lobster hummer *c* 43, 45
local lokal 36, 69
long lange 115
long-sighted langsynet 123
look for, to se efter 13
look out! giv agt! 156
look, to se 100;
loose *(clothes)* løs 115
lose, to miste 123
loss tab *nt* 131
lost faret vild 13, 156
lost and found/lost property office
  hittegodskontor *nt* 67, 156
lot *(a lot)* en masse 14
lotion lotion *c* 109
loud *(voice)* høj 135
love, to elske 95
lovely dejlig 94
low lav 141
low season lavsæson *c* 150
low tide ebbe *c* 90
lower under- 69, 71
luck lykke *c* 152
luggage bagage *c* 17, 18, 21, 26, 31, 71
luggage locker bagageboks *c* 18, 67,
  71
luggage trolley bagagevogn *c* 18, 71
lump *(bump)* klump *c* 139
lunch frokost *c* 34, 80, 94
lung lunge *c* 138

M

machine *(washable)* (vaske)maskine *c*
  114
mackerel makrel *c* 45
magazine tidsskrift *nt* 105
magnificent storartet 84
maid stuepige *c* 26
mail post 28, 133
mail, to poste 28
mailbox postkasse *c* 132
main hoved- 67
make-up remover pads vatrondeller til
  at fjerne makeup med *pl* 109
make up, to *(prepare)* gøre i stand 71
make-up sminke *c* 109
mallet kølle *c* 106
man mand 115, 155
manager direktør *c* 26
manicure manicure *c* 30

many mange 14
map kort *nt* 76, 105
March marts 150
marinated marineret 46
marjoram merian *c* 54
market torv *nt* 81, 99
marmalade appelsinmarmelade *c* 40
married gift 93
mass *(church)* messe *c* 84
matt *(finish)* mat 125
match *(matchstick)* tændstik *c* 106, 126
match *(sport)* kamp *c* 89
match, to *(colour)* passe til 112
material *(cloth)* stof *nt* 113
matinée eftermiddags forestillingen *c* 87
mattress madras *c* 106
May maj 150
may *(can)* må 12, 163
meadow eng *c* 85
meal måltid *nt* 24, 34, 39, 143
mean, to betyde 11, 26
measles mæslinger *pl* 142
measure, to tage mål af 113
meat kød *nt* 47, 61
meatball frikadelle, kødboller *c* 47
mechanic mekaniker *c* 78
mechanical pencil skrueblyant *c* 105, 112
medical certificate lægeattest *c* 144
medicine medicin *c* 83
medicine *(drug)* medicin *c* 143
medium-sized mellemstor 20
medium *(meat)* medium 48
meet, to mødes 96
melon melon *c* 55
memorial mindesmærke *nt* 81
mend, to reparere 75
menthol *(cigarettes)* mentol- 126
menu menu *c* 37
menu *(printed)* spisekort *nt* 36, 38, 39
merry glædelig 152
message besked 28, 136
metre meter *c* 111
mezzanine *(theatre)* balkon *c* 87
middle midten 69, 150
midnight fireogtyve, midnat 153
mild *(light)* mild 126
mileage kilometerpenge *c* 20
milk mælk *c* 40, 60, 64
milkshake milkshake *c* 60
milliard milliard *c* 148
million million *c* 148
mineral water mineralvand *nt* 60

minister *(religion)* protestantisk præst *c* 84
mint mynte *c* 54
minute minut 21, 69, 153
mirror spejl *nt* 115, 123
miscellaneous forskellig 127
Miss frk. 10
miss, to mangle 18, 29, 61
mistake fejltagelse *c* 31, 61, 62, 102
moccasin mokkasin *c* 117
moisturizing cream fugtighedscreme *c* 110
moment øjeblik *nt* 12, 136
monastery munkekloster *nt* 81
Monday mandag *c* 151
money penge *pl* 18, 129, 130
money order postanvisning 133
month måned *c* 16, 150
monument monument *nt* 81
moon måne *c* 94
more mere 12, 14
morning, in the om morgenen 143, 151, 153
mortgage panteret *c* 131
mosque moske *c* 84
mosquito net myggenet *nt* 106
motel motel *nt* 22
mother mor *c* 93
motorboat motorbåd *c* 91
motorway motorvej *c* 76
moustache overskæg *nt* 31
mouth mund *c* 138, 142
mouthwash mundvand *nt* 108
move, to bevæge 139
movie camera filmkamera *nt* 124
movies film, *(gå i)* biografen *pl* 86, 96
Mr. hr. 10
Mrs. fru 10
much meget 11, 14
mug krus 120
muscle muskel *c* 138
museum museum *nt* 81
mushroom champignon *c* 51
music musik *c* 83, 128
musical musical *c* 86
mussel blåmuslinge *c* 45
must *(have to)* måtte 31, 37, 61, 95, 142
mustard sennep *c* 50, 52, 54, 64
my min/mit/mine 161
myself mig selv 119

N
nail *(human)* negl c 109
nail brush neglebørste c 109
nail clippers negleklipper c 109
nail file neglefil c 109
nail polish neglelak c 109
nail polish remover neglelakfjerner c 109
nail scissors neglesaks c 109
name navn nt 23, 25, 79, 92, 131, 136
napkin serviet c 36, 105
nappy ble c 110
narrow smal 117
nationality nationalitet c 25, 92
natural natur- 83
natural history naturhistorie c 83
nausea *(nauseous)* kvalme c 140
near nær 14, 15
near(by) i nærheden 32, 77
nearest nærmeste 75, 78, 98
neat *(drink)* tør 59
neck hals c 30, 138; nakke c 138
necklace halskæde c 121
need, to have brug for 29
needle nål c 27
negative *(film)* negativ 124, 125
nephew nevø c 93
nerve nerve c 138
nervous system nervesystem nt 138
Netherlands Holland 146
never aldrig 15
new ny 14
New Year nytår 152
newsagent's bladhandler c 99
newspaper avis c 104, 105
newsstand aviskiosk c 19, 67, 99, 104
next næste 14, 21, 65, 67, 73, 76, 149, 151
next time næste gang c 95
next to ved siden af 15, 77
nice *(beautiful)* dejlig 94
niece niece c 93
night nat c 10, 24, 151
night cream natcreme c 109
night, at om natten 151
nightclub natklub c 88
nightdress/-gown natkjole c 115
nine ni 147
nineteen nitten 147
ninety halvfems 148
ninth niende 149
no nej 10
noisy støjende 25
nonalcoholic alkoholfrie 60
none ingen 15

nonsmoker ikke-ryger c 35, 70
noodle nuddel c 51
noon middag c 31, 153
normal normal 30
north nord 77
North America Nordamerika 146
Norway Norge 146
nose næse c 138
nose drops næsedråber pl 108
nosebleed næseblødning 141
not ikke 15, 163
note *(banknote)* seddel c 130
note paper brevpapir nt 105
notebook notesbog c 105
nothing ikke noget 15, 17
notice *(sign)* skilt nt 155
notify, to underrette 144
November november 150
now nu 15
number nummer nt 26, 65, 135, 136
nurse sygeplejerske c 144
nutmeg muskatnød c 54

O
o'clock klokken 153
occupation *(profession)* stilling c 25
occupied optaget 14, 70, 155
October oktober 150
office kontor nt 19, 67, 80, 99, 132, 156
office hittegodskontor nt 67
oil spiseolie c 37; olie c 75
oily *(greasy)* fedt 30, 110
old gammel 14
old town gamle by c 81
olive oliven c 41
omelet omelet c 40
on på 15
on foot til fods 76
on time rettidigt 68
once en gang 149
one en 147
one-way *(traffic)* ensrettet trafik c 77, 79
one-way ticket enkeltbillet c 65, 68
onion løg nt 51
only kun 15, 24, 80, 87, 108
onyx onyks c 122
open åben 14, 82, 155
open air udendørs 90
open, to åbne 11, 17, 82, 107, 130, 132
opera opera c 88
opera house opera 81, 88

operation operation *c* 144
operator telefonist *c* 134
opposite overfor 77
optician optiker 99, 123
or eller 15
orange appelsin *c* 55
orange *(colour)* orange 112
orange juice appelsinsaft *c* 40, 60
orangeade orangeade *c* 60
orchestra orkester *nt* 88
orchestra *(seats)* parket *nt* 87
order *(goods, meal)* bestilling *c* 36, 102
order, to bestille 36
order, to *(goods, meal)* bestille 61, 102, 103
oregano oregano *c* 54
ornithology ornitologi *c* 83
other anden, andet 74, 101
our vor, vort, vore 161
out of order virker ikke 136, 155
out of stock udsolgt 103
outlet *(electric)* stikkontakt *c* 27
outside udenfor 15, 36
oval oval 101
overdone *(meat)* for meget 61
overheat, to *(engine)* være for varm 78
overtake, to overhale 79
oyster østers *c* 45

P

pacifier *(baby's)* sut *c* 110
packet pakke *c* 126
pail spand *c* 128
pain smerte *c* 140, 141, 144
painkiller smertestillende middel *nt* 140
paint maling *c* 155
paint, to male 83
paintbox farvelade *c* 105
painter maler *c* 83
painting malerier *nt* 83
pair par *nt* 115, 117, 149
pajamas pyjamas *c* 116
palace slot *nt* 81
palpitations hjertebanken *c* 141
pancake pandekage *c* 40, 56
panties trusser *pl* 115
pants *(trousers)* bukser *pl* 115
panty girdle roll-on *c* 115
panty hose strømpebukser *pl* 115
paper papir *c* 105
paper napkin papirserviet *c* 105, 120

paperback billigbog *c* 105
paperclip papirclip 105
paraffin *(fuel)* petroleum *nt* 106
parcel pakke *c* 132, 133
pardon, I beg your undskyld 11
parents forældre *pl* 93
park park *c* 81
park, to parkere 26, 77
parking parkering *c* 77, 79
parking disc parkeringsskive *c* 77
parking meter parkometer *c* 77
parliament building Christiansborg *(folketinget)* 81
parsley persille *c* 54
part del *c* 138
partridge agerhøne *c* 49
party *(social gathering)* fest *c* 95
passport pas *nt* 16, 17, 25, 26, 156
passport photo pasbilleder *nt* 124
paste *(glue)* kliste *c* 105
pastry shop konditori *nt* 99
patch, to lappe 29
path sti *c* 85
patient patient *c* 144
pattern mønster *nt* 112
pay, to betale 17, 31, 62, 100, 102, 136
paying betaling *c* 102, 131
pea ærte *c* 51
peach fersken *c* 55
peanut jordnød *c* 55
pear pære *c* 55
pearl perle *c* 122
pedestrian fodgænger *c* 79
peg *(tent)* pløk *c* 107
pen pen *c* 105
pencil blyant *c* 105
pencil sharpener blyantsspidser *c* 105
pendant hængesmykke *nt* 121
penicilline penicillin *c* 143
penknife lommekniv *c* 120
pensioner pensionist *c* 82
pepper peber *nt* 37, 51, 54, 64
per cent procent *c* 149
per day pr. dag *c* 20, 32, 89
per hour pr. time *c* 77, 89
per person pr. person *c* 32
per week pr. uge *c* 20, 24
percentage procentsats *c* 131
perch aborre 45
perfume parfume *c* 109
perhaps måske 15
period *(monthly)* menstruation *c* 141
period pains menstruationssmerter *pl* 141
permanent wave permanent *c* 30

permit *(fishing)* fiskekort; *nt* 90; *(hunting)* jagtkort *nt* 90
person person *c* 32
personal personlig 17, 130
personal cheque personlig check *c* 130
petrol benzin *c* 75, 78
pewter tinlegering *c* 122
pharmacy apotek *nt* 108
pheasant fasan *c* 49
photo bilder *nt* 82, 124, 125
photocopy fotokopi *nt* 131
photographer fotograf *c* 99
photography fotografering *nt* 124
phrase vending *c* 12
pick up, to *(person)* hente 80, 96
picnic medbragt mad *c* 63
picnic basket madkurv *c* 106
piece stykke *nt* 18, 120
pig gris *c* 47
pigeon due *c* 49
pike gedde 45
pill pille *c* 141, 143
pillow pude *c* 27
pin nål *c* 110
pineapple ananas *c* 55
pink lyserød 112
pipe pibe *c* 126
pipe cleaner piberenser *c* 126
pipe tobacco pibetobak *c* 126
pipe tool pibekradser *c* 126
place sted *nt* 25, 76
place of birth fødested *nt* 25
place, to bestille 135
plaice rødspætte *c* 45
plain *(colour)* ensfarvet 112
plane fly *nt* 65
planetarium planetarium *nt* 81
plaster gibs *nt* 140
plastic plastic *c* 120
plastic bag plasticpose *c* 120
plate tallerken *c* 36, 61, 120
platform *(station)* perron *c* 67, 68, 69, 70
platinum platin *nt* 122
play *(theatre)* stykke *nt* 86
play, to spille 86, 88, 89, 93
playground legeplads *c* 32
playing card spillekort *nt* 105, 128
please vær venlig og 10
plimsolls lærredssko, gymnastiksko *pl* 117
plug *(electric)* stik *nt* 29, 118
plum blomme *c* 55
pneumonia lungebetændelse *c* 142
poached pocheret 46

pocket lomme *c* 116
pocket calculator lommeregner *c* 105
pocket watch lommeur *nt* 121
point of interest *(sight)* seværdighed *c* 80
point, to pege 12
poison gift *c* 142
poisoning forgiftning *c* 142
pole *(ski)* (ski)stav *c* 91
pole *(tent)* (telt)stang *c* 106
police politi *nt* 156
police station politistation *c* 99, 156
pond dam *c* 85
poplin poplin *c* 113
porcelain porcelæn *nt* 127
pork svinekød *nt* 46
port havn *c* 74
port *(wine)* portvin *c* 59
portable transportabel 118
porter drager *c* 18; portier *c* 26
portion portion *c* 37, 56, 61
Portugal Portugal 146
possible, (as soon as) (så snart som) muligt 137
post *(mail)* post *c* 28, 133
post office posthus *nt* 99, 132
post, to poste 28
postage porto *c* 132
postage stamp frimærke *nt* 28, 126, 132, 133
postcard postkort *nt* 105, 126
poste restante poste restante *c* 133
potato kartoffel *c* 50
pottery pottemageri *nt* 83
poultry fjerkræ *nt* 49
pound pund *nt* 18, 102, 130
powder pudder *nt* 109
powder compact pudderdåse *c* 121
powder puff pudderkvast *c* 109
prawn reje *c* 45
pregnant gravid 141
premium *(gasoline)* super 75
prescribe, to skrive recept på 143
prescription recept *c* 107, 143
present gave/gift *c* 17, 121
press stud tryklås *c* 116
press, to *(iron)* presse 29
pressure tryk *nt* 75, 141
pretty køn 84
price pris *c* 24, 69
priest katolsk præst *c* 84
print *(photo)* aftryk *nt* 125
private privat 23
process, to fremkalde 124
processing *(photo)* fremkaldning *c* 125

profit overskud *c* 131
programme program *nt* 87
pronounce, to udtale 12
pronunciation udtale *nt* 6
propelling pencil skrueblyant *c* 105, 121
Protestant protestant *c* 84
provide, to skaffe 131
prune sveske *c* 55
public holiday offentlig helligdag *c* 152
pull, to trække 155
pull, to *(tooth)* trække ud 145
pullover pullover *c* 116
pump pumpe *c* 106
puncture punktering *c* 75
purchase køb *nt* 131
pure ren 113
purple violet 112
push, to skubbe 155
put, to sætte 24
pyjamas pyjamas *c* 116

Q

quality kvalitet *c* 103, 112
quantity mængde *c* 14
quarter kvart *nt* 81, 149
quarter of an hour kvarter *nt* 153
question spørgsmål *nt* 11
quick(ly) hurtig(t) 14, 36, 79, 137, 156
quiet rolig 23, 25

R

rabbi rabiner *c* 84
rabbit kanin *c* 50
race væddeløb *nt* 89
race course/track væddeløbsbane *c* 90
racket *(sport)* ketsjer *c* 90
radiator *(car)* køler *c* 78
radio radio *c* 23, 28, 118
radish radise *c* 51
railway bane *c* 154
railway station jernbanestation *c* 19, 21, 67
rain regnvejr *nt* 94
raincoat regnfrakke *c* 116
raisin rosin *c* 55
rangefinder afstandsmåleren *c* 125
rare *(meat)* rødt 48, 61

rash udslet *nt* 139
raspberry hindbær *nt* 55
rate *(of exchange)* vekselkurs *c* 19, 130
rate *(price)* takst *c* 20
razor barbermaskine *c* 109
razor blades barberblade *pl* 109
reading lamp læselampe *c* 27
ready færdig 29, 117, 123, 125, 145
real *(genuine)* ægte 118, 121
rear bagerst 69
receipt kvittering *c* 103, 144
reception reception *c* 23
receptionist receptionist *c* 26
recommend, to anbefale 35, 36, 39, 80, 86, 88, 137, 145
record *(disc)* plade *c* 127, 128
record player pladespiller *c* 118
recorder båndoptager *c* 118
rectangular rektangulær 101
red rød 105, 113
red *(wine)* rødvin *c* 59
reduction rabat *c* 24, 82
refill *(pen)* patron *c* 105
refund *(to get a)* få pengene *pl* tilbage 103
regards hilsner *pl* 152
register, to *(luggage)* indskrive 71
registered mail anbefalet 133
registration indskrivning *c* 25
registration form indskrivningsblanket *c* 25, 26
regular *(petrol)* normal 75
religion religion *c* 83
religious service gudstjeneste *c* 84
rent, to leje 19, 20, 74, 90, 91, 118, 155
rental udlejning *c* 20
repair reparation *c* 125
repair, to reparere 29, 118, 121, 123, 117, 145
repeat, to gentage 12
report, to *(a theft)* anmelde 156
request anmodning *c* 73
required nødvendig 88
requirement forespørgsle 27
reservation bestilling *c* 19, 23, 65, 69
reservations office pladsreservering *c* 67
reserve, to bestille 19, 23, 35, 69, 87
reserved reserveret 155
rest rest *c* 130
restaurant restaurant *c* 19, 32, 35, 67
return ticket returbillet *c* 65, 68
return, to *(come back)* komme tilbage 21, 80
return, to *(give back)* returnere 103

reverse the charges, to modtageren betaler 135
rheumatism reumatisme *c* 141
rib ribben *nt* 48, 138
ribbon bånd *nt* 105
rice ris *c* 51
right *(correct)* rigtigt 14
right *(direction)* til højre 21, 69, 77
ring *(jewellery)* ring *c* 122
ring, to *(doorbell)* ringe 155
river flod *c* 85, 90
road vej *c* 76, 77, 85
road assistance hjælp på vejen 78
road map vejkort *nt* 105
road sign vejskilt *nt* 79
roast beef oksesteg *c* 47
roasted ovnstegt 48
roll rundstykke *nt* 40, 64
roll film rulle *c* 124
roller skate rulleskøjte *c* 128
room værelse *nt* 19, 23, 24, 25, 26, 27
room *(space)* plads *c* 32
room number værelsesnummer *nt* 26
room service service på værelset *c* 23
rope reb *nt* 106
rosary rosenkrans *c* 122
rosé *(wine)* rose 59
rosemary rosmarin *c* 54
rouge rouge *c* 109
round rund 101
round-neck rund halsudskæring *c* 116
round-trip ticket returbillet *c* 65, 68
round *(golf)* runde *c* 89
round up, to runde op 62
route rute *c* 85
rowing boat robåd *c* 91
rubber *(eraser)* viskelæder *nt* 105
rubber *(material)* gummi *nt* 117
ruby rubin *c* 122
rucksack rygsæk *c* 106
ruin ruin *c* 81
ruler *(for measuring)* lineal *c* 105
rum rom *c* 59
running water rindende vand *nt* 23
Russia Rusland *nt* 146

S
safe boks *c* 26
safe *(free from danger)* trygt 90
safety pin sikkerhedsnål *c* 109
saffron safran *c* 54
sage salvie *c* 54
sailing boat sejlbåd *c* 91

salad salat *c* 43
sale salg *nt* 131
sale *(bargains)* udsalg *nt* 100
salmon laks *c* 45
salt salt *nt* 37, 64
salty saltet 61
same samme 117
sand sand *nt* 90
sandal sandal *c* 117
sandwich sandwich *nt* 63
sanitary napkin/towel hygiejnebind *nt* 108
sapphire safir *c* 122
sardine sardin *c* 45
satin satin *c* 113
Saturday lørdag *c* 151
sauce sovs *c* 52
saucepan kasserolle *c* 120
saucer underkop *c* 120
sausage pølse *c* 40, 46, 64
scarf tørklæde *nt* 116
scarlet skarlagensrød 112
scenery landskab *nt* 92
scenic route køn rute *c* 85
school skole *c* 79
scissors saks *c* 109, 120
scooter scooter *c* 74
Scotland Skotland 146
scrambled eggs røræg *nt* 40
screwdriver skruetrækker *c* 106, 120
sculptor billedhugger *c* 83
sculpture skulptur *c* 83
sea hav *nt* 85, 90
seafood skaldyr *pl* 45
season sæson *c* 150
seasoning krydderier *pl* 37
seat plads 65, 69
seat belt sele *c* 75
second anden, andet 149
second sekund *nt* 153
second-hand shop marskandiser *c* 99
second class anden klasse *c* 69
second hand sekundviser 122
secretary sekretær *c* 27, 131
section afdeling *c* 104
see, to se 12, 25, 26, 87, 89, 96, 121
sell, to sælge 100
send, to sende 78, 102, 103, 132, 133
sentence sætning *c* 12
September september 150
seriously alvorlig 139
serve, to *(meal)* servere 39
service betjening *c* 100
service service *c* 24, 62; betjening *c* 62, 100

service *(church)* gudstjeneste c 84
serviette serviet c 36
set *(hair)* sat håret c 30
set menu dagens ret c 36
setting lotion setting lotion c 30, 110
seven syv 147
seventeen sytten 147
seventh syvende 149
seventy halvfjerds 148
sew, to sy 29
shade *(colour)* nuance c 111
shampoo shampoo c 30, 110
shampoo and set håret vasket og sat c 30
shape form c 103
share *(finance)* aktie c 131
sharp *(pain)* skarp *(smerte)* c 140
shave barbering c 31
shaver barbermaskinen c 27, 119
shaving brush barberbørste c 109
shaving cream barbercreme c 109
she hun 162
shelf hylde c 119
ship skib nt 74
shirt skjorte c 116
shivery kuldegysninger pl 140
shoe sko c 117
shoe polish skocreme c 117
shoe shop skoforretning c 99
shoelace snørebånd nt 117
shoemaker's skomager c 99
shop butik c 98
shop window vinduet nt 100, 111
shopping indkøb c 97
shopping area forretningskvarter nt 100
shopping centre indkøbscenter nt 99
short kort 30, 116, 117
short-sighted kortsynet 123
shorts shorts pl 116
shoulder skulder c 138
shovel skovl c 128
show show nt 86, 88
show, to vise 12, 13, 76, 100, 101, 103, 118, 124
shower bruser c 23, 32
shrimp reje c 45
shrink, to krybe 113
shut lukket 14
shutter *(camera)* lukker c 125
shutter *(window)* skodde c 29
side side c 30
sideboards/-burns kindskæg nt 31
sightseeing sightseeing c 80

sightseeing tour rundtur c 80
sign *(notice)* skilt nt 77, 79, 155
sign, to underskrive 26, 130
signature underskrift c 25
signet ring signetring c 122
silk silke c 113
silver sølv nt 121, 122
silver *(colour)* sølvfarvet 112
silver plated forsølvning c 122
silverware sølvtøj nt 122
since siden 15, 150
sing, to synge 88
single *(ticket)* enkelt(billet) c 65, 68
single *(unmarried)* ugift 93
single cabin enkeltkahyt c 74
single room enkeltværelse nt 19, 23
sister søster c 93
sit down, to sætte sig 95
six seks 147
sixteen seksten 147
sixth sjette 149
sixty tres 147
size størrelse 124
size *(clothes)* mål nt 113
size *(shoes)* nummer nt 117
skate skøjte c 91
skating rink skøjtebane c 91
ski ski c 91
ski boot skistøvle c 91
ski lift skilift c 91
ski run skibakke c 91
skiing skiløb 89, 91
skiing equipment skiudstyr nt 91, 106
skiing lessons undervisning i skiløb c 91
skin hud c 138
skin-diving equipment dykkerudstyr nt 91; frømandsudstyr nt 106
skirt nederdel c 116
sky himmel c 94
sleep, to sove 144
sleeping bag sovepose c 106
sleeping car sovevogn c 66, 68, 69, 70
sleeping pill sovepille c 108, 143
sleeve ærme nt 116, 142
sleeveless uden ærmer pl 115
slice skive c 119
slide *(photo)* diapositiv nt 124
slip *(underwear)* underkjole c 116
slipper tøffel c 117
slow(ly) langsom(t) 14, 21, 135
small lille 14, 20, 25, 101, 117, 130
smoke, to ryge 95
smoked røget 45
smoker ryger c 70

snack mellemmåltid *c* 63
snack bar snackbar, bar-pub *c* 34, 67
snap fastener tryklås *c* 116
sneaker lærredssko, gymnastiksko *c* 117
snorkel snorkel *c* 128
snow snevejr *nt* 94
snuff snus *c* 126
soap sæbe *c* 27, 110
soccer fodbold *c* 89
sock sokke *c* 116
socket (electric) stikkontakt *c* 27
soft blød 123
soft-boiled (egg) blødkogt (æg) *nt* 40
soft drink læskedrik *c* 64
sold out udsolgt 87
sole (shoe) sål *c* 117
soloist solist *c* 88
some noget 15
someone nogen 95
something noget 29, 36, 56, 107, 111, 112, 125, 139
somewhere et eller andet sted 87
son søn *c* 93
song sang *c* 128
soon snart 15
sore (painful) øm 145
sore throat ondt i halsen 141
sorry beklager 11, 16
sort (kind) slags *c* 119
soup suppe *c* 44
south syd 77
South Africa Sydafrika 146
South America Sydamerika 146
souvenir souvenir *nt* 127
souvenir shop souvenirbutik *c* 99
spade skovl *c* 128
Spain Spanien 146
spare tyre reservehjul *c* 75
spark(ing) plug tændingsrør *nt* 75
sparkling (wine) mousserende 59
speak, to tale 12, 16, 84, 135
speaker (loudspeaker) højttaler *c* 118
special særlig 20
special delivery ekspres 133
specialist specialist *c* 142
speciality specialitet *c* 39
specimen (medical) prøve *c* 142
spectacle case brillefutteral *nt* 123
spell, to stave 12
spend, to bruge 101
spice krydderi *nt* 53
spinach spinat *c* 51
spine rygrad *c* 138
sponge svamp *c* 110

spoon ske *c* 36, 61, 120
sport sport *c* 89
sporting goods shop sportsforretning *c* 99
sprained forstuvet 140
spring (season) forår *nt* 150
spring (water) kilde *c* 85
square firkantet 101
staff (personnel) personale *nt* 26
stain plet *c* 29
stainless steel rustfrit stål 120, 122
stalls (theatre) parket *nt* 87
stamp (postage) frimærke *nt* 28, 126, 132, 133
staple hæftestift *c* 105
star stjerne *c* 94
start, to begynde 80, 88
starter (meal) forret *c* 41
station (railway) (jernbane)station *c* 19, 21, 66, 70
station (underground, subway) S-togsstation *c* 73
stationer's papirhandel *c* 99, 104
stay være *nt* 31, 92
stay, to blive 16, 24, 26, 142
stay, to (reside) bo 93
steal, to stjæle 156
steamed dampkogt 46
stew ragout *c* 48
stewed stuvet 48
stiff neck stiv nakke 141
still (mineral water) almindelig 60
sting stik *nt* 139
sting, to stikke 139
stitch, to sy 29
stocking strømpe *c* 116
stomach mave *c* 138
stomach ache mavepine *c* 141
stools afføring *c* 142
stop (bus) busholdeplads *c* 73
stop thief! stop tyven! 156
stop! stop! 156
stop, to standse 21, 68, 70, 72
store (shop) forretning *c* 98
straight (drink) tør 59
straight ahead ligeud 21, 77
strange underlig 84
strawberry jordbær *nt* 55
street gade *c* 25, 77
street map gadekort *nt* 19;
streetcar sporvogn *c* 73
string snor *c* 105
strong stærk 126, 143
student studerende *c* 82, 93
study, to studere 93

stuffed fyldt 41
sturdy solid 101
sturgeon stør c 45
subway (railway) S-bane c 72
suede ruskind c 113, 117
sugar sukker nt 37, 64
suit (man's) sæt tøj nt 116
suit (woman's) dragt c 116
suitcase kuffert c 18
summer sommer c 150
sun sol c 94
sun-tan cream solcreme c 110
sun-tan oil sololie c 110
sunburn solforbrænding 107
Sunday søndag c 151
sunglasses solbriller pl 123
sunshade (beach) parasol c 91
sunstroke solstik nt 141
super (petrol) super 75
superb fantastisk 84
supermarket supermarked nt 99
suppository stikpille c 108
surgery (consulting room)
konsultation c 137
surname efternavn nt 25
suspenders (Am.) seler pl 116
swallow, to sluge 143
sweater sweater c 116
sweatshirt sweatshirt c 116
Sweden Sverige 146
sweet sødt 59, 61
sweet (confectionery) bolsje nt 126
sweet shop chokoladeforretning c 99
sweetener sødemiddel nt 37
swell, to hæve 139
swelling hævelse c 139
swim, to svømme 89
swimming svømning c 89, 90
swimming pool svømmebasin nt 23, 32, 90
swimming trunks badebukser pl 116
switch (electric) kontakt c 29
switchboard operator telefonist c 26
Switzerland Schweiz 146
swollen hævet 139
synagogue synagoge c 84
synthetic syntetisk 113
system system nt 138

T
T-shirt T-shirt c 116

table bord nt 35, 106
tablet (medical) tablet nt 108
tailor's skrædder c 99
take away, to tage med 63, 102
take pictures, to fotografere 82
take to, to køre til 21, 66
take, to tage 18, 25, 72, 102, 143
taken (occupied) taget 69
talcum powder talkumpudder nt 110
tampon tampon c 108
tangerine mandarin c 55
tap (water) vandhane c 28
tape recorder båndoptager c 119
tarragon estragon c 53
tax skat c 32, 102
taxi taxa c 18, 19, 21, 31, 66
taxi rank/stand taxaholdeplads c 21
tea te c 40, 60, 64
team hold nt 89
teaspoon teske c 120, 143
telegram telegram nt 133
telegraph office telecenter nt 99
telephone telefon c 28, 79, 134
telephone booth telefonboks c 134
telephone directory telefonbog c 134
telephone number telefonnummer nt 135, 136, 156
telephone, to (call) telefonere 134
telephoto lens teleobjektiv nt 125
television fjernsyn nt 23, 28, 118
telex telex nt 133
telex, to sende et telex 130
tell, to sige 13, 73, 76, 136, 153
temperature temperatur c 90
temporary midlertidig 145
ten ti 147
tendon sene c 138
tennis tennis c 89
tennis court tennisbane c 89
tennis racket tennisketsjer c 90
tent telt nt 32, 106
tent peg teltpløk c 106
tent pole teltstang c 106
tenth tiende c 149
terrace terrasse c 36
terrifying forfærdelig 84
tetanus stivkrampe c 140
than end 14
thank you tak 10
thank, to takke 10, 96
that det der 11
that's all det hele 103
theatre teater nt 82, 86
theft tyveri nt 156

their deres 161
then så 15
there der 14
thermometer termometer *nt* 108, 144
these disse 161
they de 162
thief tyv *c* 156
thigh lår *nt* 138
thin tynd 112
think, to *(believe)* tro 31, 94
third tredje *c* 149
third tredjedel *c* 149
thirsty , to be være tørstig 13, 35
thirteen tretten 147
thirty tredive 147
this det her 100
those de 161
thousand tusind *nt* 148
thread tråd *c* 27
three tre 147
throat hals *c* 138, 141
throat lozenge halstablet *c* 108
through gennem 15
through train gennemgående tog *nt* 68
thumb tommelfinger *c* 138
thumbtack tegnestift *c* 105
thunder torden *c* 94
thunderstorm tordenvejr *nt* 94
Thursday torsdag *c* 151
thyme timian *c* 54
ticket billet *c* 65, 68, 72, 87, 89
ticket office billetluge *c* 67
tide flod/ebbe *c* 90
tie slips *nt* 116
tie clip slipseklemme *c* 122
tie pin slipsenål *c* 122
tights strømpebukser *pl* 116
time tid *c* 67, 80
time *(occasion)* gang *c* 95, 142, 143
timetable *(trains)* køreplan *c* 68
tin *(container)* dåse *c* 119
tin opener dåseåbner *c* 120
tint toning *c* 110
tinted farvede 123
tire dæk *nt* 75
tired træt 13
tissue *(handkerchief)* papirslommetørklæde *pl* 110
to til 15
to get *(fetch)* få fat på 137
to get *(go)* komme 100
to get *(obtain)* få 107, 134
toast ristet brød *nt* 40
tobacco tobak *c* 126

tobacconist's tobakshandler *c* 99
today i dag 29, 151
toe tå *c* 138
toilet paper toiletpapir *nt* 110
toilet water toiletvand *nt* 110
toiletry toiletartikel *c* 109
toilets toilet *nt* 23, 27, 32, 67
tomato tomat *c* 51
tomato juice tomatsaft *c* 41; tomatjuice *c* 60
tomb gravsted *nt* 82
tomorrow i morgen 29, 96, 151
tongue tunge *c* 138
tonic water tonic water *c* 60
tonight i aften 29, 86, 87, 96
tonsils mandler *pl* 138
too *(also)* også 15
too much for meget 14
tools værktøj *nt* 120
tooth tand *c* 145
toothache tandpine *c* 145
toothbrush tandbørste *c* 110
toothpaste tandpasta *c* 110
top, at the øverst oppe 30
torch *(flashlight)* lommelygte *c* 106
torn forvredet 140
touch, to røre 155
tough *(meat)* sej 61
tour tur 74, 80
tourist office turistkontor *nt* 80
tourist tax turistskat *c* 32
towards mod 15
towel håndklæde *nt* 27, 110
towelling *(terrycloth)* frotté *nt* 113
tower tårn *nt* 82
town by *c* 19, 76, 88
town centre (byens) centrum *nt* 21, 73, 76
town hall rådhus *nt* 82
toy legetøj *nt* 128
toy shop legetøjsforretning *c* 99
track *(station)* spor *nt* 68, 69
tracksuit træningsdragt *c* 116
traffic light trafiklys *nt* 77
trailer campingvogn *c* 32
train tog *nt* 66, 68, 69, 70, 153
tram sporvogn *c* 73
tranquillizer beroligende middel *nt* 143
transfer *(finance)* overførsel *c* 131
transformer transformator *c* 118
translate, to oversætte 12
travel agency rejsebureau *nt* 99
travel guide rejsefører *c* 105

travel sickness kørosyge *c* 107
travel, to rejse 93
traveller's cheque rejsecheck *c* 18
travelling bag holdall *c* 18
treatment behandling *c* 143
tree træ *nt* 85
tremendous gevaldig 84
trim, to *(a beard)* studse 31
trip rejse 93, 152;
trolley bagagevogn *c* 18, 71
trousers bukser *pl* 116
trout forel *c* 45
try on, to prøve 114
tube tube *c* 119
Tuesday tirsdag *c* 151
tumbler vandglas *nt* 120
tuna tunfisk *c* 45
turbot pigvarre 45
turkey kalkun *c* 49
Turkey Tyrkiet 146
turn, to *(change direction)* dreje til 21;
køre til 77
turnip majroe, kålrabi *c* 51
turquoise turkis 112
turquoise *(stone)* turkis *c* 122
turtleneck højhalset 116
tweezers pincet *c* 110
twelve tolv 147
twenty tyve 147
twice to gange *pl* 149
twin beds to senge *pl* 23
two to 147
typewriter skrivemaskine *c* 27
typing paper skrivemaskinepapir *nt* 105
tyre dæk *nt* 75

U
ugly grim 14, 84
umbrella paraply *c* 116
umbrella *(beach)* parasol *c* 91
uncle onkel *c* 93
unconscious bevidstløs 139
under under 15
underdone *(meat)* letstegt 48, 61
underground *(railway)* S-bane 73
underpants underbukser *pl* 116
undershirt undertrøje *c* 116
understand, to forstå 12, 16
undress, to tage tøjet af 142
United States USA 146
university universitet *nt* 82

unleaded blyfri 75
until indtil 15
up op 14
upper over- 69
upset stomach dårlig mave *c* 107
upstairs ovenpå 15
urgent, to be haste 13, 145
urine urin *c* 142
use brug *nt* 17, 108
usually sædvanlige 94

V
V-neck V-hals *c* 116
vacancy ledigt værelse *nt* 23
vacant ledig 14, 22, 155
vacation ferie *c* 151
vaccinate, to vaccinere 140
vacuum flask termoflaske *c* 120
vaginal infection underlivsbetændelse *c* 141
valley dal *c* 85
value værdi *c* 131
value-added tax moms *c* 24, 102
vanilla vanilje *c* 54
VAT *(sales tax)* moms *c* 24
veal kalvekød *nt* 47
vegetable grøntsag *c* 39, 51
vegetable store grønthandel *c* 99
vegetarian vegetar *c* 37
vein vene *c* 138
velvet fløjl *nt* 113
venereal disease kønssygdom *c* 142
venison dyrekød *nt* 49
vermouth vermouth *c* 59
very meget 15
vest undertrøje *c* 116
vest *(Am.)* vest *c* 116
veterinarian dyrlæge *c* 99
video camera videokamera *nt* 124
video cassette videobånd *c* 119, 124, 127
video recorder videobåndoptager *c* 118
view *(panorama)* udsigt *c* 23, 25
village landsby *c* 76, 85
vinegar eddike *c* 37
visit besøg *nt* 92
visit, to besøge 95
visiting hours besøgstid *c* 144
vitamin pill vitaminpille *c* 108
vodka vodka *c* 59
volleyball volleyball *c* 89

DICTIONARY

voltage spænding c 27
vomit, to kaste op 140

W

waistcoat vest c 116
wait, to vente 21, 95, 107
waiter tjener c 26, 36
waiting room venteværelse nt 67
waitress frøken c 26, 36
wake, to vække 27, 70
Wales Wales 146
walk, to gå 74
wall mur c 85
wallet tegnebog c 156
walnut valnød c 55
want, to ville have 13, 101, 102 145
warm varm 94, 155
wash, to vaske 29, 113
washbasin håndvask c 28
washing-up liquid opvaskemiddel nt 120
washing machine vaskemaskine c 23
washing powder vaskepulver nt 120
watch ur nt 121, 122
watchmaker's urmager c 99, 121
watchstrap urrem c 122
water vand nt 23, 28, 32, 60, 75, 90
water-skis vandski pl 91
water flask feltflaske c 106
water melon vandmelon c 55
watercress brøndkarse c 53
waterfall vandfald nt 85
waterproof vandtæt 122
wave bølge c 90
way vej c 76
we vi 162
weather vejr nt 94
weather forecast vejrudsigt c 94
wedding ring vielsesring c 122
Wednesday onsdag c 151
week uge c 16, 20, 24, 80, 92, 151
weekend weekend c 20
well godt 10, 140
well-done (meat) gennemstegt 48
west vest 77
what hvad 11
wheel hjul nt 78
when hvornår 11
where hvor 11
where from hvorfra 146
which hvilken 11
whipped cream flødeskum c 56

whisky whisky c 17, 59
white hvid 59, 112
who hvem 11
whole hele 143
why hvorfor 11
wick vær c 126
wide brede 117
wide-angle lens vidvinkelobjektiv nt 125
wife kone c 93
wig paryk c 110
wild boar vildsvin nt 49
wind vind c 94
window vindue nt 28, 36, 65, 69
window (shop) vinduet nt 100, 111
windscreen/shield vindskærm c 76
windsurfer windsurfer c 91
wine vin c 17, 58, 59, 61
wine list vinliste nt 58
wine merchant's vinhandler c 99
winter vinter c 150
winter sports vintersport c 91
wiper (car) visker c 75
wish ønske nt 152
with med 15
withdraw, to (from account) få udbetalt 131
withdrawal udbetaling c 130
without uden 15
woman kvinde 114
wonderful virkelig hyggelig 96
wood skov c 85
wool uld c 113
word ord nt 12, 15, 133
work, to virke 28, 119
working day hverdag, arbejdsdag c 151
worse værre 14
worsted kamgarn nt 113
wound sår nt 139
wrap up, to indpakke 103
wrinkle-free krølfrit 113
wristwatch armbåndsur nt 122
write, to skrive 12, 101
writing pad skriveblok c 105
writing paper brevpapir nt 27, 105
wrong forkert 14, 77, 135

X

X-ray, to røntgenfotografere 140

Ordliste

Y

year år *nt* 149
yellow gul 112
yes ja 10
yesterday i går 151
yet endnu 15, 16, 24
yoghurt yoghurt *c* 40, 64
you du, De, dig, Dem 162
young ung 14
your din, dit, Deres 161

youth hostel vandrehjem *nt* 22, 32

Z

zero nul 147
zip(per) lynlås *c* 116
zoo zoologisk have *c* 82
zoology zoologi *c* 83

Dansk indholdsfortegnelse

Alder	149	Fotoforretning	124
Alfabet	9	Frimærker	132
Anvendelige udtryk	10	Frisøren	30
Apotek	107	Frugt	55
Aviser	105	Fuglekød	49
Baby	110	Grammatik	159
Bagage	18, 71	Grøntsager	51
Ballet	88	Gudstjenester	84
Bank	129	Guldsmeden	121
Beklædning	111		
Benzinstation	75	Hilsner	10, 152
Bil	75	Hittegods	156
motorstop	78	Hospital	144
parkering	77	Hotel	22
udlejning	20	afrejse	31
ulykke	79	ankomst	23
værksted	79	indskrivning	25
Billetter	68, 87	personale	26
Biograf	86	post	28
Boghandel	104	vanskeligheder	28
Bus	73	værelsesbestilling	19
Butikker og forretninger	98		
Båd	74	Indbydelser	94
		Indkøbsvejledning	97
Camping	32, 106		
Cykeludlejning	74	Jernbanestation	67
Dage	151, 152	Kassetter	127
Dato	151	Kemisk rensning	29
Dessert	56	Klokken	153
Diabetikere	37, 141	Klæder	115
Diskoteker	88	Koncert	88
Diæt	37	Krydderier	49
Drikkevarer	57	Kød	47
Elektricitetsforretning	118	Lande	146
		Landet	85
Familien	93	Legemsdele	138
Farver	112	Legetøj	128
Fisk	45	Lufthavn	16, 65
Fly	65	Læge	137
Forkortelser	154		
Forlystelser	86	Mad og drikkevarer	63, 119
Forretningsudtryk	131	Madvarer	119

Medbragt mad	63
Mellemmåltider	63
Menu	39, 40
Morgenmad	40
Musik	128
Måneder	150
Natklubber	88
Nødstilfælde	156
Offentlige helligdage	152
Omregningstabeller	157, 158
Opera	85
Optiker	123
Ost	54
Overnatning	22
Papirhandel	104
Parkering	77
Pas	16
Penge	18, 129
Plader	127
Politi	79, 156
Posthus	132
Præsentationer	92
Restaurant	33
klager	61
regning	62
spørgsmål og bestilling	36
S-bane	73
Salater	43
Seværdigheder	80
Sisevaner	34
Skaldyr	45
Skilte	79, 155
Sko	117
Souvenirer	127
Sovse	52
Spisebestik	109
Spisestel	109
Sport	89
Spørgsmål	11
Strand	91

Stævnemøde	95
Størrelser	113
Supper	44
Sygdomme	140
Tallene	147
Tandlæge	145
Taxa	21
Teater	86
Telefon	134
Telegram, telex	133
Te	60
Tobakshandleren	126
Toiletartikler	109
Told	16, 17
Transport	
billetbestilling	69
billetter	68
forespørgsler	67
med bus	73
med båd	74
med fly	65
med rutebil	72
med tog	66
Træffe mennesker	92
Tyveri	156
Tøjstof	112
Udtale	6
Ulykker	79, 139
Urmageren	121
Valuta	129
Valuta	18, 129
Vaskeri	29
Vejangivelser	76, 77
Vejret	94
Vejskilte	79
Vintersport	91
Vin	58
Årstiderne	150
År	149
Øl	55